SCREWED, BLUED, TATTOOED, AND SOLD DOWN THE RIVER

D1441727

SCREWED, BLUED, TATTOOED, AND SOLD DOWN THE RIVER

An American Saga
Remedies Included
(Some Assembly Required)

D. H. Mason

Copyright © 2016 D. H. Mason
All rights reserved.

ISBN: 1519118325
ISBN 13: 9781519118325
Library of Congress Control Number: 2016901160
CreateSpace Independent Publishing Platform
North Charleston, South Carolina

Contents

Chapter 4
Blued 95

Chapter 5
Tattooed 99

Chapter 6
Sold Down the River 113

Chapter 7
Needed Acts, Petitions, Resolutions—Federal, State, County, City 145

Conclusion   155

Declaration of Independence   157

United States Constitution   163

United States Constitution Amendments   175

Bibliography   185

Cognitive Dissonance

That's not true! I'll never believe the earth is round! The mind involuntarily rejects information not in line with previous thoughts and/or actions. If you're unaware, you are…, what's it called…, oh yeah, unaware. For many of you, the following information is wildly new. For some, somewhere along this path you're about to trek, a line from an old rock song will come to mind: "I wish I didn't know now what I didn't know then." Some of you will become so psychologically uncomfortable that you will actively avoid situations and information likely to increase your discomfort with what you will know after reading this book. Some will oppose, ridicule, and challenge the enclosed information because of ego and/or because they just do not want to believe the truth given here. That's okay. You can deny, fear, oppose, ridicule, challenge; you can hide and watch; or you can support our work from afar. Many, like me, will be "on fire" to act, and we will win.

It can be extremely difficult for well fed, comfortable and amused people to conceive of a system of plunder that they, their parents and grandparents were born into along with the plunderers, their parents and grandparents, yet such failure to see does not prove the nonexistence of that system, it only insures that it will continue until the people are stripped of all of their wealth and reduced to serfs. Throughout history, governments have plundered their citizens. Ancient governments clipped the edges of coins and melted the clippings to make new coins, which also were clipped. The serrated or milled edge of coins was intended to prevent that practice. As time passed, the plunderers progressed to debased coinage, that is, base metals were switched for all or part of the precious metals in the coins. Still later, non-redeemable paper currency was used to steal the fruits of men's labor.

The most sophisticated plunder yet inflicted on trusting citizens combines the use of controlled news media; paper and metal tokens; credit (monetized debt) and imaginary taxes. The news media and schools deceive the people to believe that copper tokens and credit are "money;" that prices are inflation and that some of the "money" must be returned to the plunderers as taxes even though the plunderers have access to unlimited "money." The plunderers' creation and financing of foreign "enemies" helps to convince the victims that taxes are needed to support government while largesse to the most robbed poor buys votes to perpetuate the plunder. The ancient Chinese carved in stone, "Disperse the money, collect the people." As the Romans had bread and circuses, we today, have food stamps, football, foosball and fools on TV ad infinitum. We must be distracted at any cost….[1]

---

1 Dave Wilber, economics writer, quoted in Archibald Roberts, *The Most Secret Science*, 101.

Definitions

SCREWED

Screw: Pressure, coercion; extortionist. Slang: jailer.

—*Roget's College Thesaurus* (1978)

To put on the screw, to bring pressure to bear on a person, often, for the purpose of getting money. To put under the screw, to influence by strong pressure; to coerce. To oppress by exactions.

—*Webster's Encyclopedic Dictionary* (1942)

BLUED

Blue: Colloq., sad, dejected, depressed, dispirited, downhearted.

—*Roget's College Thesaurus* (1978)

TATTOOED

Tattoo: To prick the skin and stain the punctured spots with a coloring substance, forming lines and figures upon the body.

—*Webster's Encyclopedic Dictionary* (1942)

Social Security number: A "tattoo" the government requires that might as well be etched on your buttocks at birth. From the cradle to the grave, without this tattoo you cannot go to school, get a job, apply for loans, acquire medical insurance, recoup Social Security money fraudulently confiscated from your paychecks, or file tax returns to get back a dime on the dollar of the illegal taxes you were forced to pay.

—D. H. Mason

SOLD DOWN THE RIVER

A term coined by slaves as a response when asked what happened to friends and family members.[2]

---

2 http://www.npr.org/sections/codeswitch/2014/01/27/265421504/what-does-sold-down-the-river-really-mean-the-answer-isnt-pretty.

Introduction

STARTING FROM SCRATCH

Thank God for evolution! My parents (William and Attie) were Arkansas sharecroppers and ranch hands when we first moved to California. My father was twelve when he saw his first car (1919). Fifty years later (1969), as the world watched Neil Armstrong set foot on the moon, I called to hear his thoughts. He said, "I don't believe everything I see on the television, do you?"

My parents were married November 11, 1942, in the Dumas, Arkansas, drugstore; the pharmacist was also the justice of the peace. My father was on a short leave from the army before heading to California for additional training. World War II was hot and heavy. After the wedding, they took a bus to Wilmot, Arkansas, near the Louisiana border. From there, my father rowed his bride a mile or so in a small boat to his brother Abe's home. They spent the night, and my father left for an army training base in California the next evening. A few days later, my mother left to join him. Dad (artilleryman and then a cook after a back injury) left for the Pacific islands in the early spring of 1943. Mom got a job as a "gasser" refueling planes at Eagle Field, a pilot-training base near Dos Palos, California. She lied about her age to get the job; she was seventeen. She worked at Eagle Field for nearly two years before returning to Arkansas. When Dad returned home in 1945, Mom had nine acres of cotton near ready for them to pick.

I was born September 8, 1946, in Dumas, Arkansas. I was born breech and have had a contrary prospective ever since. Well, so said my twin brother, who, following standard procedure, was born twenty-five minutes later. Our sister was born three years and two months later. My brother died December 14, 2007. He was my best friend (behind my wife, Linda), and no day passes that I don't think about him, miss him, and think that we travel together, have always traveled together, and some-day will travel together again (save me a place at the table, bro!).

After four years of sharecropping, our parents transplanted our family to California. We grew up working in the fields and packinghouses around Dinuba, one of many small agricultural communities dotting California's Central Valley. There were a good number of us Arkies and Okies working along-side the Mexicans in the fields. The Mexicans followed the harvests and many returned to Mexico for the winter months, when demand for field labor was low. I was brown as any Mexican from working and playing in the hot valley sun, but I learned at an early age that I couldn't work hard enough to be Mexican. At that time, a lot of the field work, like picking cotton and grapes, was piecework, so a relatively slow Arkie like me could work the fields, too.

My brother recalled that we were almost nine when we got our first cotton sacks. They were actu-ally fifty-pound burlap potato sacks with denim shoulder straps; Dad tailored them for us. We would arrive at the field before sunrise, even though you weren't allowed to start picking until a half hour or so after sunrise, the time needed for the cotton to dry from overnight dew. When we got the word, we sprang into action. Wet cotton added weight, so we were anxious to get pickin' as soon as possible. Fill your sack with as much cotton as you could carry, tote it over your shoulder to the trailer, hang it on the paymaster's scale, and get paid cash money right then and there, a nickel for every pound. Then, back over your shoulder, up a ten-foot ladder, walk out on a narrow plank spanning the top of the trailer, and empty your sack. When the trailer was nearly full, you could help pack down the cotton by jumping off the narrow plank into the trailer, sort of a "fringe benefit" for us kids.

I didn't *have* to work; I wanted to work. I begged to work, because every nickel I earned was mine to keep. Well, I didn't keep any of it—I spent every last bit. I bought comic books, model cars, model planes, bicycles, BB guns, and clothes. When I was fifteen and a half, my parents cosigned so I could buy a small motorcycle to commute to work and school. At sixteen, I had my driver's license, so during the summer months, I worked as a "swamper"[3] during the day and in the packinghouse in the evening. The swamper job paid an extra twenty-five cents per hour, bringing the hourly wage up to $1.50. All that money coming in was burning a hole in my pocket. I bought my first car—a 1950 Ford coupe, an eight-cylinder flathead with a three-speed on the column that I quickly converted to a three-speed on the floor, thanks to my cousin Ira. Driving your own car at sixteen—now, that's freedom!

I learned to read and write from my parents, my great-grandmother, Mahallie, and the church. I didn't go to kindergarten. I attended first grade in Cutler, California, then finished elementary school in Sultana, California. I graduated from Dinuba Joint Union High School in 1964. I was an average student. I did well in geometry and auto shop, played drums in the high-school band, and lettered in football and wrestling. After high school, I attended Reedley Community College for nearly ten minutes before dropping out and moving to Martinez, California. I lived with my cousin's family and got a job as a warehouseman for American Standard in Richmond. My brother got an apartment in Dinuba and was working as a carpenter's apprentice—and, by the way, he *could* work hard enough to be Mexican.

Today, many religious people would say I'm a heathen in need of redemption. I was baptized a Christian (Mennonite Brethren), April 14, 1959. Our family started attending the Cutler Bible Chapel shortly after we arrived in California (1951). At that time, Cutler was little more than an old, very old, farm-labor camp; it was mostly dilapidated housing, with the toilets and showers at the center of the camp. I was six years old before we lived in a place with an indoor toilet. Lonnie and I must have flushed five hundred gallons of water, marveling as it disappeared in a turbulent swirl. We lived in the labor camp over a year, but we stayed connected to the small chapel long after. The last time I attended the chapel, I was on leave from the Air Force (1968); it was the last time I remember being in any church to hear a sermon. Don't take that the wrong way; I didn't turn anti-Christian, and Mennonites are some of the kindest, most generous, and moral people on earth. I went searching.

Some eight years later (1976), I was an active Rosicrucian, a member of the Ancient Mystical Order of the Rosy Cross. The cross represents the hardships of traveling a spiritual path; the rose represents the budding of the spirit as a result of traveling that path. For more than four years, mostly through

---

3 A swamper loads the field boxes of fruit or vegetables onto a large truck and delivers them to the packinghouse.

home-study courses, I studied subjects such as concentration, contemplation, meditation, reincarnation, telepathy, telekinesis, and extrasensory perception. I also attended Rosicrucian University in San Jose, California, for creative writing and other courses. In recent years, I have taken some courses at the Church of Scientology in San Francisco. I'm not a churchgoing Christian, active Rosicrucian, or Scientologist. I'm a mutant mystic who has found his way, or—well, let's put it this way: I'm just another student on the path. The paths of righteousness are as abundant as sunrays, and evil lurks in every shadow along every way. I can't tell all, you can't hear all, and we cannot successfully challenge without getting into some matters of the Spirit. Know this: I expect us to win this battle, and what you expect tends to come to you. So, from the get-go, think what you want.

I recall waking early one morning before dawn; my mother was sitting on the edge of Lonnie's bed, weeping softly. I listened for a while before I whispered, "Mom, what's wrong?"

"I'm afraid," she answered, "afraid there's going to be another world war, and you boys will have to go."

It was October 1962. Vietnam was warming up, the Cold War was hot and heavy, and the United States was toe-to-toe with the Soviet Union. The United States had discovered that the USSR was attempting to install nuclear missiles in Cuba. Twenty years earlier, our mother had watched as our father shipped out to fight in the South Pacific; she lived every day for years not knowing if he would return alive. Now, it was her sons in jeopardy.

Fortunately, the Cuban Missile Crisis was averted. Unfortunately, three years later, Vietnam and the Cold War were both gaining speed. Since we'd chosen work over school, my brother and I knew the military draft was inevitable. We received our draft notices on the same day in 1965, shortly after our nineteenth birthday. Thanks to the insistence of Jim Cathy, a childhood friend, we had joined the United States Air Force a few days earlier. Not that we did not admire and appreciate the other branches of military service, but the Air Force offered a variety of technical-training schools, and Jim put it something like this: "You want to crawl through the muck or fly over the muck?" We parted company with Jim after a month in boot camp at Lackland Air Force Base (AFB) in Texas. Lonnie and I went to Chanute AFB in Illinois for training as hydraulic and pneudraulic specialists. Six months later, we were given two weeks' leave, with orders to report to Beale AFB near Marysville, California. We didn't know it at the time, but we had been investigated, cleared, and given "secret" clearances.

Our first day home on leave, Lonnie got us on with the carpenter he had worked for before we'd joined the Air Force. We worked full time those two weeks and drove to Beale AFB on the morning of the last day of our leave. When we checked in at the base, the young lieutenant looked at our orders and said, "These aren't right. They don't take any grunts[4] over there." We spent two weeks working on the B-52s before the hydraulic shop chief from "over there" tracked us down. "Over there" was the

---

4 A grunt is an airman fresh out of tech school; someone who does the "grunt" work.

SR-71s, a handful of supersonic reconnaissance aircraft the Air Force was still testing. They were taking grunts and gearing up to go operational; we happened to be the first grunts to arrive. There was a lot to learn and a short time to learn it in.

The technical manuals were evolving guides; the men training and overseeing our work were the best hydraulic specialists in the Air Force. Sergeant Dickey, our shop chief, and many others in the squadron had worked on the YF-12 (SR-71 forerunner) and the U-2 spy plane. Their enthusiasm and dedication were contagious. Under their supervision, we immediately started "wrenching" on the SR-71's hydraulic systems, hydraulic lines, pumps, servos, and actuators controlling flight controls, landing gear, and brakes. More aircraft and personnel filtered in. Eight months after our arrival, operations officially started. Spying had reached a new height; doing better than two thousand miles an hour at an altitude of eighty thousand feet, the SR-71 took excellent pictures. We spent the next three years flying over the muck. It was a long way from the cotton patch.

Linda and I were married in 1967; we'd met when I was living in Martinez (1964–65). Our son, Todd, was born a few months before I left for temporary duty on Okinawa. One of the first thoughts I had upon landing on Okinawa was that my father had been there some twenty-five years earlier, a part of one of the hardest-fought battles of World War II. My brother and I were honorably discharged from active duty on May 16, 1969; he moved to Visalia, California, got a job in a battery plant, and was soon married and making a good living. My wife, son, and I moved to Crockett, California. I quickly got a job as a Southern Pacific Railroad (SP) switchman and started making a good living.

I worked almost exclusively on the graveyard shift for the next twenty-three years. Our daughter was born (1972), and we bought our first home (1974) in Benicia, California, a home where we raised our children and lived for the next twenty-five years. Buying the home was a bit scary. The payment was going to be double what we had paid in rent, and I didn't know how the heck we were going to cover a mortgage of two hundred dollars a month.

I also went back to school, with help from the GI Bill. I went part time, took evening classes, and accumulated over a hundred college credits, getting the education I wanted. I did well in college, including my business, history, child-development, psychology, and creative-writing courses.

Linda and I both got a different kind of education in the early eighties, our "illegal tax-protester" years—an ironic classification, since we were refusing to voluntarily pay an illegal tax.[5] I'd read and researched Irwin Schiff's book, *How Anyone Can Stop Paying Income Taxes*, and a few other such books. I was on fire and very, very naive.

We didn't file federal or state income-tax returns for three years (1981–83). And we filed amended returns for the previous three years (1978–80), demanding back all taxes erroneously paid on our labor

---

5 See my American Free Labor Act, reproduced herein.

(wages) as income (gain/profit). I claimed exempt on a W-4 at work. Early on, before I had my own copy of the Internal Revenue Code, I went to the Internal Revenue Service (IRS) field office in Walnut Creek, California. I took a number and waited my turn to talk to a lone woman behind a twelve-foot-long counter. When it was my turn, I asked politely to see a copy of the Internal Revenue Code, noting I had some things I wanted to look up. She took a quick glance up and down the long counter and said, "We got one of those things around here somewhere, but I'll be darned if I know where it's at. What did you want to look up?"

"Well," I started, nervously. "I've heard that the Internal Revenue Code notes that filing an income-tax return is voluntary."

"Yeah, filing an income-tax return is voluntary, but you still gotta do it!" she answered, irritation creeping into her voice.

That was not an answer I had expected. I decided to move on. I asked, "What if you don't make enough income to require you to file a return? What if you only receive wages for your labor?"

Now she was getting excited. "What are you talking about? Wages are income!"

"No," I responded. "Congress and the Supreme Court define income as gains and profits. Wages are what I receive for the time I spend working, a value-for-value exchange."

She quickly retorted, "Your time has no value!"

Again, an answer I hadn't expected, and I asked without thinking, "If your time has no value, then why does the IRS pay you to work here?"

"I don't have time to answer those kinds of questions!" she shot back defiantly and called the next number.

My exempt status lasted about eight months, until the IRS required my employer to withhold the maximum from my paychecks, plus penalties. My wife was self-employed, so neither the IRS nor the Franchise Tax Board (FTB) could get to her labor. But the IRS calculated income-tax liabilities on my labor (wages) and began collecting by attacking my paychecks, after draining our checking and savings accounts. We had filed a joint return for fourteen years and claimed two children for nine years, but the IRS, "using all available information," demanded that my employer withhold at the much higher "single" rate and assessed yearly taxes at that same rate, using only the standard deduction. The FTB also calculated state income-tax liabilities on my labor and placed a lien on our home to secure the assessed debts.

All of the above was accomplished with no judicial involvement whatsoever. There was no day in court, no judgment rendered; form letters sent from the IRS and FTB to my employer, bank, and credit union were sufficient. Some illegal tax-protesters were not so "lucky"; some lost their jobs and homes, some were prosecuted by the State (FTB) for failure to file and went to jail, and some fled the State to evade prosecution and imprisonment.

After nearly four years, Linda and I could see we were not going to defeat the Federal or State collection agencies. They were collection machines. We might as well been talking to our vacuum cleaner. Nothing we said had any impact whatsoever; all those who tried had been neutralized; they didn't have a pot to piss in—how were they going to challenge now? Before all this got started, Linda was very much afraid of what I wanted us to do (not file, file amended returns for years past). What would happen to our two children if we went to jail? I argued that we had to do this for our children's future. Linda understood that, too, but she was still not ready to act. We had some very long discussions and debates, some heated, but they ended when I said, "I can't let this pass." Linda conceded, and we spent the next four years living with the consequences, together. We learned it firsthand: "Yeah, filing an income-tax return is voluntary, but you still gotta do it!" We claimed our labor (wages) as profit (income), and we filed, "voluntarily."

I was still working the graveyard shift for SP, so I took evening classes at Saint Mary's College of California in Moraga, earning my paralegal certification in June 1987. I received an honors grade in most of my classes, with the advantage of having spent many hours researching and writing from the law libraries during our illegal tax-protestor years. The teachers were lawyers, and some genuinely encouraged me to go to law school. Family, life, and survival have taken precedence.

GREETINGS, FELLOW SLAVES

> *Employ your time in improving yourself by other men's writings, so that you shall gain easily what others have labored hard for.*

> —SOCRATES (469–399 BC), GREEK PHILOSOPHER—
> ONE OF THE FOUNDERS OF WESTERN PHILOSOPHY

Today, the masses are like a pinball in an old arcade game, bouncing from immediate crisis to immediate crisis. Most people are honestly too busy trying to make ends meet to stop, observe, and see what has been lost: our freedom, our liberty, our security. All of us alive today were born into servitude. Conventional wisdom tells us we are free, but deep down, many, like me, know better. We are slaves, one and all.

How did I come across all this information? I'm a nosey paralegal, researcher, and writer with some traditional, some rare, and some unique sources of education, training, and information. As my dearly departed pappy would have said (good-humoredly), "Even a blind hog finds an acorn once-n-a-while." I started rooting around off the beaten paths with gusto some thirty-plus years ago; now I'm passing on my experiences and grim political discoveries (with remedies) to you.

To get to the truth of this matter, there are some rules. Don't accept conclusions based on authority. Do not rely on what others have said or are saying; just because the "expert" says so don't make it so. You have this thing…what's it called…oh, yeah, a brain. You can think for yourself, so do it! Make your own observations. Challenge convention. Now, this does not mean you should not respect those with specific expertise, but you should ask mass quantities of questions. Look where questioning got Socrates. Oh, yeah, it got him killed. Hey! You're gonna die anyway! While you're here this time, might as well kick some evil ass, take some names, and leave your earthly existence knowing you stood in the light, knowing you did good in this life.

What is life? It is the flash of a firefly in the night. It is the breath of a buffalo in the wintertime. It is the little shadow which runs across the grass and loses itself in the sunset.

—GREAT BLACKFOOT WARRIOR, CROWFOOT (1890)

We hold from God the gift which includes all others. This gift is life—physical, intellectual, and moral life. But life cannot maintain itself alone. The Creator of life has entrusted us with the responsibility of preserving, developing, and perfecting it. In order that we may accomplish this, He has provided us with a collection of marvelous faculties. And He has put us in the midst of a variety of natural resources. By the application of our faculties to these natural resources we convert them into products, and use them. This process is necessary in order that life may run its appointed course.

Life, faculties, production—in other words, individuality, liberty, property—this is man. And in spite of the cunning of artful political leaders, these three gifts from God precede all human legislation, and are superior to it.

Life, liberty, property do not exist because men have made laws. On the contrary, it was the fact that life, liberty, and property existed beforehand that caused men to make laws in the first place.

But, unfortunately, law by no means confines itself to its proper functions. And when it has exceeded its proper functions, it has not done so merely in some inconsequential and debatable matters. The law has gone further than this; it has acted in direct opposition to its own purpose. The law has been used to destroy its own objective: It has been applied to annihilating the justice that it was supposed to maintain; to limiting and destroying rights which its real purpose was to respect. The law has placed the collective force at the disposal of the unscrupulous who wish, without risk, to exploit the person, liberty, and property of others. It has converted plunder into a right, in order to protect plunder. And it has converted lawful defense into a crime, in order to punish lawful defense. How has this perversion of the law been accomplished? And what have been the results?

—FREDERIC BASTIAT, *THE LAW* (1850)[6]

---

6 *The Law* is only seventy-five pages long; PLEASE get it, read it, and then read it again.

What you are about to read in the following pages may be, at first, confusing. Well, at least I know it took me some time to research and understand what you are about to read. Do not pass a word you do not understand. Please, use a few dictionaries, including a legal dictionary. The more sources of clarification you can use, the better. If you have questions, comments, or need further clarification about anything herein, contact me at my website/blog, SqueakyWheelPolitics.com. What we do not want here is a failure to communicate.

The greatest obstacle to discovery is not ignorance but the illusion of knowledge.

—Socrates

KARL MARX WAS A VERY GOOD BOY

When I joined the Air Force in 1966, I took an oath to "preserve, protect and defend the Constitution of the United States against all enemies, foreign and domestic." I was nineteen. I'd known enough about the Constitution to pass the required high-school exams, but what I *understood* about the Constitution could have been mistaken for a dust mite. In the early 1980s, I became *very* interested in the Constitution during our "illegal tax protestor" years. As my research continued, I learned that the illegal taxation we were challenging was the good news.

You are about to read the saga of how we Americans were screwed, blued, tattooed, and sold down the river. Remedies are included (some assembly required). We were screwed in 1913 with passage of the Sixteenth and Seventeenth Amendments to the United States Constitution and especially by the passage of the Federal Reserve Act. We were blued starting in 1929 with the so-called Great Depression. We were tattooed in 1935 with passage of the Social Security Act. And, we've been sold down the river ever since with the covert establishment and implementation of a socialist form of government.

Throughout our history, we Americans have been able to protect our freedom and liberty and form of government from obvious, overt attacks. But the obscure, piecemeal attacks on our freedom and liberty and form of government from within, for well more than a hundred years, have gone undetected by the public at large and have been very successful. Substantial but fractured opposition has been no match. Limited government is history, free enterprise is chained up in the dungeon, and individual freedom is little more than illusion…or delusion—hard to tell from this angle. Representative government has been severely diluted, and separation of powers is just a vulgar joke. Herein are the links in our evolution from self-governance to governmental servitude; herein are the details of how it came to be that we Americans were disfranchised and now all serve an up-and-functioning socialist government. Who does our socialist government serve? You will soon know the answer.

Do not be disheartened; there are viable solutions. The United States Constitution is not dead… more like buried alive. A hundred-fifty-some years ago, English philosopher Herbert Spencer wrote, "The

Republican form of government is the highest form of government, but because of this it requires the highest type of human nature—a type nowhere at present existing." Sixty-some years before Herbert wrote these words, a republican form of government had been institutionalized with ratification of the United States Constitution.[7] It's been lost. But we can get it back. As my wise wife has repeatedly told me over the years when I'm frustratingly taking twice as long as I should to finish a "some assembly required" project, "When all else fails, read the instructions!" I've included a copy of the Declaration of Independence and United States Constitution for easy reference. It's not too late to excavate, educate, and legislate.

I know many of you refuse to accept that such a drastic change in *your* government has happened. You would have noticed—well, maybe not. Our political trek from a republican form of government through the muck of democracy into the insanity of a socialist form has taken better than a hundred years. Your education and ego tell you this is not so, but reality doesn't give a hoot about education or ego.

Do you know the difference between a republican, democratic, and socialist form of government?[8] If you don't know the difference, how do you know you have one form of government and not another? Oh, some millionaire politician, school book or teacher told you so? The quotes I give below offer some insight into why a socialist form of government appeals to many "educated" Americans as a solution to problems that are blamed on the democratic government they think we have.

> Joseph Goebbels, Nazi propaganda minister, 1933–45: "If you tell a lie big enough, and keep repeating it, people will eventually come to believe it."

Explaining how and why the federal government seized control of education via the Department of Education and the former National Institute of Education, Charlotte Thomson Iserbyt, who was the senior policy advisor in the Department of Education during the Reagan administration, offered the following:

> You think the purpose of education is reading, writing and arithmetic? The purpose of education is to change the thoughts, actions and feelings of students. Hitler wanted to control the education system in Germany; Stalin did in Russia; Mao Tse Tung in China. You have to get a hold of the minds of the young where you break the person's values; you break their understanding of their individuality; you bring them to a consensus with the group; they become a member of the collective.

> It's soviet education basically, might as well say it; it's soviet education. You cannot expect to have a smoothly running world socialist system if you have people out there who are going to object to what you are trying to do, so you have to brainwash them.

---

7 The Constitution was certainly not perfect, except in form; it set us up with the uniquely republican form of government that survived the Civil War, expedited the end of slavery, and (eventually) institutionalized women's right to vote.

8 I'm talking about the *form* of government, not political parties.

Also:

It's hard to make your wits kick out things which have been accepted, unquestioned, from earliest childhood—hard to suspect them.

—L. Ron Hubbard

And:

The Communists[9] in neighboring countries like to brag how they teach the peasants and the children how to read and write. But if you teach people to read and write using the sentence, "Karl Marx was a very good boy," chances are good when they learn to read and write they will think, Karl Marx was a very good boy.

—Anonymous captain, Costa Rican National Guard, 1984

PLEASE PASS THE HACKSAW

America's trek from self-governance to governmental servitude has been relatively nonviolent. Here in America, we have trusted our elected officials to represent our best interests, trusted our textbooks and teachers to educate us, and trusted our so-called free press to alert us—but hey, they attended the same schools we did, and then some. More and more Americans are overcoming their "education" via the increased ease of communication—with a computer, we now have each other, and the world, just a click away.

It may seem like the odds are stacked against us, but this is mere illusion. Great efforts have been made to suppress us, and to stifle our true power and potential in order to control us. We've been conditioned into a state of potential apathy, distraction, fear and ignorance. We've been dumbed down, brainwashed and misled. There has been an ongoing assault on our perception of reality, on our boundaries of possibility and on our collective sense of self. Most importantly though, we have been divided. The opposition of the many by the few has only been possible because we've been manipulated into fighting amongst each other, over trivial differences such as race, gender, age and religion, to divert us from the fact that we're all in the same boat—a boat which is rapidly sinking, and will continue to at an ever increasing rate until we abandon our petty differences and perceptions of each other, realize that we all have the same enemy and start working together to take back responsibility and control of our own lives.

---

9 Ah, communism: the beloved commune where human nature has evolved to the point where government is no longer needed. Dialectic materialism (conflict in motion): "First, you must be my slave, then I shall set you free! Honest!" A so-called, self-proclaimed communist is in reality a lying, deceitful, dishonest, two-faced, insincere, mendacious, double-dealing socialist—or just a plain stupid, ignorant, and/or evil person—but still an imposer of a socialist form of government. (Sorry to be so vague; I will try to be more descriptive in the future.)

Realize that the climate of paranoia and fear perpetuated by the mainstream media, which turns us against each other, paints every single person a potential criminal, pedophile or "terrorist" and makes us too scared to leave our own houses, is illusionary, and serves only one purpose—to terrify us into docility and division. A nation of terrified and divided citizens is a manipulator's wet dream. Stop giving your mind away to the mainstream media. Stop giving away your responsibility away to the government. Unfortunately, the highest levels of government, as well as most other institutions, such as banking and mainstream education—are overrun by corruption and deception, and are a large part of the reason we're in this mess in the first place.

Fortunately millions are now beginning to wake up. We need to start coming together and doing everything in our power as a collective to raise awareness on these issues. The methods and structure of manipulation can only be effective when the majority of people are kept in ignorance of them. Change that and the entire system of deception and control will collapse.

We can all do something—make leaflets, websites and YouTube videos, write articles, form or join activist organizations, arrange public documentary viewings, give lectures, or even just go out of your way to talk about these issues to friends, family and complete strangers. At first, many will not want to listen, but as things get worse and the methods of control become increasingly more blatant and desperate, it will prove harder to ignore what is happening, and denial would cease to be an option.

This system that seeks to enslave us is held together by the cooperation of ordinary people. As soon as we refuse to cooperate with our own enslavement—in a large scale, nonviolent way, it will collapse like a house of cards. It is *essential* that we come together as one and stop allowing the few to dictate the lives of the many. Individually we can be picked off, one by one, but en-masse we are extremely powerful and our manipulators know that.[10]

Albert Einstein said:

> The strength of the Constitution lies entirely in the determination of each citizen to defend it. Only if every single citizen feels duty bound to do his share in this defense are the constitutional rights secure.

The British historian Edward Gibbon chronicled the rise and fall of the first great Western civilization: in the end, more than freedom, the Athenians wanted security. They wanted a comfortable life, and they lost it all—security, comfort, and freedom. When the Athenians finally wanted not to give

---

10 Bill Hicks (1961–1994), American stand-up comedian, social critic, satirist, and musician, quoted in *Wake Up Call (YouTube:* https://www.youtube.com/watch?v=UVQvlG59sJ8).

to society but for society to give to them, when the freedom they wished for most was freedom from responsibility, then Athens ceased to be free—and was never free again.

LET US NOW TRY LIBERTY

God has given to men all that is necessary for them to accomplish their destinies. He has provided a social form as well as a human form. And these social organs of persons are so constituted that they will develop themselves harmoniously in the clean air of liberty. Away, then, with quacks and organizers! Away with their rings, chains, hooks, and pincers! Away with their artificial systems! Away with the whims of governmental administrators, their socialized projects, their centralization, their tariffs, their government schools, their bank monopolies, their regulations, their restrictions, their equalization by taxation, and their pious moralizations!

And now that the legislators and do-gooders have so futilely inflicted so many systems upon society, may society finally end where they should have begun: May they reject all systems, and try liberty; for liberty is an acknowledgment of faith in God and His Works.

—FREDERIC BASTIAT, *THE LAW* (1850)

A GOOD GOVERNMENT

Alexander Hamilton or James Madison, *Federalist Paper* #62:

A good government implies two things: first, fidelity to the object of government, which is the happiness of the people; secondly, a knowledge of the means by which that object can be best attained. Some governments are deficient in both these qualities; most governments are deficient in the first. I scruple not to assert, that in American governments too little attention has been paid to the last. The Federal Constitution avoids this error; and what merits particular notice, it provides for the last in a mode which increases the security for the first.

To trace the mischievous effects of a mutable government would fill a volume. I will hint a few only, each of which will be perceived to be a source of innumerable others.

In the first place, it forfeits the respect and confidence of other nations, and all the advantages connected with national character. An individual who is observed to be inconstant to his plans, or perhaps to carry on his affairs without any plan at all, is marked at once, by all prudent people, as a speedy victim to his own unsteadiness and folly. His more friendly neighbors may pity him, but all will decline to connect their fortunes with his; and not a few will seize the opportunity of making their fortunes out of his. One nation is to another what one individual is to another; with this melancholy distinction perhaps, that the former, with fewer of the benevolent emotions than the latter, are under fewer restraints also from taking undue advantage from the indiscretions of each other. Every nation, consequently, whose affairs betray a want of wisdom and stability, may calculate on every loss which can be sustained from the more systematic policy of their wiser neighbors. But the best instruction on this subject is unhappily conveyed to America by the example of her own situation. She finds that she is held in no respect by her friends; that she is the derision of her enemies; and that she is a prey to every nation which has an interest in speculating on her fluctuating councils and embarrassed affairs.

The internal effects of a mutable policy are still more calamitous. It poisons the blessing of liberty itself. It will be of little avail to the people, that the laws are made by men of their own choice, if the laws be so voluminous that they cannot be read, or so incoherent that they cannot be understood; if they be repealed or revised before they are promulgated, or undergo such incessant changes that no man, who knows what the law is today, can guess what it will be tomorrow. Law is defined to be a rule of action; but how can that be a rule, which is little known, and less fixed?

Another effect of public instability is the unreasonable advantage it gives to the sagacious, the enterprising, and the moneyed few over the industrious and uniformed mass of the people. Every new regulation concerning commerce or revenue, or in any way affecting the value of the different species of property, presents a new harvest to those who watch the change, and can trace its consequences; a harvest, reared not by themselves, but by the toils and cares of the great body of their fellow citizens. This is a state of things in which it may be said with some truth that laws are made for the *few*, not for the *many*.

In another point of view, great injury results from an unstable government. The want of confidence in the public councils damps every useful undertaking, the success and profit of which may depend on a continuance of existing arrangements. What prudent merchant will hazard his fortunes in any new branch of commerce when he knows not but that his plans may be rendered unlawful before they can be executed? What farmer or manufacturer will lay himself out for the encouragement given to any particular cultivation or establishment, when he can have no assurance that his preparatory labors and advances will not render him a victim to an inconstant government? In a word, no great improvement or laudable enterprise can go forward which requires the auspices of a steady system of national policy.

But the most deplorable effect of all is that diminution [lessening] of attachment and reverence which steals into the hearts of the people, towards a political system which betrays so many marks of infirmity, and disappoints so many of their flattering hopes. No government, any more than an individual, will long be respected without being truly respectable; nor be truly respectable, without possessing a certain portion of order and stability.

1

Forms of Government

REPUBLICAN FORM OF GOVERNMENT

> A government limited and governed by written laws formulated by the
> people, but written laws not easily changed, even by the majority.

Solon was an Athenian statesman, lawmaker, and poet. History shows that laws and principles formulated in Greece by Solon (638–558 BC) paved the way for future republican forms of government. Will Durant (1885–1981), a prolific American writer, historian, and philosopher, noted that Solon introduced the principle of "government by written and permanent law" instead of "government by incalculable and changeable decrees." Durant, in simple terms, stated that within a well-governed state, "the people obey the rulers and the rulers obey the laws." What a concept! Rule by written laws even kings must heed? That is so…Western!

The distinguishing feature of a republican form is the right of the people to choose their own officers for governmental administration, and pass their own laws in virtue of the legislative power reposed in representative bodies, whose legitimate acts may be said to be those of the people themselves; but while the people are thus the source of political power, their governments, national and state, have been limited by written constitutions, and they have themselves thereby set bounds to their own power, as against the sudden impulses of mere majorities.

—Duncan v. McCall 139 U.S. 449, 461 [1891][11]

George Washington (1732–1799)—American Founding Father; Continental Army Commander-in-Chief during the Revolutionary War; presided over the Constitutional Convention (1787), which drafted the United States Constitution to replace the Articles of Confederation; first president of the Republic (1789–1797):

Happiness is more effectually dispensed to mankind under a republican form of government than any other.

John Adams (1735–1826)—American Founding Father; second United States president (1797–1801); first vice-president (1789–1797); statesman; diplomat; leading advocate for American independence from Great Britain:

All good government is and must be republican. But at the same time, you can or will agree with me, that there is not in lexicography a more fraudulent word…Are we not, my friend, in danger of rendering the word republican unpopular in this country by an indiscreet, indeterminate, and equivocal use of it? Whenever I use the word republic with approbation, I mean a government in which the people have collectively, or by representation, an essential share in the sovereignty….

---

11 *Constitution of the United States of America, Revised and Annotated,* 549.

James Madison (1751–1836)—American Founding Father; "Father of the Constitution"; champion and author of the Bill of Rights; one of three authors of *The Federalist Papers*[12] (1788); fourth United States president (1809–1817):

The first question that offers itself is whether the general form and aspect of the government be strictly republican. It is evident that no other form would be reconcilable with the genius of the people of America; with the fundamental principles of the Revolution; or with that honorable determination which animates every votary of freedom to rest all our political experiments on the capacity of mankind for self-government. If the plan of the convention, therefore, be found to depart from the republican character, its advocates must abandon it as no longer defensible.

What, then, are the distinctive characters of the republican form? Were an answer to this question to be sought, not by recurring to principles but in the application of the term by political writers to the constitutions of different States, no satisfactory one would ever be found. Holland, in which no particle of the supreme authority is derived from the people, has passed almost universally under the denomination of a republic. The same title has been bestowed on Venice, where absolute power over the great body of the people is exercised in the most absolute manner by a small body of hereditary nobles. Poland, which is a mixture of aristocracy and of monarchy in their worst forms, has been dignified with the same appellation.

The government of England, which has one republican branch only, combined with a hereditary aristocracy and monarchy, has with equal impropriety been frequently placed on the list of republics. These examples, which are nearly as dissimilar to each other as to a genuine republic, show the extreme inaccuracy with which the term has been used in political disquisitions.

If we resort for a criterion to the different principles on which different forms of government are established, we may define a republic to be, or at least may bestow that name on, a government which derives all its powers directly or indirectly from the great body of the people, and is administered by persons holding their offices during pleasure for a limited period, or during good behavior. It is *essential* to such a government that it be derived from the great body of the society, not from an inconsiderable proportion or a favored class of it; otherwise a handful of tyrannical nobles, exercising their

---

12 Starting in fall 1787, using the pen name "Publius," John Jay (1745–1829), Alexander Hamilton, and James Madison wrote a series of essays (*The Federalist Papers*) explaining and promoting the Constitution and had them published in New York City newspapers. John Jay wrote five, Alexander Hamilton wrote fifty-one, James Madison wrote twenty-six, and three were joint efforts of Hamilton and Madison. This body of work is considered the most valuable source on the Constitution ever written, revealing the Founders' logic and political knowledge (philosophy and theory) used to create the Constitution. "Father of the Constitution" James Madison played a key part in guiding the Constitution through the Continental Congress; he also helped form and ensure passage of the Bill of Rights. He certainly knew the difference between republican and democratic forms of government, as well as the historical evils and perils of a democratic form of government.

oppressions by a delegation of their powers, might aspire to the rank of republicans and claim for their government the honorable title of republic.

It is *sufficient* for such a government that the persons administering it be appointed, either directly or indirectly by the people; and that they hold their appointments by either of the tenures just specified; otherwise every government in the United States as well as every other popular government that has been or can be well organized or well executed, would be degraded from the republican character.[13]

General Joseph P. Hoar (1934–)—United States Marine Corps, retired; former Commander-in-Chief, United States Central Command:

In their great wisdom, our Founding Fathers, gathered in Philadelphia to draft the new United States Constitution, gave the sole authority to declare war to the United States Congress. Our Founders understood that it was essential, to secure a representative form of republican self-government, that the power to declare war must be in the hands of Congress, and not in the Executive Branch.

James Madison, Virginia Ratifying Convention, June 20, 1788:

But I go on this great republican principle, that the people will have virtue and intelligence to select men of virtue and wisdom. Is there no virtue among us? If there be not, we are in a wretched situation. No theoretical checks—no form of government can render us secure. To suppose that any form of government will secure liberty or happiness without any virtue in the people, is a chimerical idea. If there be sufficient virtue and intelligence in the community, it will be exercised in the selection of these men. So that we do not depend on their virtue, or put confidence in our rulers, but in the people who are to choose them.

George Washington, Farewell Address 1796:

While, then, every part of our country thus feels an immediate and particular interest in Union, all the parts combined cannot fail to find in the united mass of means and efforts greater strength, greater resource, proportionally greater security from external danger, a less frequent interruption of their peace by foreign nations…Hence, likewise, they will avoid the necessity of those overgrown military establishments, which, under any form of government, are inauspicious to liberty, and which are to be regarded as particularly hostile to Republican Liberty. In this sense it is, that your Union ought to be considered as a main prop of your liberty, and that the love of the one ought to endear to you the preservation of the other.

---

13 *Federalist Paper* #39.

Thomas Jefferson (1743–1826)—American Founding Father; principal author of the Declaration of Independence (1776); third United States president (1801–1809).

In a letter to Wm. Hunter, Esq., Alexandria Mayor, dated March 11, 1796, he wrote:

> Convinced that the republican is the only form of government which is not eternally at open or secret war with the rights of mankind, my prayers and efforts shall be cordially distributed to the support of that we have so happily established. It is indeed an animating thought that, while we are securing the rights of ourselves and our posterity, we are pointing out the way to struggling nations who wish, like us, to emerge from their tyrannies also. Heaven help their struggles, and lead them, as it has done us, triumphantly through them.

DEMOCRATIC FORM OF GOVERNMENT

> A government governed by the whims and prejudices of the majority;
> ochlocracy (government by the mob; mob rule; mobocracy)

And so, it is here today, and we have surpassed mob rule (democracy) and now dwell in the house of a socialist dictatorship. The mob demanded more of what we had (mob rule) to cure what it thought we were supposed to have (democracy). Socrates keenly explained America's blurred political thinking when he said, "It's fuzzy thinking gelled into accepted truth by people living in the dark, seeing only shadowy representations of reality, and fearful of going out into the sunlight." Knowing the history and evils of democracy, the Founders created a Constitution offering protection from democracy. Here's what some, including Founders, thought of democracy:

Lucius Annaeus Seneca (5 BC–65 AD)—Roman Stoic philosopher; statesman; dramatist; humorist; tutor; and advisor to emperor Nero:

> Democracy is more cruel than wars and tyrants.

> It is proof of a bad cause when it is applauded by the mob.

Marcus Tullius Cicero (106–43 BC)—Roman philosopher; statesman; lawyer; orator; political theorist; consul; and constitutionalist:

> For out of such an ungoverned populace one is usually chosen as leader…someone bold
> and unscrupulous…who curries favor with the people by giving them other men's property.

Cicero's statement, as summarized by Dr. Will Durant: "Without checks and balances, monarchy becomes despotism, aristocracy becomes mob rule, chaos, and dictatorship."

Alexander Hamilton (1755–1804)—American Founding Father; soldier in the Revolutionary War; economist; political philosopher; one of America's first constitutional lawyers; first United States Treasury Secretary; a leader of the Federalist Party, opposed by the Democratic-Republican Party led by Thomas Jefferson and James Madison:

> It has been observed that a pure democracy if it were practicable would be the most perfect government. Experience has proved that no position is more false than this. The ancient democracies in which the people themselves deliberated never possessed one good feature of government. Their very character was tyranny; their figure deformity.

> We are a Republican Government. Real liberty is never found in despotism or in the extremes of Democracy.

Elbridge Gerry (1744–1814)—American statesman; diplomat; fifth vice-president (1813–1814), serving with President James Madison (Democratic-Republican party); known for being the namesake of "gerrymandering"; actively involved in drafting and passage of the Bill of Rights:

> The evils we experience flow from the excess of democracy. The people do not want (lack) virtue; but are the dupes of pretended patriots.

Edmund Jennings Randolph (1753–1813)—Attorney; seventh Virginia Governor; second Secretary-of-State; first United States Attorney General; joined Continental army as aide-de-camp to General George Washington; Virginia delegate at Constitutional Convention (1787). During that convention, Randolph noted the reason the delegates had met:

> To provide a cure for the evils under which the United States labored; that in tracing these evils to their origin every man had found it in the turbulence and trials of democracy.

James Madison:

> From this view of the subject it may be concluded that a pure democracy, by which I mean a society consisting of a small number of citizens, who assemble and administer the government in person, can admit of no cure for the mischiefs of faction. A common passion or interest will, in almost every case, be felt by a majority of the whole; a communication and concert result from the form of government itself; and there is nothing to check the inducements to sacrifice the weaker party or an obnoxious individual. Hence it is that such democracies have ever been spectacles of turbulence and contention; have ever been found incompatible with personal security or the rights of property; and have in general been as short in their lives as they have been violent in their deaths. Theoretic politicians, who have patronized this species of government, have erroneously supposed that by reducing mankind to a perfect equality in their

political rights, they would, at the same time, be perfectly equalized and assimilated in their possessions, their opinions, and their passions.[14]

John Adams:

Remember democracy never lasts long. It soon wastes, exhausts, and murders itself. There never was a democracy yet that did not commit suicide.[15]

And:

Democracy will soon degenerate into an anarchy, such an anarchy that every man will do what is right in his own eyes and no man's life or property or reputation or liberty will be secure, and every one of these will soon mould itself into a system of subordination of all the moral virtues and intellectual abilities, all the powers of wealth, beauty, wit and science, to the wanton pleasures, the capricious will, and the execrable cruelty of one or a very few.[16]

John Marshall (1755–1835)—Supreme Court Chief Justice (1801–1835):

Between a balanced republic and a democracy, the difference is like that between order and chaos.

H. L. Mencken (1880–1956)—American journalist, essayist, magazine editor, satirist, acerbic critic of American life and culture, American English scholar:

The most popular man under a democracy is not the most democratic man, but the most despotic man. The common folk delight in the exactions of such a man. They like him to boss them. Their natural gait is the goose step.

Under democracy one party always devotes its chief energies to trying to prove that the other party is unfit to rule, and both commonly succeed, and are right.

Benjamin Disraeli (1804–1881)—Chancellor of the Exchequer of the United Kingdom (1866–1868); prime minister; played a central role in creation of the modern UK Conservative Party:

If you establish a democracy, you must in due time reap the fruits of a democracy. You will in due season have great impatience of public burdens, combined in due season with great increase of public expenditure. You will in due season have wars entered into from passion and not from reason; and you will in due season submit to peace

---

14 From *Federalist Paper* #10.
15 John Adams, *letter to John Taylor*, 1814.
16 John Adams, *An Essay of Man's Lust for Power* (1763).

ignominiously sought and ignominiously obtained, which will diminish your authority and perhaps endanger your independence. You will in due season find your property is less valuable and your freedom less complete.

Archibald E. Stevenson (1884–1961)—American attorney, legislative researcher:

De Tocqueville once warned us that: If ever the free institutions of America are destroyed, that event will arise from the unlimited tyranny of the majority. But a majority will never be permitted to exercise such "unlimited tyranny" so long as we cling to the American ideals of republican liberty and turn a deaf ear to the siren voices now calling us to democracy. This is not a question relating to the form of government. That can always be changed by constitutional amendment. It is one affecting the underlying philosophy of our system—a philosophy which brought new dignity to the individual, more safety for minorities and greater justice in the administration of government. We are in grave danger of dissipating this splendid heritage through mistaking it for democracy.

Sir Winston Churchill (1874–1965)—British statesman; led United Kingdom during World War II; prime minister 1940–1945 and 1951–1955; won Nobel Prize for Literature, 1953:

The best argument against democracy is a five minute conversation with the average voter.

Alexis de Tocqueville (1805–1859)—French political thinker, historian:

Above this race of men stands an immense and tutelary power, which takes upon itself alone to secure their gratifications and to watch over their fate…After having thus successively taken each member of the community in its powerful grasp and fashioned him at will, the supreme power then extends its arm over the whole community…The will of man is not shattered, but softened, bent, and guided…It does not tyrannize, but it compresses, enervates, extinguishes, and stupefies a people, till each nation is reduced to nothing better than a flock of timid and industrious animals, of which the government is the shepherd.[17]

Bertrand Russell (1872–1970)—British philosopher; logician; mathematician; historian; social critic:

Envy is the basis of Democracy.

Oscar Wilde (1854–1900)—Irish playwright, novelist, essayist, and poet; one of London's most popular playwrights in the early 1890s; remembered for his epigrams, novels, and plays, as well as circumstances surrounding his imprisonment and early death:

---

17 Alexis de Tocqueville, *Democracy in America* (1840).

Democracy means simply the bludgeoning of the people by the people for the people.

Arthur Melvin Spander (1938-present)—Award-winning American sports writer:

The great thing about democracy is that it gives every voter a chance to do something stupid.

James Russell Lowell (1819–1891)—American romantic poet, critic, editor, diplomat:

Democracy gives every man the right to be his own oppressor.

Walter Williams (1936–present)—American economist, commentator, academic; John M. Olin Distinguished Professor of Economics at George Mason University; syndicated columnist; author:

Democracy and liberty are not the same. Democracy is little more than mob rule, while liberty refers to the sovereignty of the individual.

Westbrook Pegler (1894–1969)—American journalist, writer, columnist:

Did I say "Republic?" By God, yes, I said "Republic!" Long live the glorious Republic of the United States of America. Damn democracy. It is a fraudulent term used, often by ignorant persons but no less often by intellectual fakers, to describe an infamous mixture of socialism, graft, confiscation of property and denial of personal rights to individuals whose virtuous principles make them offensive.

SOCIALIST FORM OF GOVERNMENT

A government governed by the whims and prejudices of a small group of people powerful enough to take and hold office. An arrogant, dictatorial form of government, doomed for failure, as it claims ownership and control of the means of production and distribution.

Socialists wish to play God—well, they don't believe in God, so it's dictator they wish to play. Socialists despise mankind, force conformity, and defend compulsory labor for the benefit of the state. Socialists make the state yo' daddy and yo' mama! Three laws of life govern all of us: the Law of Averages, the Law of Tendency, and the Law of Capillary Attraction:

The Law of Averages, under which man in the mass is no better off than the animals, his chances of happiness and success in life but little better than one in a hundred.

The Law of Tendency, which is towards Life-GIVING. To the extent that a man allies himself with this great fundamental force of nature, to that extent he improves his chances of success.

The Law of Capillary Attraction, which gives to every nucleus the power to draw to itself those things necessary for its growth and fulfillment. It is through this third law that man is able to rise above the Law of Averages. It is by using it with the Law of Tendency that he is able to reach any height, attain any goal.

Under the Law of Averages, man in the mass is subject to alternate feast or famine, happiness or misery—just as the animals are. Nature seems carelessly profligate. She brings forth enough fish to choke the sea—then lets the many die that the few may live. She gives life with a prodigal hand—then seems entirely careless of it, letting the mass suffer or perish so long as the few survive.[18]

Socialists only believe in the Law of Averages. True, die-hard socialists firmly believe we are dumb animals; we have nothing to contribute except doing what we are trained and instructed to do. Socialists mandate equality of wealth, impose philanthropic tyranny and dictatorship, all the while ignoring facts and reason. Anything can be capital. Socialists and lying socialists (communists) talk about the evils of capitalism. But they don't hate capital—they worship capital. What they hate is anyone but themselves controlling it.

Stephen Leacock (1869–1944)—Canadian economist, humorist; noted publisher, author, lecturer:

But this socialism, this communism, would only work in Heaven where they don't need it, or in Hell where they have it already.

Thomas Sowell (1930–present)—American economist, social theorist, political philosopher, author; National Humanities Medal winner; advocate of laissez-faire economics; takes a conservative and libertarian perspective. Currently a Rose and Milton Friedman Senior Fellow on Public Policy, Hoover Institution at Stanford University:

Socialism in general has a record of failure so blatant that only an intellectual could ignore or evade it.

Sir Winston Churchill (1874–1965):

Socialism is a philosophy of failure, the creed of ignorance, and the gospel of envy, its inherent virtue is the equal sharing of misery.

Frederic Bastiat French classical liberal theorist, political economist, Freemason, and member of the French National Assembly:

---

18 Robert Collier, *The Law of the Higher Potential 1947* (Tarrytown: Book Of Gold, 1947).

Socialism, like the ancient ideas from which it springs, confuses the distinction between government and society. As a result of this, every time we object to a thing being done by government, the socialist conclude that we object to its being done at all. We disapprove of state education. Then the socialist say that we are opposed to any education. We object to a state religion. Then the socialists say that we want no religion at all. We object to a state-enforced equality. Then they say that we are against equality. And so on, and so on. It is as if the socialists were to accuse us of not wanting people to eat because we do not want the state to raise grain.[19]

Margaret Thatcher (1925–2013)—Prime minister of the United Kingdom (1979–1990); Conservative Party leader (1975–1990); called the "Iron Lady" because of her uncompromising politics and leadership style:

The problem with Socialism is that you eventually run out of other people's money.

Ludwig Mises (1881–1973)—Austrian philosopher, economist, sociologist, classical liberal; prominent figure in the Austrian School of economic thought; best known for his work on praxeology.[20] Mises immigrated to the United States in 1940; he had a significant influence on the libertarian[21] movement. Mises predicted the downfall of *all* Socialist economies, for a precise reason: without a free-market pricing system, there's no way to make proper economic decisions. For any of the following books, go to Mises.org. Please take note of his wisdom:

Socialism (1922):

Liberalism and capitalism address themselves to the cool, well-balanced mind. They proceed by strict logic, eliminating any appeal to the emotions. Socialism, on the contrary, works on the emotions, tries to violate logical considerations by rousing a sense of personal interest and to stifle the voice of reason by awakening primitive instincts (53).

The nationalization of intellectual life, which must be attempted under Socialism, must make all intellectual progress impossible (167).

No censor, no emperor, no pope, has ever possessed the power to suppress intellectual freedom which would be possessed by a socialist community (169).

---

19 From *The Law* (1850).

20 Praxeology: the study of human conduct.

21 Libertarian: 1. a person who advocates liberty, especially with regard to thought or conduct. 2. a person who maintains the doctrine of free will (distinguished from *necessitarian*). 3. advocating liberty or conforming to principles of liberty.

For it is an essential difference between capitalist and socialist production that under capitalism men provide for themselves, while under Socialism they are provided for (405).

Liberalism (1927):

There is simply no other choice than this: either to abstain from interference in the free play of the market, or to delegate the entire management of production and distribution to the government. Either capitalism or socialism: there exists no middle way (79).

Bureaucracy (1944):

Capitalism means free enterprise, sovereignty of the consumers in economic matters, and sovereignty of the voters in political matters. Socialism means full government control of every sphere of the individual's life and the unrestricted supremacy of the government in its capacity as central board of production management (10).

Omnipotent Government (1944):

The salesman thanks the customer for patronizing his shop and asks him to come again. But the socialists say: Be grateful to Hitler, render thanks to Stalin; be nice and submissive, then the great man will be kind to you later too (53).

Human Action (1949):

A man who chooses between drinking a glass of milk and a glass of a solution of potassium cyanide does not choose between two beverages; he chooses between life and death. A society that chooses between capitalism and socialism does not choose between two social systems; it chooses between social cooperation and the disintegration of society. Socialism is not an alternative to capitalism; it is an alternative to any system under which men can live as human beings (676, 680).

Every socialist is a disguised dictator (689, 693).

Planning for Freedom (1952):

Tyranny is the political corollary of socialism, as representative government is the political corollary of the market economy (218).

The Anti-Capitalistic Mentality (1956):

Capitalism and socialism are two distinct patterns of social organization. Private control of the means of production and public control are contradictory notions and not merely contrary notions. There is no such thing as a mixed economy, a system that would stand midway between capitalism and socialism (64–65).

John Maynard Keynes noted, "Capitalism is the astounding belief that the wickedest of men will do the wickedest of things for the greatest good of everyone." Really John? Anything and everything can be "capital." The poorest of people need and use "capital." In its implementation, Keynes's economic philosophy has caused more socialist misery, more heartache, and given us poor people as far as the eye can see. Any person who shares his opinion cannot be trusted to answer any question truthfully or assess any problem correctly. Keynes's economic philosophy is, "When you're in a hole, keep digging!" He is known as the father of modern economics. Yes! And what sprang from his loins was a Grand Canyon of "modern" economic pain and misery for working Americans.

What does a country with a socialist form of government look like? The old USSR, Cuba, China, and North Korea are perfect examples of overtly socialist countries. You see dictatorship, fear, slavery, pain, and misery for the peons. Exempt and living a life of luxury are those powerful enough to hold power and their fellow travelers. A note about China: come on, Communists (lying socialists)? Allegedly, Communists hate capitalism. Well, you wouldn't know it, looking at China. China is the largest capitalist country in the world—a dictatorship but still a true-blue capitalist country. Then there are the covert socialist countries: the United States and other so-called free nations. Okay, it's "socialist light"—which is like saying "slavery light." The rule of law will return. There will be some monumental obstacles. But our trek from the slavery of socialism to the freedom of our once grand republican form of government must be traveled. At the end of the road, life, liberty, and justice for all.

2

Psyched Out

PSYCHOPOLITICS

And then there is psychopolitics: the art and science of asserting and maintaining power over people's thoughts and loyalties and conquering nations via "mental healing." Have Americans been brainwashed? Have Americans been "mentally healed"? Google and read "*Brain-Washing—A Synthesis of the Russian Textbook on Psychopolitics.*" These methods have been and are being used against America and the world.[22] Think not? Please, read on.

On the next page is a picture of the cover of the copy of the book I obtained from the O'Grady files (discussed later). On the following page is a picture of the cover of a copy furnished by Wikipedia, which it alleges was "a book published by the Church of Scientology in 1955." I have little doubt it was "published" by the church—it very well could be that L. Ron Hubbard came across the information and published it, so that Americans could see the extent of their situation. Dianetics is mentioned in the exposé as a technology that must be discredited and destroyed, as it is noted as one of the methods of escape from the attempted mind control (brainwashing) being foisted upon the American people.[23]

---

22 Please see the quote by the anonymous Costa Rican National Guard captain on page xxii.

23 I'm not a Scientologist. I have taken some courses (Learning to Learn was an excellent course) at the Church of Scientology in San Francisco. I do have great respect for L. Ron Hubbard; I'm not one to shoot the messenger.

BRAIN-WASHING

A Synthesis of the Russian Textbook on Psychopolitics

●

PSYCHOPOLITICS— the art and science of asserting and maintaining dominion over the thoughts and loyalties of individuals, officers, bureaus, and masses, and the effecting of the conquest of enemy nations through "mental healing."

●

Published by

TRUTH, Inc.

P. O. Box 10188
FORT WORTH 14, TEXAS
Per copy, $1.00

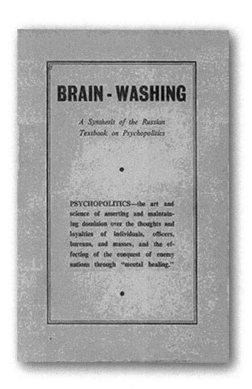

According to Wikipedia, the cover shown above is that of "*Brain-Washing* as published by the Church of Scientology in 1955." Wikipedia at one time noted:

> It purports to be a condensation of the work of Lavrentiy Beria, the Soviet secret police chief. The book states Kenneth Goff as author. Its true authorship is not clear, the three common hypotheses being: scientology founder L. Ron Hubbard, Kenneth Goff (alias Oliver Kenneth Goff), or both swiping a common U.S. agency report.

> It is also sometimes referred to as "The Communist Manual of Psycho-Political Warfare" or the "Communist Manual of Instructions of Psychopolitical Warfare." Morris Kominsky in "The Hoaxers: Plain Liars, Fancy Liars and Damned Liars" (1970) attributes *Brain-Washing* authorship to Rev. Kenneth Goff (alias Oliver Kenneth Goff) of Englewood, Colorado, an assistant of Gerald L. K. Smith. Chapter twelve of Kominsky's book is devoted to analysis of the text and the author's correspondence with others to determine the authenticity of the text or points within it, and other publications which make reference to it. Kominsky's copy of the book had an introduction by Goff [as does mine], but he doesn't give the publication date, though one of the publications referencing Goff's introduction is dated 1956. Goff claimed the book came to him from the Communist Party. Goff's claim is reasonable since Goff was a card-carrying very active Communist operative.

Wikipedia (today) does not mention Kenneth Goff's extensive 1939 Congressional testimony, some of which I have here. First, take a look at Goff's "Editorial Note" from inside the cover of my copy of *Brain-Washing*:

From May 2, 1936, to October 10, 1939, I was a dues-paying member of the Communist party, operating under my own name Kenneth Goff, and also the alias John Keats. In 1939, I voluntarily appeared before the Un-American Activities Committee in Washington, D.C., which was chaired at that time by Martin Dies, and my testimony can be found in Volume 9 of that year's Congressional Report.

During the period that I was a member of the Communist Party, I attended their school which was located at 113 E. Wells St., Milwaukee, Wisconsin, and operated under the name Eugene Debs Labor School. Here we were trained in all phases of warfare, both psychological and physical, for the destruction of the Capitalistic society and Christian civilization. In one portion of our studies we went thoroughly into the matter of psychopolitics. This was the art of capturing the mind of a nation through brainwashing and fake mental health—the subjecting of whole nations of people to the rule of the Kremlin by the capturing of their minds. We were taught that the degradation of the populace is less inhuman than their destruction by bombs, for to an animal who lives only once any life is sweeter than death. The end of a war is the control of a conquered people. If a people can be conquered in the absence of war the end of the war will have been achieved without the destructions of war.

During the past few years I have noted with horror the increase of psychopolitical warfare upon the American public. First in the brainwashing of our boys in Korea, and then in the well-financed drive of mental health propaganda by left-wing pressure groups, wherein many of our States have passed Bills which can well be used by the enemies of America to subject to torture and imprisonment those who preach the gospel of our Lord and Saviour Jesus Christ, and who oppose the menace of Communism. A clear example of this can be seen in the Lucille Miller case. In this warfare the Communist have definitely stated: "You must recruit every agency of the nation marked for slaughter into a foaming hatred of religious healing."

Another example of the warfare that is being waged can be seen in the attempt to establish a mental Siberia in Alaska, which was called for in the Alaskan Mental Health Bill. A careful study of this Bill will make you see at once that the land set aside under the allotment could not be for that small territory, and the Bill within itself establishes such authority that it could be turned into a prison camp under the guise of mental health for everyone who raises their voice against Communism and the hidden government operating in our nation.

This book was used in underground schools, and contains the address of Beria to the American students in the Lenis University prior to 1936. The text of the book in general is from the Communist Manual of Instructions of Psychopolitical Warfare and was used in America for the training of Communist cadre. The only revision in this book is the summary, which was added by the Communist after the atomic bomb came into being. In its contents you can see the diabolical plot of the enemies of Christ and America, as they seek to conquer our nation by subjecting the minds of our people to their will by various sinister means. This manual of the Communist Party should be in the hands of every loyal American, that they may be alerted to the fact that it is not always by armies and guns that a nation is conquered.

DEM COMMIE BASTARDS!

I was going to include the entire Goff testimony as an exhibit, but it's 144 pages. I've given you a few pages, enough for you to get a good idea as to the extent of the infiltration and the successful use of psychopolitics. The Congressional Investigation of Un-American Propaganda Activities in the United States was extensive; the testimony includes reams of original documents. I have volume 9 in PDF at my website. See it there or go straight to the Congressional Record to read more about this revealing and chilling investigation. Goff's testimony: "Investigation of Un-American Propaganda Activities in the United States," Volume 9, p. 5644–5681.

Reading Mr. Goff's testimony, I was amazed and certainly impressed how organized, methodical, and dedicated "dem commie bastards" were. The Communist Party came to America in 1919. By the time the investigation quoted here came about (1939), they had been active in the United States for twenty years. Like a virus, they infiltrated important organizations: the Young Democrats, the AFL and the CIO (before the merger), teachers' unions and organizations, farm-labor organizations, churches and their charitable affiliations, and virtually every trade union. The Progressive Party is mentioned and certainly rooted in the Communists' agenda; after all, the term "Progressive" is used to shield the true nature of the Progressives—they are Socialists!

INVESTIGATION OF UN-AMERICAN PROPAGANDA ACTIVITIES IN THE UNITED STATES

HEARINGS

BEFORE A

SPECIAL

COMMITTEE ON UN-AMERICAN ACTIVITIES

HOUSE OF REPRESENTATIVES

SEVENTY-SIXTH CONGRESS

FIRST SESSION

ON

H. Res. 282

TO INVESTIGATE (1) THE EXTENT, CHARACTER, AND OBJECTS OF UN-AMERICAN PROPAGANDA ACTIVITIES IN THE UNITED STATES, (2) THE DIFFUSION WITHIN THE UNITED STATES OF SUBVERSIVE AND UN-AMERICAN PROPAGANDA THAT IS INSTIGATED FROM FOREIGN COUNTRIES OR OF A DOMESTIC ORIGIN AND ATTACKS THE PRINCIPLE OF THE FORM OF GOVERNMENT AS GUARANTEED BY OUR CONSTITUTION, AND (3) ALL OTHER QUESTIONS IN RELATION THERETO THAT WOULD AID CONGRESS IN ANY NECESSARY REMEDIAL LEGISLATION

VOLUME 9

SEPTEMBER 28, 29, 30, AND OCTOBER 5, 6, 7, 9, 11, 13, AND 14, 1939
AT WASHINGTON, D. C.

Printed for the use of the Special Committee on Un-American Activities

UNITED STATES
GOVERNMENT PRINTING OFFICE
WASHINGTON : 1939

SPECIAL COMMITTEE ON UN-AMERICAN ACTIVITIES
WASHINGTON, D. C.

MARTIN DIES, Texas, *Chairman*

JOHN J. DEMPSEY, New Mexico   NOAH M. MASON, Illinois
JOE STARNES, Alabama   J. PARNELL THOMAS, New Jersey
JERRY VOORHIS, California
JOSEPH E. CASEY, Massachusetts

ROBERT E. STRIPLING, *Secretary*
RHEA WHITLEY, *Counsel*
J. B. MATTHEWS, *Director of Research*

CONTENTS

Goff ✳

Partial Testimony, Oliver Kenneth Goff (aka John Keats), Hearings before a Special Committee on Un-American Activities, House of Representatives, Volume 9 (1939):

Goff testimony, page 5644

Mr. Matthews. That is right. This continues:

The North American Congress has taken on two new people. One, a Negro social worker. A conference of leading Negro people is being called for Spanish work. The second is a person to make contacts and get into the trade-union field on the question of aid for Spain. We should wait until the fall before setting up the broader coordinating committee for general work. At present it is best, to have it work only on the relief ship. After the World Youth Congress we can throw more of our forces back of this whole

Spanish work. That is page three of the minutes. Do you identify that as the minutes of your national committee?

Mr. Goff (after examining). Yes; that is true.

Mr. Matthews. At your suggestion, Mr. Chairman, we will have the entire minutes incorporated in the record.

The Chairman. Yes; I think they are very important.

Mr. Matthews. There is one further point here on the Young Democrats.

The Chairman. Yes; give us that—how they tried to work with them.

Mr. Matthews. Mr. Goff, did you know anything first hand about the attempts of the Young Communist League to bore from within the Young Democrats?

Mr. Goff. Well, we decided, you know, that at the time that there was a feeling that the building of the Farmer-Labor Party was not necessary in America as long as the leftist groups are supporting the New Deal; therefore, that the most progressive organization to work within and bring around our way would be the Young Democrats.

The Chairman. In other words, before this you were trying to build up a national farmer-labor party.

Mr. Goff. Yes; and Farmer-Labor Juniors.

The Chairman. When did you abandon that strategy; what year, about, did you quit that?

Mr. Goff. Well, in about 1935.

The Chairman. In 1935 you decided it was no longer necessary to try to build up a Farmer-Labor Party and then decided to work through the Young Democrats; is that right?

Mr. Goff. That is right.

Mr. Matthews. In this section on the Young Democrats rally, we have the following words: It is necessary to draw conclusions from the national rally and indicate the developments that have taken place and the tasks before the Y. C. L. in the near future. In California, in the southern part of the state, the comrades play an important role in a large and growing movement of the Young Democrats which is actually a youth movement. In Washington and Oregon our comrades are influencing the movement considerably. In Michigan and western Pennsylvania our comrades with the party have begun to take up the problem of working within and in closer collaboration with the Young Democrats. Governor Murphy is displaying a growing interest in the youth problem and the Young Democrats and has indicated a desire to come forward with a progressive youth program in the coming elections. Every state organization of the league and party must begin to pay increased attention to the Young Democrats movement and to working more closely with it. The problem is that of sending more forces into the Young Democrats clubs down below and transform them into active and live organizations involving young people in the membership. In the South we have raised the question of building a movement among the white youth. It is necessary to utilize the Young Democratic clubs in the South as a menu of developing this progressive movement.

Page 5645:

The Chairman. By the way, the Young Communist League have worked completely underground in the South, have they not?

Mr. Goff. Yes: that is true. We very seldom meet any of the leaders of the Young Communist League in the South and find no members in the South, because it is an underground movement there.

The Chairman. All right; proceed.

Mr. Matthews (reading): We must now actively, with the assistance of the party, begin to put into practice this policy in the South. Throughout the South there is the possibility of entering into and transforming the young Democratic clubs into a strong basis for New Deal policies in the Democratic Party of the South.

And one final paragraph: The main job of the young Democrats is to break the stranglehold of the office seekers. In local and state organizations there should be an emphasis on the principles of the organization and thus making it impossible for office seekers to manipulate the organization for their own ends. There should be emphasis on fighting for democratic structure of the organization. In places like New York, Chicago, and Boston where there is machine policies, we should think in term of building Roosevelt Young Democratic Clubs so that they are not identified with the machine. We should also concentrate on small towns where progressives have come into power in the Democratic Party. Does that correctly describe the efforts of the Young Communists League to get into the young Democrats' movement, Mr. Goff?

Mr. Goff. Yes; it does.

Mr. Matthews. Do you have any further comments to make on that?

Mr. Goff. I think there are other ones along the same line there in regard to the young Democrats' rally.

The Chairman. What is the date of that report?

Mr. Goff. July 23, 1938. In this last campaign we set up a committee of these "first voters' clubs" and "young citizenship clubs." We got the endorsement of leading Democrats and then carried on our campaign there.

Mr. Thomas. And how active was the Young Communist League in the National Progressive Party out in Wisconsin?

Mr. Goff. In the new National Progressive Party?

Mr. Thomas. Yes.

Mr. Goff. Later on I have statements to show that they conducted that as a Fascist movement.

The Chairman. Conducted what?

Mr. Goff. That the National Progressive Party, the early Progressive Party—they worked in the youth movement there and tried to do their best to control the youth movement, and they carried on their main activity. Then later, if you will recall, the Progressive Party and the Socialist Party merged in Wisconsin, along with some other labor groups and farm groups, in setting up what they called the Farmer-Labor Progressive Federation in the State of Wisconsin, and that is where they did a great deal of their work. One of their biggest campaigns there was to have them affiliate the C.I.O. with the Farmer-Labor Progressive Federation, in the hopes that by affiliating the C.I.O. they would bring hundreds and hundreds of Communist leaders into the federation.

Page 5646

The Chairman. By the way, what is the situation with reference to the Communists and labor; what is the labor situation in Wisconsin?

Mr. Goff. Well, in Wisconsin, the Communists control considerable labor groups, especially in the C.I.O. Take, for instance, Amos Castello; he was a member of the state board of the Communist Party and one of the leading men in the C.I.O. there. Up until about a month ago he was the state president of the C.I.O.; but they withdrew in the election this time to bring about a unity; but, in withdrawing, they put in a man whom they control, this Gunnel Michaelson, who was formerly a big Communist but who never attends a Communist meeting since he has been with the C.I.O., but his wife always attends the Communist meetings, and he has worked with me in many campaigns.

Mr. Matthews. To what union did Mr. Michaelson belong?

Mr. Goff. Mr. Michaelson was formerly with the Newspaper Guild. Now he is state secretary of the C.I.O. Following was the Minutes of National Resident Board Meeting, Young Communist League, U.S.A., July 23, 1938.

Page 5649

Mr. Matthews. Coming back to the Young Communists, we have here a six-page memorandum which deals exclusively with the plans of the young Communist League to get into and work in the Young Democrats clubs, Mr. Chairman.

Mr. Mason. That is a report, is it?

Mr. Matthews. Will you identify this, Mr. Goff?

Mr. Goff (after examining). This was sent out as a memorandum of the national rally of Young Democrats. It was sent out by the national committee of the Young Communist League. It is another one of those "Please destroy after reading" documents.

Mr. Matthews. This outlines in considerable detail the manner in which the Young Communist League expected to bore within the Young Democrats.

Mr. Mason. What is the date of that?

Mr. Matthews. This is July 1938. I will take the time to read only one statement on the matter of the tactics: A warning is necessary against a sectarian and narrow approach to this work. Known Communists should not be asked to join Young Democratic clubs.

Mr. Goff, was that a practice followed in getting Young Communist League members into Young Democratic clubs?

Mr. Goff. Yes.

Mr. Matthews. To get only those who were not known to be such?

Mr. Goff. That is true. It would be dangerous to try to put somebody else in, because we could not work successfully and would expose those who were not known in the organization.

Mr. Matthews. Is it your desire that this entire memorandum be incorporated in the record, Mr. Chairman?

The Chairman. Yes; I think the entire memorandum should go in.

The memorandum reads as follows:

Please destroy after reading.

Memorandum on National Rally of Young Democrats, July 14-15-16, 1938, Seattle

1. Why the rally was held in Seattle: Since the organization of the Young Democrats of America, the western state organizations have felt themselves neglected in the national set-up. Conventions, big doings, and officers were monopolized by the East and Midwest. The Washington delegation went to the third biennial convention held last year at Indianapolis, with the idea of bringing the next convention to Seattle. Although they made a strong bid for it, it was thrown to Pittsburgh and the national rally was given to Seattle as a solace concession.

2. Object and character of the rally: According to Pitt Tyson Manor, national president, Gerald Shucklin (former Washington State chairman), and the arrangements committee, the gathering was to be a big pre-election pep rally to enthuse the Young Democrats for active participation in the 1938 congressional campaign, and to boost the growth of the organization. As a rally, and not a convention, its body was to be composed of any Young Democrats from anywhere in the U. S. who could manage to get to Seattle, pay the initiation fee and expenses, together with as much of the local population that could be interested in the rally. In many cases, state and local organizations assisted in financing the groups coming. In such conditions it was but natural that most of the representation would be from the Western States. Utah had 60; California, 18; Oregon, 12; Idaho, about 8; Washington, about 75—most other States from the East and Midwest that had people, had groups of from 1 or 2 up to about 8. Furthermore, as it was a rally, no business was to be transacted on the floor. There took place

a national committee meeting, a women's breakfast meeting, state chairmen's advisory committee, regional directors, and public relations committee meetings. Most of the "delegates" not taking part in those meetings, either attended the rally sessions or went sightseeing, party hunting, or just having a good time.

3. Progressive objectives and results: The objective of the rally as such, that is its pre-election pep character, was the objective of the progressives as well. The latter, of course, were mainly concerned with a strong follow-up on the last fireside chat of President Roosevelt, in his call for a "liberal congress" with endorsement of progressive legislation, and in building the movement. From the roster of speakers as well as the general national set-up at the moment, there was good reason to believe that this particular note would be strongly sounded at the rally. This proved correct, especially insofar as the main speech delivered by [James Aloysius] Farley was concerned. The rally can definitely be classified as a strong New Deal rally, one that called for a New Deal Congress and stimulated the progressives in their struggle against the Tories in the Democratic Party.

Some excerpts from Farley's speech would indicate this:

We are at the beginning of a campaign which will determine whether we shall go on with Roosevelt, or go back to Hooverism. After six years of unprecedented achievement for popular government and the people's economic and social rights, that has attracted the admiration of the entire world, we are going to determine this fall whether that is what we want, or whether we want reaction.

No one in America is so deeply concerned in the reforms made and proposed by the Roosevelt administration for the preservation of democracy, liberty, and human rights: for today we are necessarily building for tomorrow; and tomorrow belongs to you.

End of Memo—Communist Memorandum on National Rally of Young Democrats, July 14–16, 1938, Seattle

DON'T WASTE THAT CRISIS!

The psychological and physical methods developed and employed over the decades have helped undermine our unique American way of life, including the rule of law, capitalism, freedom of religion, liberty, and the right of the individual to own property. I know what you're thinking. You're thinking that nothing like this could work on you. Please, you have got to set your ego aside here. And, by the way, I do believe that at one time most of you believed in Santa Claus and the Tooth Fairy. You were lied too. Misled. I understand. It happens to the best of us.

People should really think before they think. Don't you think? Few things in life are absolute, there are certainly exceptions: Good people not thinking but caught up in the magma of the hype, the "climate of opinion." As Dumont says in *The Master Mind*,[24] "They are simply allowing the stream of memory to flow through their field of consciousness, while the Ego stands on the banks and idly watches the passing waters of memory flow by. They call this 'thinking,' while in reality there is no process of thought under way."

In the middle of the subprime mortgage crisis (November 2008), President Obama's chief of staff, Rahm Emanuel, was videoed before a *Wall Street Journal* conference of top corporate executives, saying, "You never want a serious crisis to go to waste. And what I mean by that is it's an opportunity to do things you think you could not do before."[25] He meant that the economic crisis of the day should be used to implement programs people would not otherwise consider. This is a perfect example of the three-step Hegelian method of implementing change: thesis, antithesis, and synthesis. The first step (thesis): create a problem, or use an existing problem. Second step (antithesis): generate opposition to the problem. Third step (synthesis): offer a solution that would never have been considered or accepted without the conditioning of the first two steps.

I was filling my truck at the Crockett, California gas station back when we had first gone into Iraq. A young man in his twenties, monitoring the self-service fill-ups and making change, was wearing an Air Force fatigue shirt. Since I'd spent four years wearing one just like it, I asked, "Were you in the Air Force?"

"No," he responded quickly, with a sourpuss look on his face. "It belongs to a friend of mine. I wouldn't join the military and fight for oil!"

"But," I responded, "you're workin' in a gas station." From the look on his face, I could tell a small light had come on, but it soon dimmed as he turned and walked away.

A major goal of psychopolitics is to destroy existing loyalties; that's been working pretty well, given our system of public "education" and the impact of the "screwed" stage of our progression from freedom to slavery. President Obama made great strides in his effort to help destroy representative government. He spoke of our elected representatives (Congress) as if it were a dirty word. As dictator, President Obama bypassed Congress throughout his reign, and made his socialist agenda the law of the land via executive orders. Sadly, Congress sat and let it happen.

I know many of you have had the feeling that things seem to be twisted around, a deep-down feeling something is wrong, but you just can't quite get a handle on it. I know because that's the way I felt until after my Rosicrucian studies and my tutoring under Mrs. O'Grady and Mrs. Wilt. I'll tell you more about Mrs. O'Grady and Mrs. Wilt in a bit.

---

24   Theron Q. Dumont was one of the aliases of the American writer William Walker Atkinson (1862–1932), who was editor of the popular magazine *New Thought* from 1901 to 1905 and of the journal *Advanced Thought* from 1916 to 1919. He authored dozens of mind-power books under numerous pseudonyms, including Yogi Ramacharaka, Theron Q. Dumont, and some that are likely still unknown today. See *www.psitek.net/pages/PsiTek-the-master-mindContents.html*.

25   *www.youtube.com/watch?v=1yeA_kHHLow*.

Mainstream educators, media, politicians—they all have a lot invested in their beliefs. They are "highly educated," but they are not as free thinking as we need them to be. They are fast learners, though. Still, some may never admit they have been duped (too much ego); they will defend their misunderstandings to the bitter end. We certainly need mainstream educators, media and politicians on our side, but it is common sense solutions as outlined herein that need to be implemented. And, we need to remember the advice Sir Winston Churchill gave to the boys at Harrow in 1941:

> Never give in, never give in, never, never, never, never, in nothing, great or small, large
> or petty; never give in except to convictions of honor and good sense.

3

Screwed

Screw: Pressure, coercion; extortionist. Slang: jailer.

—ROGET'S COLLEGE THESAURUS.

To put on the screw, to bring pressure to bear on a person, often, for the purpose of getting money. To put under the screw, to influence by strong pressure; to coerce. To oppress by exactions.

—WEBSTER'S ENCYCLOPEDIC DICTIONARY (1942)

ONCE UPON A TIME...THE SCREWING BEGAN

The law can be anything.

Daniel Webster, James Otis and Sir Edward Coke all pointed out that the mere fact of enactment does not and cannot raise statutes to the standing of Law. Not everything which may pass under the form of statutory enactment can be considered the Law of the Land.

—16TH AMERICAN JURISPRUDENCE, 2ND ED., SEC. 547

The beginning of the end of our constitutional, republican form of government was just about 1913. My father was six years old. The Federal Reserve Act, along with the Sixteenth and Seventeenth Amendments to the United States Constitution, put us under the screw, but good.

It was under the Wilson[26] command that huge parts of Marxian programs began. Presidents always get more credit and blame than they deserve. President Wilson was certainly a leader of the progressive movement. He had the right Congress. And, we owe that 1913 Congress for the push down the slide from republican into the muck of a democratic form of government. It was quite a push: the progressive income tax,[27] direct election of senators,[28] and the Federal Reserve Act. So it came to pass that what the Romans would have called our "mixed constitution" was aggressively pushed out of American politics. A little brainwashing always helps. Was our slide into mob rule a conspiracy? You can bet your buttocks, yes! A conspiracy does not have to be covert. These three acts together were in-your-face, out-and-out, bold "progressive" moves to help make our republic history. And, it is an ongoing conspiracy.

SIXTEENTH AMENDMENT

The Congress shall have the power to lay and collect taxes on Incomes, from whatever source derived, without apportionment among the several States, and without regard to any census or enumeration.

INCOME TAX

The Revenue Act of 1934 (680 Stat 277, 48) raised individual income tax rates marginally on higher incomes, but left the top individual income tax rate at 63 percent. Imagine working your buttocks to the bone and giving the government 63 percent. It was signed into law by President Roosevelt. In 1935–1936, the median family income was $1,160.

The only serious argument I remember my parents having concerned income taxes. It was April 1956; I was nine years old. My mother worked full time at a poultry-processing plant in Dinuba, California. My father worked there part time during the winter months, but his primary job was on the ranch where we lived. Our great-grandmother Mahallie lived with our family and watched us

---

26 Thomas Woodrow Wilson (1856–1924)—28th president of the United States (1913–1921).

27 Sixteenth Amendment to the United States Constitution.

28 Seventeenth Amendment to the United States Constitution.

children while our parents worked. My father was fit to be tied because my mother demanded that he include the wages he earned working on the ranch as income on their joint tax return. He did.

I love old, fat books (they remind me of...me). One of my favorites is the *Constitution of the United States of America, Revised and Annotated* (1938):

Page 284–287:

Article I, Sec. 9 (Powers denied to Congress), Cl. 4 (Capitation and direct taxes):
No capitation, or other direct, Tax shall be laid, unless in Proportion to the Census of Enumeration herein before directed to be taken.

In General.
It was with the idea that the power of direct taxation should be exercised only in cases of "absolute necessity" that the framers of the Constitution inserted this clause limiting the taxing power of Congress.[29]

The original draft of the instrument did not contain the words "or other direct tax"; this phrase was inserted to avoid any possible misconstruction which would narrow the intention.[30]

In Knowlton v. Moore,[31] the Court said that the requirement that direct taxes should be apportioned among the several States "contemplated the protection of the States, to prevent their being called upon to contribute more than was deemed their due share of the burden."

Definition.
A capitation tax is a direct tax, but the term "direct taxes" comprehends also taxes on lands and taxes on personal property by general valuation. A tax upon property holders in respect of their estates, real or personal, or of the rents therefrom which cannot be avoided, is a direct tax, while a tax paid primarily by persons who can shift the burden upon others, or who are not under compulsion, is an indirect tax.[32]

Distinction Between Direct Taxes and Indirect Taxes or Excises.
A tax levied on property because of its ownership is direct; one levied on property because of its use is an excise duty or impost.[33] To levy a tax by reason of ownership of property is the same as taxing the property itself.[34]

---

29 Pollock v. Farmers' Loan & Trust Co., 157 U.S. 429, 574 [1895].
30 Documentary Hist. Const., vol. III, 578, 747.
31 178 U.S. 41, 89 [1900].
32 Pollock v. Farmers Loan & Trust Co., 157 U.S. 429, 558 [1895].
33 Brushaber c. Union P.R. Co., 240 U.S. 1, 14 [1916].
34 Dawson v. Kentucky Distilleries & Warehouse Co., 255 U.S. 288, 294 [1921].

What Constitutes a Direct Tax.

It was held in Pollock v. Farmers Loan & Trust Co.,[35] that a tax on the income from either real estate or personal property was not an indirect tax but was a direct tax subject to the requirement of apportionment. Prior to the Pollock decision the Supreme Court had held the following taxes levied by Congress to be indirect and therefore not required to be apportioned: On carriages kept for pleasure;[36] on receipts of insurance companies;[37] on the circulating notes of state banks;[38] on succession to real estate;[39] on all gains and profits, whether divided or undivided, derived from manufacturing companies;[40] on all income.[41]

A tax on the net income of a corporation is not a tax on the franchise or property of the corporation, but a tax upon doing business in the corporate capacity.[42] A tax on the conduct of business in a corporate capacity, measured by net income, is not a direct tax.[43] The inclusion for tax purposes of the rental value of property where taxpayer made deductions for taxes, expenses and depreciation thereon, does not constitute a direct tax on the rental value of such property.[44]

The Sixteenth Amendment qualifies this clause,[45] but "income" as used in that amendment does not include common stock dividends declared in favor of common stockholders, and any taxation of them must be in accordance with this clause and clause 3 of section 2 of article I.[46]

Page 1025–26:

Income Tax.

Amendment 16

The Congress shall have the power to lay and collect taxes on Incomes, from whatever source derived, without apportionment among the several States, and without regard to any census or enumeration.

---

35 157 U.S. 429 [1895]; 158 U.S. 601 [1895].

36 Hylton v. United States, 3 Dall171 [1796].

37 Pacific Ins. Co. v. Soule, 7 Wall. 433 [1869].

38 Veazie Bank v. Fenno, 8 Wall. 533 [1869].

39 Scholey v. Rew, 23 Wall. 331 [1875].

40 Brainard c, Hubbard, 12 Wall. 1 [1871].

41 Springer v. United States, 102 U.S. 586 [1881].

42 Flint v. Stone Tracy Co., 220 U.S. 107 [1911]. See also Doyle v. Mitchell Bros. Co., 247 U.S. 179 [1918].

43 Stratton's Independence v. Howpert, 231 U.S. 399 [1914].

44 Helvering v. Indep. Life Ins Co., 292 U.S. 371 [1934].

45 United States Constitution, Article I, Sec. 9, Cl. 4.

46 Eisner v. Macomber, 252 U.S. 189 [1920]; Koshland v. Helvering, 298 U.S. 441 [1936]; Helvering v. Gowran, 302 U.S. 238 [1937].

Purpose of Amendment

This Amendment permits Congress to levy income taxes without the necessity of apportionment among the States according to population. Prior to its adoption, Congress had power to levy income taxes without apportionment, provided they were indirect. But, in Pollock v. Farmer's Loan & T. Co.[47] the Supreme Court had held that a tax on income from property was direct, and subject to apportionment under Article I, section 2, clause 4. Therefore, the purpose of this amendment (adopted in 1913) is to remove the necessity of apportioning such income taxes as are direct. The amendment does not extend the power of Congress to tax income which, prior to 1913, it had no power to tax.[48] The amendment, like other laws authorizing or imposing taxes, is not to be extended beyond the meaning clearly indicated by its words.[49]

Meaning of "Income."

Income may be defined as the gain derived from capital, from labor, or from both combined, provided it be understood to include profit gained through the sale or conversion of capital assets.[50]

Substance and not form should control in the application of the Sixteenth Amendment and the income tax laws enacted under it.[51] A common stock dividend declared in favor of common stockholders is not taxable income. It is a mere exchange of form and not the realization of income. Such a dividend is capital, and a statute attempting to treat it as income for taxation is unconstitutional.[52]

So, what is the difference between "substance" and "form"?

Webster's Encyclopedic Dictionary (1942) offers the following definitions:

Substance. That of which a thing consists or is made up; matter; material; a distinct portion of matter; a body; that which is real; that which constitutes a thing really a thing.

Form. The shape or external appearance of a body, as distinguished from its material.

Black's Law Dictionary (5th ed.) offers these definitions:

---

47 157 U.S. 429 [1895]; 158 U. S. 601 [1895].

48 Brushaber v. Union P. R. Co., 240 U. S. 1 [1916]; Stanton v. Battle Min. Co., 240 U. S. 103 [1916]; Tyee Realty Co. v. Anderson, 240 U. S. 115 [1916]; Peck (Wm. E.) & Co. v. Lowe, 247 U. S. 165 [1918]; Evans v. Gore, 253 U. S. 245 [1920]; Edwards v. Cuba R. Co., 268 U. S. 628 [1925]; Bowers v. Kerbaugh-Empire Co., 271 U. S. 170 [1926].

49 Edwards v. Cuba R. Co., 268 U. S. 628 [1925].

50 Eisner v. Macomber, 252 U. S. 189 [1920]; Bowers v. Kerbaugh-Empire Co., 271 U. S. 170 [1926].

51 Eisner v. Macomber, 252 U. S. 189 [1920]; United States v. Phellis, 257 U. S. 156 [1921]; Burk-Waggoner Oil Assoc. V. Hopkins, 269 U. S. 110 [1925]; Bowers v. Kerbaugh-Empire Co., 271 U. S. 170 [1926].

52 Eisner v. Macomber, 252 U.S. 189 [1920]. See also Towne v. Eisner, 245 U.S. 418 (1918); Koshland v. Helvering, 298 U.S. 441 [1936]; Helvering v. Gowran, 302 U.S. 238 [1937].

Substance. Essence; the material or essential part of a thing, as distinguished from "form." That which is essential.

Form. Antithesis of "substance."

From Gary Allen's *None Dare Call It Conspiracy*, (1972):

Two months prior to the passage of the Federal Reserve Act, the conspirators had created the mechanism to collect the funds to pay the interest on the national debt. That mechanism was the progressive income tax, the second plank of Karl Marx' *Communist Manifesto* which contained ten planks for SOCIALIZING a country.

...Actually, very few of the proponents of the graduated income tax realized they were playing into the hands of those they were seeking to control. As Ferdinand Lundberg notes in *The Rich and the Super-Rich*:

"What it [the income tax] became, finally, was a siphon gradually inserted into the pocketbooks of the general public. Imposed to popular huzzas as a class tax, the income tax was gradually turned into a mass tax in a jiujitsu turnaround...."

On October 3, 1913, the Underwood Tariff Bill passed the Senate.[53] It lowered tariffs and imposed a graduated tax on income. It had been eighteen years since the federal government was stopped from collecting taxes on income from property.[54] That Court decision took the guts out of Congress's Income Tax Act of 1894. Democrats threw a tizzy: "A tax on income is a tax on wealth! Wealth should pay its fair share!" So progressive Democrats really celebrated as passage of the Sixteenth Amendment gave Congress the power to impose a direct tax—that is, a tax on income WITHOUT apportionment. Income (gain/profit), or "wealth," as Democrats disgustingly referred to it, would finally pay its "fair share."

Congress can lawfully lay and collect taxes on incomes. The problem? Government, via the Internal Revenue Service (IRS), continues to use its expanded and illegal definition of income, except as it applies to stock dividends. The Eisner court blasted and outlawed government's interruption of income in 1920. To clearly explain to government why a stock dividend is not income derived from property but evidence of a measure of the growth of capital, the court succinctly clarified the meaning of income. The Court did such a good job that the decision has been a neglected signpost for courts ever since. The Court did not define or redefine income; it merely looked to dictionaries of the day and previous court decisions for a clarification of the term, and then, so government could not expand it, said, "Nothing else answers the description." However, government left the courtroom with the erroneous definition of income it came in with, except as applied to stock dividends. In the American Free Labor Act, you will find more of the succinct definition of income the Eisner Court gave us.

---

53 Sixty-Third Congress, Session 1, chapter 16.
54 Pollock v. Farmers' Loan & T. Co., 157 U.S. 429; 158 U.S. 601 (1895).

Government's definition of income remains erroneously expanded to include labor and other changes in the form of capital. Reading through the Congressional Record leading up to passage of the Sixteenth Amendment, I could see the glee when Democrats got their way in 1913 and taxes on income began in earnest. It doesn't matter if most of Congress thought wages were income. Just because a person thinks apple trees are apples don't make it so. But the Democrats were after "wealth," and thus, the $3,000 ($4,000, if married filing jointly) exemption. The average annual wage in 1913 was less than $500. Notwithstanding that wages are labor (apple trees), not income (apples), the monumental inflation created by the Federal Reserve banking system put middle-class wage earners into the taxing brackets in a little over thirty years (See USInflationCalculator.com). Had Congress kept the personal exemption adjusted for inflation, that $3,000 of 1913 would be $70,626.97 today, with the $4,000 exemption for married couples coming in at $94,169.29. They're talking gain and profit here, not labor (wages). That's a fair amount of gain and profit before any tax would be due. The tax on income (should it continue to exist) should not be a graduated progressive tax, but a uniform, fair tax for all.

Yes, some statutes and court cases seem to dictate that wages, salaries, and compensation for services are taxable income (profit). The government is thereby saying a person's labor has no intrinsic value. In other words, the government is taxing fruit trees as fruit. There were once statutes and court cases dictating that slavery was legal. Anything can be made legal. But laws will never be able to make fruit trees fruit. When a slave petitioned the United States Supreme Court for his freedom, the Court ruled against him and ruled that the Bill of Rights didn't apply to African Americans. If it did, the majority ruling argued, then African Americans would be permitted "the full liberty of speech in public and in private," "to hold public meetings upon political affairs," and "to keep and carry arms wherever they went." In 1856, both the justices in the majority and the white aristocracy they represented found this idea too frightful to contemplate.[55]

Following is the American Free Labor Act, an Act I wrote to clarify that trees are not fruit. The Act frees our labor from the illegal taxation we have long endured.

---

55 Dred Scott v. Sandford, 1856.

AMERICAN FREE LABOR ACT

Be it enacted by the Senate and House of Representatives of the United States of America in Congress assembled.

Definitions:

WAGES. A compensation given to a hired person for his or her services. Compensation of employees based on time worked or output of production.

SALARY. A reward or recompense for services performed. In a more limited sense, fixed periodical compensation paid for services rendered. A stated compensation paid periodically as by the year, month, or other fixed period, in contrast to wages which are normally based on an hourly rate.

COMPENSATION. Indemnification; payment of damages; making amends; making whole; giving an equivalent or substitute of equal value. That which is necessary to restore an injured party to his former position. Remuneration for services rendered, whether in salary, fees, or commissions.

FOR. In behalf of, in place of, in lieu of, instead of, representing, as being which, or equivalent to which…. —Medler v. Henry, 44 N.M. 63, 97 P.2d 661, 662.
In consideration for; as an equivalent for; in exchange for; in place of; as where property is agreed to be given "for" other property or "for" services.

SERVICE. "Service" as used in contracts: Duty or labor to be rendered by one person to another, the former being bound to submit his will to the direction and control of the latter. The act of serving the labor performed or the duties required.

LIVELIHOOD. Means of support or subsistence.

MEANS. That through which, or by the help of which, an end is attained.

SUPPORT. That which furnishes a livelihood; a source or means of living; subsistence, sustenance, or living.

SUBSISTENCE. Support. Means of support, provisions, or that which procures provisions or livelihood. See Necessaries.

NECESSARIES. An article which a party actually needs. Things indispensable, or things proper and useful, for the sustenance of human life. Necessaries consist of food, drink, clothing, medical attention, and a suitable place of residence, and they are regarded as necessaries in the absolute sense of the word.

LABOR. Work; toil; service; mental or physical exertion. Term normally refers to work for wages as opposed to work for profits, though the word is sometimes construed to mean service rendered or part played in production of wealth.

GAIN. Profits; winnings; increment of value. Difference between cost and sale price.

PROFIT. Most commonly, the gross proceeds of a business transaction less the cost of the transaction (i.e., net proceeds). Excess of revenues over expenses for a transaction; sometimes used synonymously with net income for a period. Gain realized from business or investment over and above expenditures.

SLAVERY. The condition of a slave; that civil relation in which one man has absolute power over the life, fortune, and liberty of another.[56]

INCOME. "Income may be defined as the gain derived from capital, from labor, or from both combined, provided it be understood to include profit gained through the sale or conversion of capital assets."

—EISNER V. MACOMBER, 252 U.S. 189 (1920); BOWERS V. KERBAUGH-EMPIRE CO., 271 U.S. 170 (1926)

WHEREAS, according to truth and substance, without regard to form:

(1) INCOME IS GAIN OR PROFIT.
(2) LABOR FOR WAGES[57] IS A VALUE-FOR-VALUE EXCHANGE.
(3) WAGES ARE LABOR, NOT INCOME.

WHEREAS, the Sixteenth Amendment of the United States Constitution states:

The Congress shall have power to lay and collect taxes on incomes, from whatever source derived, without apportionment among the several states, and without regard to any census or enumeration.

WHEREAS, concerning the meaning of "income," as used in the Sixteenth Amendment, the Eisner Court[58] stated:

In order, therefore, that the clauses cited from Article 1 of the Constitution may have proper effect, save only as modified by the Amendment, and that the latter also may have proper effect, it becomes essential to distinguish between what is and what is

---

56 Source for above definitions: *Black's Law Dictionary*, 5th ed. (Saint Paul, Minn.: West Publishing Company, 1979).

57 For brevity, as used herein, *wages* means "wages, salaries, and/or compensation for services."

58 Eisner v. Macomber, 252 U. S. 189 [1920].

not "income," as the term is there used; and to apply the distinction, as cases arise, according to truth and substance, without regard to form. Congress cannot by any definition it may adopt conclude the matter, since it cannot by legislation alter the Constitution, from which alone it derives its power to legislate, and within whose limitations alone that power can be lawfully exercised.

The fundamental relation of "capital" to "income" has been much discussed by economists, the former being likened to the tree or the land, the latter to the fruit or the crop. After examining dictionaries in common use (*Bouv. L. ED.*; *Standard Dict.*; *Webster's International Dict.*; *Century Dict.*) we find little to add to the succinct definition adopted in two cases arising under the Corporation Tax Act of 1909 (Stratton's Independence v. Howbert, 231 U.S. 399, 415; Doyle v. Mitchell Bros. Co., 247 U.S. 179, 185)—"Income" may be defined as the gain derived from capital, from labor, or both combined, provided it be understood to include profit gained through a sale or conversion of capital assets...Brief as it is, it indicates the characteristic and distinguishing attribute essential for a correct solution of the present controversy.

WHEREAS, concerning government's interruption of "income," the Eisner Court stated:

The Government, although basing its argument upon the definition as quoted, placed chief emphasis upon the word "gain," which was extended to include a variety of meanings; while the significance of the next three words was either overlooked or misconceived. "DERIVED FROM CAPITAL"; "THE GAIN DERIVED FROM CAPITAL," etc. Here we have the essential matter; not a gain accruing to capital, not a growth or increment of value in the investment; but a gain, a profit, something of exchangeable value proceeding from the property, severed from the capital however invested or employed, and coming in, being "derived," that is, received or drawn by the recipient (the taxpayer) for his separate use, benefit and disposal; that is income derived from property. Nothing else answers the description.

WHEREAS, the first income-tax legislation after passage of the Sixteenth Amendment (Underwood Tariff Bill) states at Chapter 16, Section II (B): "That, subject only to such exemptions and deductions as are hereinafter allowed, the net income of a taxable person shall include gains, profits, and INCOME DERIVED FROM [emphasis added] salaries, wages, compensation for personal service" INCOME (GAIN) DERIVED FROM salaries, wages, compensation for services, NOT salaries, wages, compensation for services. The disparity is the difference between the crop and the land, the fruit and the tree. It is the difference between freedom and slavery.

WHEREAS, "The property which every man has in his own labor, as it is the original foundation of all other property, it is the most sacred and inviolable. The patrimony of the poor man lies in the strength and dexterity of his own hands, and to hinder his employing this strength and dexterity in what manner he thinks proper, without injury to his neighbor, is a plain violation of this most sacred property."

—Butchers Union v. Crescent City Co., 111 U.S. 764 (1883)

Whereas, "this most sacred property" has been violated. Wages are not a "gain derived from capital, from labor, or both combined," any more than the land is the crop or the tree is the fruit. Wages are "something of exchangeable value," but not "proceeding from the property" or "severed from the capital." Wages *are* the property, *the* capital, but more specifically, **Wages *are* Labor**. No gain is realized in the exchange of labor for wages, there is merely a change in form. **Wages are labor**, *the* property and capital of the laborer, transformed into a medium-of-exchange, something of value, for which labor of equal value was given.

Whereas, American wage-earners have been misled and coerced into "voluntarily" filing tax returns and thereon erroneously claim their wages as taxable income, with mandatory payments deducted from their paychecks. American wage-earners have therefore long endured the pains and expense of an infamous, complicated, "voluntary" process in order to figure and pay a tax they do not owe.

Whereas, according to substance, without regard to form, **wages *are* labor**, *the* livelihood, *the* means of support, *the* subsistence, *and the* necessaries for life. Every individual has an inalienable right to exchange labor *for* life, to work *for* a living, to use his or her labor to provide *for* self and family the necessities and pleasures of life and liberty.

Whereas, government's denial and suppression of each individual's inalienable right to freely exchange labor for life is tantamount to slavery.

Therefore, without regard to form, wages, salaries, and compensation for services are not income, and cannot be taxed as income by *any* government body; all such taxation and collection of said tax will cease immediately.

End of Act

UNITED STATES CONSTITUTION
AMENDMENT SEVENTEEN

United States Constitution, Article I, Section 3: The Senate of the United States shall be composed of two Senators from each State, chosen by the Legislature thereof, for six Years, and each Senator shall have one Vote.

United States Constitution, Amendment Seventeen: The Senate of the United States shall be composed of two Senators from each state, elected by the people thereof, for six Years, and each Senator shall have one Vote.

Popular election of senators—what's wrong with that? Why did the Founders have it otherwise? Show of hands. How many of you know why the Founders set it up so that the state legislatures chose the senators and not the people directly? In Philadelphia, July 16, 1787, the Founders reached the "Great Compromise," the result of a battle between larger- and smaller-population states over apportionment of seats; they agreed on a two-house national legislature, but the fight was over how each chamber would be established. This was the most argued-over issue at the Constitutional Convention and nearly caused its crumbling. The "nationalist" principle of population-based representation was favored by the larger states; smaller states favored the "federal" principle, thereby ensuring *representation by states.*[59] The smaller states rightfully feared that the larger states would rule the roost if representation in the Senate was based on population. When the dust settled, the framers agreed that House seats would be apportioned among the states based on population, with representatives directly elected by the people. The Senate would be composed of two senators per state, regardless of size or population, elected by the state legislature, not directly by the people. It is also well-argued that the elected state legislators are better equipped to choose who would best serve the state as United States Senators over the public.

James Madison, *Federalist Paper* #39:

The House of Representatives will derive its powers from the people of America…. The Senate, on the other hand, will derive its powers from the States, as political and co-equal societies; and these will be represented on the principle of equality in the Senate.

Alexander Hamilton or James Madison, *Federalist Paper* #62:

It is equally unnecessary to dilate [to describe or develop at length] on the appointment of senators by the state legislatures. Among the various modes which might have been

---

59 "Representation by states" means that the people shall be represented as one unit (a State), thereby ensuring smaller states had voting power equal to that of the larger states in the Senate.

devised for constituting this branch of the government, that which has been proposed by the convention is probably the most congenial with the public opinion....

In this spirit it may be remarked that the equal vote allowed to each state is at once a constitutional recognition of the portion of sovereignty remaining in the individual States and an instrument for preserving that residuary sovereignty....

Another advantage accruing from this ingredient in the constitution of the Senate is the additional impediment it must prove against improper acts of legislation. No law or resolution can now be passed without the concurrence, first, of a majority of the people, and then of a majority of the States....

Not so after passage of the Seventeenth Amendment. The "...constitutional recognition of the portion of sovereignty remaining in the individual States and an instrument for preserving that residuary sovereignty" was history. The change undermined the sovereignty of the states. Senators therefore do not represent the State. Senators represent the best interest of the small group of people that elects them.

Alexander Hamilton or James Madison, *Federalist Paper* #63:

In answer to all these arguments, suggested by reason, illustrated by examples, and enforced by our own experience, the jealous adversary of the Constitution will probably content himself with repeating, that a senate appointed not immediately by the people, and for the term of six years, must gradually acquire a dangerous pre-eminence in the government, and finally transform it into a tyrannical aristocracy.

To this general answer, the general reply ought to be sufficient, that liberty may be endangered by the abuses of liberty as well as by the abuses of power; that there are numerous instances of the former as well as of the latter; and that the former, rather than the latter, are apparently most to be apprehended by the United States. But a more particular reply may be given.

Before such a revolution can be effected, the Senate, it is to be observed, must in the first place corrupt itself; must next corrupt the state legislatures; must then corrupt the House of Representatives; and must finally corrupt the people at large.

No need for all that corrupting. Not when you have a socialist dictatorship in tow. The Seventeenth Amendment helped grease the skids used to slide us from a republican form of government into the dregs of democracy, and beyond. It has to go. To get rid of an amendment, you create another amendment that repeals it. For example, the Twenty-First Amendment repealed the Eighteenth Amendment.

Please take note:

United States Constitution, Article V:

> The Congress, whenever two thirds of both Houses shall deem it necessary, shall propose Amendments to this Constitution, or, on the Application of the Legislatures of two thirds of the several States, shall call a Convention for proposing Amendments, which, in either Case, shall be valid to all Intents and Purposes, as Part of this Constitution, when ratified by the Legislatures of three fourths of the several States, or by Conventions in three fourths thereof, as the one or the other Mode of Ratification may be proposed by the Congress.

I gleaned the following information from the Federal Register:

The Constitutional Amendment Process

The authority to amend the Constitution of the United States is derived from Article V of the Constitution. As noted, an amendment may be proposed either by the Congress with a two-thirds majority vote in both the House of Representatives and the Senate or by a constitutional convention called for by two-thirds of the state legislatures. None of the 27 amendments to the Constitution have been proposed by constitutional convention. The Congress proposes an amendment in the form of a joint resolution. Since the President does not have a constitutional role in the amendment process, the joint resolution does not go to the White House for signature or approval. The original document is forwarded directly to the National Archives and Records Administration (NARA), Office of the Federal Register (OFR) for processing and publication. The OFR adds legislative history notes to the joint resolution and publishes it in slip law format. The OFR also assembles an information package for the states which includes formal "red-line" copies of the joint resolution, copies of the joint resolution in slip law format, and the statutory procedure for ratification under 1 U.S.C. 106b.

The Archivist submits the proposed amendment to the states for their consideration by sending a letter of notification to each Governor along with the informational material prepared by the OFR. The Governors then formally submit the amendment to their state legislatures. In the past, some state legislatures have not waited to receive official notice before taking action on a proposed amendment. When a state ratifies a proposed amendment, it sends the Archivist an original or certified copy of the state action, which is immediately conveyed to the Director of the Federal Register. The OFR examines ratification documents for facial legal sufficiency and an authenticating signature. If the documents are found to be in good order, the Director acknowledges receipt and maintains custody of them. The OFR retains these documents until an amendment is adopted or fails, and then transfers the records to the National Archives for preservation.

A proposed amendment becomes part of the Constitution as soon as it is ratified by three-fourths of the states (38 of 50 states). When the OFR verifies that it has received the required number of authenticated ratification documents, it drafts a formal proclamation for the Archivist to certify that the amendment is valid and has become part of the Constitution. This certification is published in the Federal Register and United States Statutes at Large and serves as official notice to the Congress and to the Nation that the amendment process has been completed.

No need for elaborate pomp and circumstance; short and sweet—Congress assembles and after two-thirds each of the House of Representatives and Senate deems abolishing the Seventeenth Amendment necessary, we push for state legislatures to concur. Send the following proposed constitutional amendment to your United States representative and senator and your state representative and senator:

Amendment XXVIII

Section 1
The Seventeenth Amendment to the United States Constitution is hereby abolished.

Section 2
Therefore, as is directed by United States Constitution, Article I, Section 3, the Senate of the United States shall be composed of two senators from each state, chosen by the legislature thereof, for six years; and each senator shall have one vote.

Do you think it was just coincidence that the Seventeenth Amendment came along with the Sixteenth Amendment and the Federal Reserve Act in 1913? Nay, nay! It was part of the scheme. And now it is part of our plan to help return America to a Republican form of government by abolishing the Seventeenth Amendment.

THE FEDERAL RESERVE
Really Screwed

It all started when people first created various mediums of exchange (money) to ease the exchange of their wares. You got carrots. I got potatoes. I don't need so many carrots. You need lots of spuds. Hey, how 'bout we make some coins from gold and silver and use them to count the value of what we trade? Or we can just use pieces of paper. We'll call it…oh, yeah…money! We agree on a material (paper's cheap) and its name (United States Note[60]) and get down to business. You give me four notes for the spuds. I'll give you two notes for the carrots. Hey, Melvin, how many notes you want for that chicken?

Just about from the get-go, priests of ancient civilizations (claiming God had endowed them with authority to bless the fiat of the day) created a medium of exchange that people would accept and use. Then the kings kicked butt on the priests and turned over the "money"-making power to central banks. Smooth move on the sovereign's part; it's hard to borrow from yourself. But with a central bank, whoop-de-do, who has better credit than the king and his friends? To the serfs of the day, it was pretty much voodoo science, a mystical happening; an easy come, easy go kind of a deal.

Hey, is that a pocket full of gold coins you got there or are you just happy to see me? Now seriously, have I got a deal for you! I'm going to lighten your load, brother. Can I call you brother? Of course I can! We're all brothers here in the good, old U S of A. Now listen to this! I'm going to take those heavy gold coins out of your saggin' pockets and give you my piece of paper. It's called a "Note," isn't it pretty? And so convenient! Try it out. Now, really, doesn't my piece of paper feel a lot more comfortable in your pocket than all that heavy gold? Sure it does! And look, right here on my piece of paper, in bold letters, it says I promise to give you back your gold, anytime you want.

—Friendly Fed the Flim-Flam Man, December 22, 1913.

President Wilson signed the Federal Reserve Act into law December 23, 1913. Wilson had no trouble (like Roosevelt) patting himself on the back for being a personal representative of the people. In reality, both Roosevelt and Wilson did the bidding of international bankers. Allegedly conservative, Wilson and Roosevelt were progressives (socialists). In 1917, international bankers gleefully celebrated as Wilson proclaimed that America was joining World War I with the goal "Make the world safe for democracy." During the Wilson reign (1913–1921), the national debt expanded 800 percent.

The Federal Reserve was named in such a way as to give the public the idea that it was a government agency. This shielded and protected the Fed's true identity as a private corporation.

---

60 The paper (United States note) I suggest we use is not actually a "note" but fiat paper that we all agree to use, and it certainly will have particular requirements and restrictions as noted herein. We could still use the familiar term "note" with the understanding that the paper we are calling a note is not actually a note. Like your personal check, a lawful note must spell out (1) who pays, (2) who gets paid, (3) when that person will be paid, and (4) the amount of payment.

Nothing new here. The Bank of England, the Bank of France, nor the Bank of Germany was owned by their governments, despite what most people would logically think, given their names. Like the Federal Reserve (Fed), they were/are privately-owned monopolies with charters granted by government. The Fed not being a governmental entity but a private corporation was affirmed by the Supreme Court in 1982. The Federal Reserve is no more a branch of the Federal Government than is Federal Express.

That is correct; the Federal Reserve is a privately owned for profit corporation which again has no reserves, at least, no reserves available to backup Reserve Notes which are our common currency.

—Henry Pasquet, Economist

Absolutely, the Federal Reserve is neither Federal and has doubtful reserves. It's a private bank owned by member banks and it was chartered under the guise of deceit by an Act of Congress in 1913.

—Larry Bates, Economist

In Lewis v. United States 680 F.2d 1239 (9th Cir. 1982), the United States Court of Appeals for the Ninth Circuit stated that "the Reserve Banks are not federal instrumentalities for purposes of the FTCA [Federal Tort Claims Act], but are independent, privately owned and locally controlled corporations."

Those who create and issue the money and credit direct the policies of government and hold in their hands the destiny of the people.

—Reginald McKenna, president, Midlands Bank of England

Half a dozen men at the top of the Big Five Banks could upset the whole fabric of government finance by refraining from renewing Treasury Bills.

—London Financial Times, September 26, 1921

Inflation? Deflation? At the Oregon Museum of Science and Industry in Portland, I saw an exhibit entitled "Moneyville." The exhibit noted (as is taught in schools) that inflation is caused by rising prices and deflation by decreasing prices. Rising prices are an *effect* of inflation; inflation is simply an increase in the money supply, and deflation, a decrease in the money supply. This confusion and misdirection runs interference as the Fed harvests profits via inflating and deflating the money supply.

Ron Paul, *End The Fed* (2009), pp. 182–83:

If it's only a price problem, then blame can be placed on profiteers, speculators, labor unions, oil companies, and price gougers. This deflects attention from the real source of the problem, the Federal Reserve and its money machine. It's because so many are convinced that consumer and producer price increases are caused by these extraneous reasons that wage and price controls are resorted to, while the Fed's role in the inflation is ignored.

After passage of the Act, Federal Reserve notes came into circulation alongside United States notes. Back then, a note was truly a note, meaning that the pieces of paper people carried around in their pockets could actually be redeemed at banks for gold or silver coin. As is well documented, some banker-type folks over in England gathered up a whole bunch of those redeemable-in-gold notes and came calling to collect. Apparently, the notes were not hard to find, since the Fed had inflated issuance of its notes to more than six times the amount of monetary gold there was in the world. From inception, it took only fifteen years for the Fed to bankrupt America (and this was when we had notes redeemable in gold or silver). Bankrupting America was good business for the Fed. Everything was on sale for pennies on the dollar.

All Fed claims are cow pies! I recognize those claims as cow pies because there's too much of them to be BULLSHIT! The Fed is the biggest taxer of them all. Increasing supply (inflation), thereby diluting the dollar's value, has been a long-term sinister tax on the poor and middle class. The Fed equals boom-bust cycles, recession, depression, and ever-growing, endless government debt. Economic experts and professors have lined up around the block and beyond to condemn or praise the Fed from inception to present. But all you need to see the truth of this matter is your own personal observations and comparisons. Everything costs more every time you blink. Inflation from 1913 to 2014 - 2,291.3 percent. What cost $20 in 1913 cost $478.25 in 2014. See USInflationCalculator.com.

The Fed owns America. We are the slaves and the Fed is our Master.

And the Fed said, "Let there be money! And there was money. And it was bad." Here's how it works:

- The Federal Government wants to do a little deficit spending; it needs $1,000.
- The Federal Reserve, through its Open Market Committee, sets the prime interest rate and what bank reserves shall be.
- The United States Treasurer then tells the Bureau of Engraving and Printing to print $1,000 in United States interest-bearing bonds.
- At the same time, the Federal Reserve Bank directs the same Bureau of Engraving and Printing to print $1,000 in Federal Reserve notes. The Fed does pay for the paper and ink.
- The Federal Reserve Bank then "swaps" the $1,000 in Federal Reserve notes for the Government's $1,000 in interest-bearing bonds.

A bit of paper, a little ink, a printing press, and presto, you got interest-bearing bonds and notes! Those Government bonds supply the flimflam Fed owners with whatever interest the market will bear.

Interest can be collected a second time when the Fed lends the notes to member banks. Unbelievably, the banks today are required to hold only 10 percent in reserve. Here is how that works: Bank A receives $1,000, holds $100 (10 percent) in reserve, and lends out $900 at interest. The borrower deposits the $900 in Bank B; Bank B holds 10 percent ($90) in reserve and lends out the remaining $810, collecting interest thereon. The borrower deposits the $810 in Bank C; Bank C retains $80 (10 percent) and lends the remaining $720 at interest. I think you get the picture.

Where does the Federal Reserve get the money with which to create bank reserves? Answer: It doesn't get money, it creates it. When the Federal Reserve writes a check for a government bond it does exactly what any bank does, it creates money…It created money purely and simply by writing a check. And the recipient of the check wants cash, then the Federal Reserve can oblige him by printing the cash—Federal Reserve Notes—which the receiver's commercial bank can hand over to him. The Federal Reserve, in short, is a total money-making machine.

—Murray N. Rothbard, *What has Government Done to Our Money?* (1963)

In the United States the Federal Reserve Act compels the banks to keep the minimum ratio of reserves to deposits and, since 1917, these reserves could only consist of deposits at the Federal Reserve Bank. Gold could no longer be part of a bank's legal reserves; it had to be deposited in the Federal Reserve Bank.

In addition to removing the checks on inflation, the act of establishing a Central Bank has a direct inflationary impact. Before the Central Bank began, banks kept their reserves in gold; now gold flows into the Central Bank in exchange for deposits with the bank, which are now reserves for the commercial banks. But the Bank itself keeps only a fractional reserve of gold to its own liabilities! Therefore, the act of establishing a Central Bank greatly multiplies the inflationary potential of the country.

Precisely how does the Central Bank go about its task of regulating the private banks? By controlling the banks' "reserves"—their deposit accounts at the Central Banks tend to keep a certain ratio of reserves to their total deposit liabilities, and in the United States Government control is made easier by imposing a legal minimum ratio on the bank. The Central Bank can stimulate inflation, then, by pouring reserves into the banking system, and also by lowering the reserve ratio, thus permitting a nationwide bank credit-expansion. If the banks keep a reserve/deposit ratio of 1:10, then "excess reserves" (above the required ratio) of ten million dollars will permit and encourage a nationwide bank inflation of 100 million. Since banks profit by credit expansion, and since government has made it almost impossible for them to fail, they will usually try to keep "loaned up" to their allowable maximum.

—Congressman Wright Patman[61]

---

61 John William Wright Patman (1893–1976) was a United States Congressman from Texas (1st congressional district and chair [1965–75] of the United States House Committee on Banking and Currency). He was a self-styled "populist" who energetically attacked the banks, the banking system, and the Federal Reserve.

In 2014, interest on the national debt totaled $430,812,121,372.05. Under the current system, "our" government is more than $18 trillion in debt, a debt growing faster than weeds in spring. Under the current money system, we can't get rid of that debt without diminishing our money supply. The current money system—that is, the Fed—is an evil, ingenious system designed to keep us buried in debt from the cradle to the grave. Paying off government debt without revamping our banking system cannot be done. The solution is a dead Fed, not trying to fix the government-debt problem. Addressing the former (killing the Fed) will solve the latter.

> Senator Charles A. Lindbergh (R-MN), 1923:
>
> The financial system has been turned over to…the Federal Reserve Board. That board administers the finance system by authority of…a purely profiteering group. The system is private, conducted for the sole purpose of obtaining the greatest possible profits from the use of other people's money.
>
> Senator Barry Goldwater (R-AZ), a frequent critic of the Fed:
>
> Most Americans have no real understanding of the international moneylenders…The accounts of the Federal Reserve System have never been audited. It operates outside the control of Congress and…manipulates the credit of the United States. The Federal Reserve really, even though it is not part of the United States Government, is more powerful than the Federal Government, more powerful than the President, Congress and the Courts.
>
> The rich ruleth over the poor, and the borrower is servant to the lender (Proverbs 22:7).

Is there any doubt that a debt of $18 trillion and perpetual borrowing makes "our" government a servant to the lender?

Could the Founders have had it wrong? Is a gold-backed currency not the way to go? When researching the Fed and the alternatives, I was looking for evidence and assurance that going back to the gold standard was our best option. After reading Rothbard's *What Has Government Done to Our Money?* and several books by Ron Paul, I was left with this nagging problem: returning to the gold standard, thus necessitating a fixed price for gold, bugged me. The price of gold, like every other commodity, has ebb and flow, down and up, dictated by demand and supply. What if you set the price of gold at $1,200 an ounce—a "dollar" being 1/20th of an ounce, as was once dictated—and the demand or supply of gold changed? Say that gold drops to $1,000 an ounce or rises to $1,500 an ounce? I think the international bankers and financial elite of the world have the ability to corner the market on gold and silver, killing any viable attempt to have a currency backed by those commodities.

The Fed must go. But does it need to be replaced with gold- and silver-backed notes as our money? Or with a fiat currency owned and operated by the United States Government, with strict written laws and monitoring? I lean toward the latter—but, for sure, repeat after me: "The Fed is dead!" And, just as important, fractional-reserve banking is deader than a maple leaf in late fall.

Congressman Louis T. McFadden - Remarks in Congress, 1934

To follow is extensive, insightful testimony from speeches made in 1934 on the floor of the House of Representatives by Congressman Louis T. McFadden[62] of Pennsylvania. He served in Congress for twenty years (1915–1935) and as Chairman of the Committee on Banking and Currency for ten years (1920–1931). He was there to watch the twenties roar, and there when the Great Depression began in 1929. He was in a position to witness and then speak with authority on the evils of the Fed. Although his testimony before Congress was given over eighty years ago, it's applicable today. Change a few names, add a row of zeros, and you would think it was spoken today.

> Mister Chairman, we have in this Country one of the most corrupt institutions the world has ever known. I refer to the Federal Reserve Board and the Federal Reserve Banks, hereinafter called the Fed. The Fed has cheated the United States Government and the people of the United States out of enough money to pay the Nation's debt. The depredations and iniquities of the Fed have cost this Country enough money to pay the National debt several times over.

> This evil institution has impoverished and ruined the people of these United States, has bankrupted itself, and has practically bankrupted our Government. It has done this through the defects of the law under which it operates, through the maladministration of that law by the moneyed vultures who control it. Some people think the Federal Reserve Banks are United States Government institutions. They are not Government institutions. They are private monopolies, which prey upon the people of these United States for the benefit of themselves and their foreign customers; foreign and domestic speculators, swindlers, and rich and predatory moneylenders. In that dark crew of financial pirates there are those who would cut a man's throat to get a dollar out of his pocket. There are those who send money into States to buy votes to control our legislatures. There are those who maintain International propaganda for the purpose of deceiving us into granting new concessions, which will permit them to cover up their past misdeeds, and set again in motion their gigantic train of crime.

> These twelve private credit monopolies were deceitfully and disloyally foisted upon this Country by the bankers who came here from Europe and repaid our hospitality by undermining our American institutions. Those bankers took money out of this Country to finance Japan in a war against Russia. They created a reign of terror in Russia with our money in order to help that war along. They instigated the separate peace between

---

62 What's with the anti-Semitic crap? McFadden was anti-Semitic, but that does not mean his observations and information on the Fed are invalid. His details on the Fed are confirmed via mass quantities of sources. It is my firm belief that anti-Semitic propaganda and other false information is generously fed to any and all who dare work to expose the Fed as the American people's number-one enemy. It doesn't matter one gnat's worth who brought the Fed to us. It was carried in on the backs of now-dead evil, despicable individuals. As we gut the Fed, those who are Fed-fed will hungrily rise to challenge; they will be lawfully neutralized.

Germany and Russia and thus drove a wedge between the Allies in the World War. They financed Trotsky's passage from New York to Russia so that he might assist in the destruction of the Russian Empire. They fomented and instigated the Russian Revolution, and placed a large fund of American dollars at Trotsky's disposal in one of their branch banks in Sweden, so that through him, Russian homes might be thoroughly broken up and Russian children flung far and wide from their natural protectors. They have since begun the breaking up of American homes and the dispersal of American children.

Mister Chairman, there should be no partisanship in matters concerning banking and currency affairs in this Country, and I do not speak with any. In nineteen-twelve the National Monetary Association under the chairmanship of the late Senator Nelson W. Aldrich made a report and presented a vicious Bill called the National Reserve Association Bill. This Bill is usually spoken of as the Aldrich Bill. Senator Aldrich did not write the Aldrich Bill. He was the tool, if not the accomplice of the European bankers, who for nearly twenty years had been scheming to set up a central bank in this Country, and who in nineteen-twelve had spent and were continuing to spend vast sums of money to accomplish their purpose.

We were opposed to the Aldrich plan for a central bank. The men who rule the Democratic Party then promised the people if they were returned to power there would be no central bank established here while they held the reins of government. Thirteen months later that promise was broken, and the Wilson administration, under the tutelage of those sinister Wall Street figures who stood behind Colonel House,[63] established here in our free Country the worm-eaten monarchical institution of the "King's Bank" to control us from the top downward, and to shackle us from the cradle to the crave.

The Federal Reserve Bank destroyed our old and characteristic way of doing business. It discriminated against our one-name commercial paper, the finest in the world, and it set up the antiquated two-name paper, which is the present curse of this Country and which wrecked every country which has ever given it scope; it fastened down upon the Country the very tyranny from which the framers of the Constitution sought to save us.

One of the greatest battles for the preservation of this Republic was fought out here in Jackson's time; when the second Bank of the United States, founded on the same false principles of those which are here exemplified in the Fed was hurled out of existence. After that, in eighteen thirty-seven, the Country was warned against the dangers that might ensue if the predatory interests, after being cast out, should come back in

---

63 Edward Mandell House (1858–1938)—politician, diplomat, presidential advisor. "Colonel" was a false title; House had no military experience. He had enormous personal influence with President Wilson as his foreign-policy advisor, but Wilson removed him in 1919. House was the founder of the Council on Foreign Relations (CFR), of which Rockefeller was a permanent member.

disguise and unite themselves to the Executive, and through him acquire control of the government. That is what the predatory interests did when they came back in the livery of hypocrisy and under false pretenses obtained the passage of the Fed.

The danger that the Country was warned against came upon us and is shown in the long train of horrors attendant upon the affairs of the traitorous and dishonest Fed. Look around you when you leave this Chamber and you will see evidence of it on all sides. This is an era of misery and for the conditions that caused that misery, the Fed is fully liable. This is an era of financed crime and in the financing of crime the Fed does not play the part of a disinterested spectator.

It has been said the draughtsman who was employed to write the text of the Fed used the text of the Aldrich bill because that had been drawn up by lawyers, by acceptance bankers of European origin in New York. It was a copy, in general a translation, of the statutes of the Richsbank and other European central banks. One-half million dollars was spent on the part of the propaganda organized by these bankers for the purpose of misleading public opinion, and giving Congress the impression that there was an overwhelming popular demand for it and the kind of currency that goes with it, namely, an asset currency based on human debts and obligations.

Doctor H. Parker Willis had been employed by Wall Street and propagandists, and when the Aldrich measure failed, he obtained employment with Carter Glass, to assist in drawing the banking bill for the Wilson administration. He appropriated the text of the Aldrich bill. There is no secret about it. The text of the Federal Reserve Act was tainted from the first.

A few days before the bill came to a vote, Senator Henry Cabot Lodge, of Massachusetts, wrote to Senator John W. Weeks as follows:

New York City, December 17, 1913
My Dear Senator Weeks,

Throughout my public life I have supported all measures designed to take the Government out of the banking business. This bill puts the Government into the banking business as never before in our history. The powers vested in the Federal Reserve Board seem to me highly dangerous especially where there is political control of the Board. I should be sorry to hold stock in a bank subject to such dominations. The bill as it stands seems to me to open the way to a vast inflation of the currency.[64]

---

64 The Federal Reserve Act put government in the banking business, not in control but as collateral. The composition of the Board only gives the appearance of some kind of government control; it's an illusion.

I had hoped to support this bill, but I cannot vote for it as it stands, because it seems to me to contain features and to rest upon principles in the highest degree menacing to our prosperity, to stability in business, and to the general welfare of the people of the United States.

Very Truly Yours, Henry Cabot Lodge

In eighteen years that have passed since Senator Lodge wrote that letter of warning all of his predictions have come true. The Government is in the banking business as never before. Against its will it has been made the backer of horse thieves and cardsharps, bootleggers, smugglers, speculators, and swindlers in all parts of the world. Through the Fed the riffraff of every country is operating on the public credit of the United States Government.

Meanwhile and on account of it, we ourselves are in the midst of the greatest depression we have ever known. From the Atlantic to the Pacific, our Country has been ravaged and laid waste by the evil practices of the Fed and the interests which control them. At no time in our history, has the general welfare of the people been at a lower level or the minds of the people so full of despair.

Recently in one of our States, sixty thousand dwelling houses and farms were brought under the hammer in a single day. Seventy-one thousand houses and farms in Oakland County, Michigan were sold and their erstwhile owners dispossessed. The people who have thus been driven out are the wastage of the Fed. Their children are the new slaves of the auction blocks in the revival of the institution of human slavery.

In nineteen thirteen, before the Senate Banking and Currency Committee, Mr. Alexander Lassen made the following statement: "The whole scheme of the Fed with its commercial paper is an impractical, cumbersome machinery—is simply a cover to secure the privilege of issuing money, and to evade payment of as much tax upon circulation as possible and then control the issue and maintain, instead of reducing interest rates. It will prove to be to the advantage of the few and the detriment of the people. It will mean continued shortage of actual money and further extension of credits, for when there is a shortage of money people have to borrow to their cost."

A few days before the Fed passed, Senator Root denounced the Fed as an outrage on our liberties. He predicted, "Long before we wake up from our dream of prosperity through an inflated currency, our gold, which alone could have kept us from catastrophe, will have vanished and no rate of interest will tempt it to return." If ever a prophecy came true, that one did.

The Fed became law the day before Christmas Eve nineteen thirteen, and shortly afterwards, the German International Bankers, Kuhn, Loeb and Company sent one of their partners here to run it.

The Fed note is essentially unsound. It is the worst currency and the most dangerous that this Country has ever known. When the proponents of the Act saw that the Democratic doctrine would not permit them to let the proposed banks issue the new currency as bank notes, they should have stopped at that. They should not have foisted that kind of currency, namely, an asset currency, on the United States Government. They should not have made the Government liable on the private debts of individuals and corporations, and, least of all, on the private debts of foreigners.

...If this United States is to redeem the Fed notes, when the general public finds it costs to deliver this paper to the Fed, and if the Government has made no provisions for redeeming them, the first element of unsoundness is not far to seek.

Before the Banking and Currency Committee, when the Bill was under discussion Mister Crozier of Cincinnati said, "The imperial power of elasticity of the public currency is wielded exclusively by the central corporations owned by the banks. This is a life and death power over all local banks and all business. It can be used to create or destroy prosperity, to ward off or cause stringencies and panics. By making money artificially scarce, interest rates throughout the Country can be arbitrarily raised, and the bank tax on all business and cost of living increased for the profit of the banks owning these regional central banks, and without the slightest benefit to the people. The twelve corporations together cover the whole Country and monopolize and use for private gain, every dollar of the public currency and all public revenue of the United States. Not a dollar can be put into circulation among the people by their Government, without the consent of and on terms fixed by these twelve private money trusts."

In defiance of this and all other warnings, the proponents of the Fed created the twelve private credit corporations and gave them an absolute monopoly of the currency of these United States, not of the Fed notes alone but of all other currency! The Fed Act provided the ways and means by which the gold and general currency in the hands of the American people could be obtained by the Fed in exchange for Fed notes, which are not money but mere promises to pay.

Since the evil day when this was done, the initial monopoly has been extended by vicious amendments to the Fed and by the unlawful and treasonable practices of the Fed.

Mister Chairman, if a Scottish distiller wishes to send a cargo of Scotch whiskey to these United States, he can draw his bill against the purchasing bootlegger in dollars, and after the bootlegger has accepted it by writing his name across the face of it, the Scotch distiller can send that bill to the nefarious open discount market in New York City, where the Fed will pay the Scotch distiller for the whiskey before it is shipped. And if it is lost on the way, or if the Coast Guard seizes it and destroys it, the Fed simply writes off the loss and the Government never recovers the money that was paid to the Scotch distiller.

While we are attempting to enforce prohibition here, the Fed is financing the distillery business in Europe and paying bootlegger bills with public credit of these United States.

Mister Chairman, by the same process, they compel our Government to pay the German brewer for his beer. Why should the Fed be permitted to finance the brewing industry in Germany either in this way or as they do by compelling small and fearful United States Banks to take stock in the Isenbeck Brewery and in the German Bank for brewing industries?

...Mister Chairman, why should the currency of these United States be issued on the strength of German beer? Why should it be issued on the crop of unplanted beans to be grown in Chili for Japanese consumption? Why should these United States be compelled to issue many billions of dollars every year to pay the debts of one foreigner to another foreigner?

Was it for this that our National Bank depositors had their money taken out of our banks and shipped abroad? Was it for this that they had to lose it? Why should the public credit of these United States and likewise money belonging to our National Bank depositors be used to support foreign brewers, narcotic drug venders, whiskey distillers, wig makers, human hair merchants, Chilean bean growers, to finance the munitions factories of Germany and Soviet Russia?

Mister Chairman, there is nothing like the Fed pool of confiscated bank deposits in the world. It is a public trough of American wealth in which the foreigners claim rights, equal to or greater than Americans. The Fed is the agent of the foreign central banks. They use our bank depositors' money for the benefit of their foreign principals. They barter the public credit of the United States Government and hire it out to foreigners at a profit to themselves.

All this is done at the expense of the United States Government and at a sickening loss to the American people. Only our great wealth enabled us to stand the drain of it as long as we did.

The United States has been ransacked and pillaged. Our structures have been gutted and only the walls are left standing. While this crime was being perpetrated, everything the world could rake up to sell us was brought in here at our expense by the Fed, until our markets were swamped with unneeded and unwanted imported goods, priced far above their value and made to equal the dollar volume of our honest exports, and to kill or reduce our favorable balance of trade. As Agents of the foreign central banks the Fed has used every means in their power to reduce our favorable balance of trade. They act for their foreign principals and they accept fees from foreigners for acting against the best interest of these United States. Naturally there has been great competition among foreigners for the favors of the Fed.

What we need to do is to send the reserves of our National Banks home to the people who earned and produced them and who still own them and to the banks which were compelled to surrender them to predatory interests.

We need to destroy the Fed wherein our national reserves are impounded for the benefit of the foreigners.

We need to save America for Americans.

Mister Chairman, when you hold a ten dollar Fed note in your hand, you are holding a piece of paper which sooner or later is going to cost the United States Government ten dollars in gold, unless the Government is obliged to go off the gold standard. It is based on limburger cheese, reported to be in foreign warehouses, or in cans purported to contain peas, but may contain salt water instead, or horse meat, illicit drugs, bootleggers fancies, rags and bones from Soviet Russia, of which these United States imported over a million dollars' worth last year, on wines, whiskey, natural gas, goat and dog fur, garlic on the string, and Bombay ducks.

If you like to have paper money…which is secured by such commodities…you have it in the Fed note. If you desire to obtain the thing of value upon which this paper currency is based, that is, the limburger cheese, the whiskey, the illicit drugs, or any of the other staples…you will have a very hard time finding them.

Many of these worshipful commodities are in foreign countries. Are you going to Germany to inspect her warehouses to see if the specified things of value are there? I think not. And what is more, I do not think that you would find them there if you did go.

On April twenty-seventh, nineteen thirty-two, the Fed outfit sent gold worth seven hundred fifty thousand dollars belonging to American bank depositors to Germany. A week later gold worth three hundred thousand dollars was shipped to Germany. About the middle of May gold worth twelve million dollars was shipped to Germany by the Fed. Almost every week there is a shipment of gold to Germany. These shipments are not made for profit on the exchange since the German marks are below parity with the dollar.

Mister Chairman, I believe that the National Bank depositors of these United States have a right to know what the Fed is doing with their money. There are millions of National Bank depositors in the Country who do not know that a percentage of every dollar they deposit in a Member Bank of the Fed goes automatically to American agents of the foreign banks, and that all their deposits can be paid away to foreigners, without their knowledge or consent, by the crooked machinery of the Fed and the questionable practices of the Fed.

...The Fed has been International Bankers from the beginning, with these United States as their enforced banker and supplier of currency. But it is none the less extraordinary to see these twelve private credit monopolies, buying the debts of foreigners against foreigners, in all parts of the world and asking the Government of these United States for new issues of Fed notes in exchange for them.

The magnitude of the acceptance racket as it has been developed by the Fed, their foreign correspondents, and the predatory European born bankers, who set up the Fed here and taught your own, by and of pirates, how to loot the people. I say the magnitude of this racket is estimated to be in the neighborhood of nine billion dollars per year. In the past ten years it is said to have amounted to ninety billion dollars. In my opinion it has amounted to several times that much. Coupled to this you have, to the extent of billions of dollars, the gambling in the United States securities, which takes place in the same open discount market, a gambling on which the Fed is now spending one hundred million per week.

Fed notes are taken from the United States Government in unlimited quantities. Is it strange that the burden of supplying these immense sums of money to the gambling fraternity has at last proven too heavy for the American people to endure? Would it not be a national calamity if the Fed should again bind down this burden on the backs of the American people and by means of a long rawhide whip of the credit masters, compel them to enter another seventeen years of slavery?

They are trying to do that now. They are trying to take one hundred million dollars of the public credit of the United States every week, in addition to all their other seizures and they are sending that money to the nefarious open market in a desperate gamble to reestablish their graft as a going concern.

They are putting the United States Government in debt to the extent of one hundred million dollars a week, and with the money they are buying our Government securities for themselves and their foreign principals. Our people are disgusted with the experiences of the Fed. The Fed is not producing a loaf of bread, a yard of cloth, a bushel of corn, or a pile of cordwood by its check-kiting operations in the money market.

Mister Speaker, on the thirteenth of January of this year I addressed the House on the subject of the Reconstruction Finance Corporation. In the course of my remarks I made the following statement, "In nineteen twenty-eight the member banks of the Fed borrowed sixty billion, five hundred ninety-eight million, six hundred ninety thousand dollars from the Fed on their fifteen-day promissory notes. Think of it. Sixty billion dollars payable on demand in gold in the course of one single year. The actual amount of such obligations called for six times as much monetary gold as there is in the world. Such transactions represent a grant in the course of one single year of about seven million to every member of the Fed."

Is it any wonder that American labor which ultimately pays the cost of all banking operations of this Country has at last proved unequal to the task of supplying this huge total of cash and credit for the benefit of the stock market manipulators and foreign swindlers?

In nineteen thirty-three the Fed presented the staggering amount of sixty billion, five hundred ninety-eight million, six hundred ninety thousand dollars to its member banks at the expense of the wage-earners and taxpayers of these United States. In nineteen twenty-nine, the year of the stock market crash, the Fed advanced fifty-eight billion to member banks.

In nineteen thirty while the speculating banks were getting out of the stock market at the expense of the general public, the Fed advanced them thirteen billion, twenty-two million, seven hundred eighty-two thousand dollars. This shows that when the banks were gambling on the public credit of these United States as represented by the Fed currency they were subsidized to any amount they required by the Fed. When the swindle began to fall, the bankers knew it in advance and withdrew from the market. They got out with whole skins…and left the people of these United States to pay the piper.

My friend from Kansas, Mister McGugin, has stated that he thought the Fed lent money on rediscounting. So they do, but they lend comparatively little that way. The real discounting that they do has been called a mere penny in the slot business. It is too slow for genuine high flyers. They discourage it. They prefer to subsidize their favorite banks by making them sixty billion dollar advances and they prefer to acquire assistance in the notorious open discount market in New York, where they can use it to control the price of stocks and bonds on the exchanges.

For every dollar they advanced on discounts in nineteen twenty-eight, they lent thirty-three dollars to their favorite banks for whom they do a business of several billion dollars every year, and pay no income tax on their profits to these United States.

This is the John Law swindle over again. The theft of Teapot Dome was trifling compared to it. What King ever robbed his subject to such an extent as the Fed has robbed us? Is it any wonder that there have been lately ninety cases of starvation in one of the New York hospitals? Is there any wonder that the children are being abandoned?

The government and the people of these United States have been swindled by swindlers deluxe, to whom the acquisition of America for a parcel of Fed notes, presented no more difficulty than the drawing up of a worthless acceptance in a Country not subject to the laws of these United States, by sharpers not subject to the jurisdiction of these United States. Sharpers with strong banking "fence" on this side of the water, a "fence" acting as a receiver of a worthless paper coming from abroad, indorsing it, and getting the currency out of the Fed for it as quickly as possible, then exchanging that currency for gold and in turn transmitting the gold to its foreign confederates.

...A few days ago, the President of the United States with a white face and shaking hands, went before the Senate on behalf of the moneyed interests and asked the Senate to levy a tax on the people, so that foreigners might know that these United States would pay its debt to them.

Most Americans thought it was the other way around. What does these United States owe to foreigners? When and by whom was the debt incurred? It was incurred by the Fed, when they peddled the signature of the Government to foreigners...for a price. It is what the United States Government has to pay to redeem the obligations of the Fed.

Are you going to let these thieves get off scot free? Is there one law for the looter who drives up to the door of the United States Treasury in his limousine and another for the United States Veterans who are sleeping on the floor of a dilapidated house on the outskirts of Washington?

The Baltimore and Ohio Railroad is here asking for a large loan from the people, and the wage earners and the taxpayers of these United States. It is begging for a handout from the Government. It is standing, cap in hand, at the door of the RFC where all the jackals have gathered to the feast. It is asking for money that was raised from the people by taxation and wants this money of the poor for the benefit of Kuhn, Loeb and Company, the German International Bankers.

Is there one law for the Baltimore and Ohio Railroad and another for the hungry veterans it threw off its freight cars the other day? Is there one law for the sleek and prosperous swindlers who call themselves bankers and another law for the soldiers who defended the flag?

The RFC is taking over these worthless securities from the Investment Trusts with United States Treasury money at the expense of the American taxpayer and the wage earner. It will take twenty years to redeem our Government. Twenty years of penal servitude to pay off the gambling debts of the traitorous Fed and to earn again that vast flood of American wages and savings, bank deposits, and United States Government credit which the Fed exported out of this country to their foreign principals.

The Fed lately conducted an anti-hoarding campaign here. Then they took that extra money which they had persuaded the American people to put into the banks…they sent it to Europe…along with the rest. In the last several months, they have sent one billion three hundred million dollars in gold to their foreign employers, their foreign masters, and every dollar of that gold belonged to the people of these United States and was unlawfully taken from them.

Mister Chairman, within the limits of the time allowed me; I cannot enter into a particularized discussion of the Fed. I have singled out the Fed currency for a few remarks because there has lately been some talk here of "fiat money."

…Fiat money,[65] indeed!

What Mister Mills is fighting for is the preservation, whole and entire, of the banker's monopoly of all the currency of the United States Government.

Mister Chairman, last December, I introduced a resolution here asking for an audit of the Fed[66] and all related matters. If the House sees fit to make such an investigation, the people of these United States will obtain information of great value. This is a Government of the people, by the people, for the people. Consequently, nothing should be concealed from the people. The man who deceives the people is a traitor to these United States. The man who knows or suspects that a crime has been committed and who conceals and covers up that crime is an accessory to it. Mister Speaker, it is a monstrous thing for this great nation of people to have its destinies presided over by a traitorous government board acting in secret concert with international usurers.

---

65 Fiat money of the Fed is not the United States fiat money proposed herein. Fed fiat requires interest to be paid and comes with fractional-reserve banking; government fiat costs us nothing, and fractional-reserve banking is to be outlawed.

66 This was over eighty years ago! A testament to the power of the Fed is that it has never been audited. I say, audit the Fed to figure what it owes the American people for its fraud, and then abolish it.

Every effort has been made by the Fed to conceal its powers…but the truth is…the Fed has usurped the Government. It controls everything here and it controls all our foreign relations. It makes and breaks governments at will.

No man and no body of men are more entrenched in power than the arrogant credit monopoly which operates the Fed. What the National Government has permitted the Fed to steal from the people should now be restored to the people. The people have a valid claim against the Fed. If that claim is enforced Americans will not need to stand in the bread line, or to suffer and die of starvation in the streets. Women will be saved, families will be kept together, and American children will not be dispersed and abandoned.

Here is a Fed note. Immense numbers of these notes are now held abroad. I am told that they amount to upwards of a billion dollars. They constitute a claim against our Government and likewise a claim against our peoples' money, gold, to the extent of one billion three hundred million dollars, which has within the last few months, been shipped abroad to redeem Fed notes and to pay other debts of the traitorous Fed. The greater part of our money stock had been shipped to other lands.

Why should we promise to pay the debts of foreigners to foreigners? Why should the Fed be permitted to finance our competitors in all parts of the world? Do you know why the tariff was raised? It was raised to shut out the flood of Fed goods pouring in here from every quarter of the globe…cheap goods, produced by cheaply paid foreign labor, on unlimited supplies of money and credit sent out of this Country by the dishonest and unscrupulous Fed.

The Fed is spending one hundred million dollars a week buying government securities in the open market and is making a great bid for foreign business. They are trying to make rates so attractive that the human hair merchants and the distillers and other business entities in foreign lands will come here and hire more of the public credit of the United States Government to pay the Fed outfit for getting it for them.

Mister Chairman, when the Fed was passed, the people of these United States did not perceive that a world system was being set up here which would make the savings of the American school teacher available to a narcotic-drug vendor in Acao. They did not perceive that these United States was to be lowered to the position of a coolie country which has nothing but raw materials and heavy goods to export, that Russia was destined to supply the man power and that this Country was to supply the financial power to an "international super-state." A super-state controlled by international bankers, and international industrialists acting together to enslave the world for their own pleasure![67]

---

67 Please know that the financial and industrial elite of the world have continually worked to this end—that is, creating a new world order, a one-world government, one they will control and use as they please. Every issue discussed herein furthers that goal.

The people of these United States are being greatly wronged. They have been driven from their employments. They have been dispossessed from their homes. They have been evicted from their rented quarters. They have lost their children. They have been left to suffer and die for lack of shelter, food, clothing and medicine.

The wealth of these United States and the working capital have been taken away from them and has either been locked in the vaults of certain banks and the great corporations, or exported to foreign countries for the benefit of the foreign customers of these banks and corporations. So far as the people of the United States are concerned, the cupboard is bare.

It is true that the warehouses and coal yards and grain elevators are full, but these are padlocked, and the great banks and corporations hold the keys.

The sack of these United States by the Fed is the greatest crime in history.

Mister Chairman, a serious situation confronts the House of Representatives today. We are trustees of the people and the rights of the people are being taken away from them. Through the Fed the people are losing the rights guaranteed to them by the Constitution. Their property has been taken from them without due process of law. Mister Chairman, common decency requires us to examine the public accounts of the Government and see what crimes against the public welfare have and are being committed.

What is needed here is a return to the Constitution of these United States. The old struggle that was fought out here in Jackson's time must be fought out over again. The independent United States Treasury should be re-established and the Government should keep its own money under lock and key in the building the people provided for that purpose.[68]

Asset currency, the device of the swindler, should be done away with. The Fed should be abolished and the state boundaries should be respected. Bank reserves should be kept within the boundaries of the states whose people own them, and this reserve money of the people should be protected so that the International Bankers and acceptance bankers and discount dealers cannot draw it away from them.

The Fed should be repealed, and the Fed Banks, having violated their charters, should be liquidated immediately. Faithless Government officials who have violated their oaths of office should be impeached and brought to trial.

---

68   And this is exactly what we will do when the Fed is dead and control of the money is returned to the people via their government.

Unless this is done by us, I predict, that the American people, outraged, pillaged, insulted and betrayed as they are in their own land, will rise in their wrath, and will sweep the money changers out of the temple.[69]

Mister Chairman, the United States is bankrupt. It has been bankrupted by the corrupt and dishonest Fed. It has repudiated its debts to its own citizens. Its chief foreign creditor is Great Britain, and a British bailiff has been at the White House and British Agents are in the United States Treasury making inventories and arranging terms of liquidation!

Mister Chairman, the Fed had offered to collect the British claims in full from the American public by trickery and corruption, if Great Britain will help conceal its crimes. The British are shielding their agents, the Fed, because they do not wish that system of robbery to be destroyed here. They wish it to continue for their benefit! By means of it, Great Britain has become the financial mistress of the world. She had regained the position she occupied before the World War.

For several years she has been a silent partner in the business of the Fed. Under threat of blackmail, or by their bribery, or by their native treachery to the people of the United States, the officials in charge of the Fed unwisely gave Great Britain immense gold loans running into hundreds of millions of dollars. They did this against the law! Those gold loans were not single transactions. They gave Great Britain a borrowing power in the United States of billions. She squeezed billions out of this Country by means of her control of the Fed.

As soon as the Hoover Moratorium was announced, Great Britain moved to consolidate her gains. After the treacherous signing away of American rights at the seven-power conference at London in July, nineteen thirty-one, which put the Fed under the control of the Bank of International Settlements, Great Britain began to tighten the hangman's noose around the neck of the United States.

She abandoned the gold standard and embarked upon a campaign of buying up the claims of foreigners against the Fed in all parts of the world. She has now sent her bailiff, Ramsey MacDonald, here to get her war debt to this country cancelled. But she has a club in her hands! She has title to the gambling debts which the corrupt and dishonest Fed incurred abroad.

Ramsey MacDonald, the labor party deserter, has come here to compel the President to sign on the dotted line, and that is what Roosevelt is about to do! Roosevelt will endeavor to conceal the nature of his action from the American people. But he will

---

69 Well, unfortunately, that didn't happen. That's why I'm here toiling over getting this information to you instead of being somewhere in the mountains, fishing.

obey the International Bankers and transfer the war debt that Great Britain should pay to the American people, to the shoulders of the American taxpayers.

Mister Chairman, the bank holiday in the several States was brought about by the corrupt and dishonest Fed. These institutions manipulated money and credit, and caused the States to order bank holidays.

These holidays were frame-ups! They were dress rehearsals for the national bank holiday which Franklin D. Roosevelt promised Sir Ramsey MacDonald that he would declare. There was no national emergency here when Franklin D. Roosevelt took office, excepting the bankruptcy which has been going on under cover for several years, and which has been concealed from the people, so that the people would continue to permit their bank deposits, and their bank reserves, and their gold, and the funds of the United States Treasury to be impounded in these bankrupt institutions.

Under cover, the predatory International Bankers have been stealthily transferring the burden of the Fed debts to the people's Treasury and to the people themselves. They have been using the farms and the homes of the United States to pay for their thievery! That is the only national emergency that there has been here since the depression began.

The week before the bank holiday was declared in New York State, the deposits in the New York savings bank were greater than the withdrawals. There were no runs on New York Banks. There was no need of a bank holiday in New York, or of a national holiday.

Roosevelt did what the International Bankers ordered him to do!

Do not deceive yourself, Mr. Chairman, or permit yourself to be deceived by others into the belief that Roosevelt's dictatorship is in any way intended to benefit the people of the United States; he is preparing to sign on the dotted line!

He is preparing to cancel the war debts by fraud!

He is preparing to internationalize this Country and to destroy our Constitution itself in order to keep the Fed intact as a money institution for foreigners!

Mister Chairman, I see no reason why citizens of the United States should be terrorized into surrendering their property to the International Bankers who own and control the Fed. The statement that gold would be taken from its lawful owners if they did not voluntarily surrender it, and given to private interests, shows that there is an anarchist in our Government.

The statement that it is necessary for the people to give their gold…the only real money… to the banks in order to protect the currency is a statement of calculated dishonesty!

By his unlawful usurpation of power on the night of March fifth, nineteen thirty-three, and by his proclamation, which in my opinion was in violation of the Constitution of the United States, Roosevelt divorced the currency of the United States from gold, and the United States currency is no longer protected by gold. It is therefore sheer dishonesty to say that the people's gold is needed to protect the currency.

Roosevelt ordered the people to give their gold to private interest…that is, to banks, and he took control of the banks so that all the gold and gold values in them, or given to them, might be handed over to the predatory International Bankers who own and control the Fed.

Roosevelt cast in his lot with the usurers. He agreed to save the corrupt and dishonest Fed at the expense of the United States. He took advantage of the people's confusion and weariness and spread the dragnet over the United States to capture everything of value that was left in it. He made a great haul for the International Bankers.

The Prime Minister of England came here for money! He came here to collect cash! He came here with Fed Currency and other claims against the Fed which England had bought up in all parts of the world. And he has presented them for redemption in gold.

Mister Chairman, I am in favor of compelling the Fed to pay their own debts. I see no reason why the general public should be forced to pay the gambling debts of the International Bankers.

By his action in closing the banks of the United States, Roosevelt seized the gold value of forty billion or more of bank deposits in the United States banks. Those deposits were deposits of gold values. By his actions he has rendered them payable to the depositors in paper only, if payable at all, and the paper money he proposes to pay out... being based on nothing into which the people can convert it, the said paper money is of negligible value altogether.

It is the money of slaves, not of free men. If the people of the United States permit it to be imposed upon them at the will of their credit masters, the next step in their downward progress will be their acceptance of orders on company stores for what they eat and wear. Their case will be similar to that of starving coal miners. They, too, will be paid with orders on Company stores for food and clothing, both of indifferent quality and be forced to live in company-owned houses from which they may be evicted at the drop of a hat. More of them will be forced into conscript labor camps under supervision.

At noon on the fourth of March, nineteen thirty-three, FDR, with his hand on the Bible, took an oath to preserve, protect and defend the Constitution of the United States. At midnight on the fifth of March nineteen thirty-three he confiscated the property of American citizens. He took the currency of the United States off the gold standard. He repudiated the internal debt of the Government to its own citizens. He destroyed the value of the American dollar. He released, or endeavored to release, the Fed from their contractual liability to redeem Fed currency in gold or lawful money on a parity with gold. He depreciated the value of the national currency.

The people of the United States are now using unredeemable paper slips of money. The Treasury cannot redeem that paper in gold or silver. The gold and silver in the Treasury has unlawfully been given to the corrupt and dishonest Fed. And the Administration had since had the effrontery to raid the country for more gold for the private interests by telling our patriotic citizens that their gold is needed to protect the currency. It is not being used to protect the currency! It is being used to protect the corrupt and dishonest Fed.

The directors of these institutions have committed criminal offenses against the United States Government, including the offense of making false entries on their books, and the still more serious offense of unlawfully abstracting funds from the United States Treasury!

Roosevelt's gold raid is intended to help them out of the pit they dug for themselves when they gambled away the wealth and savings of the American people.

The International Bankers set up a dictatorship here because they wanted a dictator who would protect them. They wanted a dictator who would issue a proclamation giving the Fed an absolute and unconditional release from their special currency in gold or lawful money of any Fed Bank.

Has Roosevelt released any other class of debtors in this country from the necessity of paying their debts? Has he made a proclamation telling the farmers that they need not pay their mortgages? Has he made a proclamation to the effect that mothers of starving children need not pay their milk bills? Has he made a proclamation relieving householders from the necessity of paying rent? Not he! He has issued one kind of proclamation only, and that is a proclamation to relieve international bankers and the foreign debtors of the United States Government.

Mister Chairman, the gold in the banks of this country belongs to the American people who have paper money contracts for it in the form of national currency. If the Fed cannot keep their contracts with United States citizens to redeem their paper money, then the Fed must be taken over by the United States Government and their officers must be put on trial.

There must be a day of reckoning. If the Fed has looted the Treasury so that the Treasury cannot redeem the United States currency for which it is liable in gold, then the Fed must be driven out of the Treasury.

Mister Chairman, a gold certificate is a warehouse receipt for gold in the Treasury, and the man who had a gold certificate is the actual owner of a corresponding amount of gold stacked in the Treasury subject to his order.

Now comes Roosevelt who seeks to render the money of the United States worthless by unlawfully proclaiming that it may Not be converted into gold at the will of the holder.

Roosevelt's next haul for the International Bankers was the reduction in the pay of all federal employees.

Next in order are the veterans of all wars, many of whom are aged and infirm, and others sick and disabled. These men had their lives adjusted for them by acts of Congress determining the amounts of the pensions, and, while it is meant that every citizen should sacrifice himself for the good of the United States, I see no reason why those poor people, these aged Civil War Veterans and war widows and half-starved veterans of the World War, should be compelled to give up their pensions for the financial benefit of the International vultures who have looted the Treasury, bankrupted the country and traitorously delivered the United States to a foreign foe.

There are many ways of raising revenue that are better than that barbaric act of injustice.

Why not collect from the Fed the amount they owe the United States Treasury in interest on all the Fed currency they have taken from the Government? That would put billions of dollars into the United States Treasury.

If FDR is as honest as he pretends to be, he will have that done immediately. And in addition, why not compel the Fed to disclose their profits and to pay the Government its share?

Until this is done, it is rank dishonesty to talk of maintaining the credit of the United States Government....

The Democratic platform advocated a change in the personnel of the Fed. These were campaign bait. As a prominent Democrat lately remarked to me, "There is a new deal. The same old crowd is in control."

...The American people should have their gold in their own possession where it cannot be held under secret agreement for any foreign controlled bank, or world bank, or foreign nation. Our own citizens have the prior claim to it. The paper money they have in their possession deserves redemption far more than United States currency and credit which was stolen from the United States Treasury and bootlegged abroad.

Why should the foreigners be made preferred creditors of the bankrupt United States? Why should the United States be treated as bankrupt at all? This Government has immense sums due it from the Fed. The directors of these institutions are men of great wealth. Why should the guilty escape the consequences of their misdeeds? Why should the people of these United States surrender the value of their gold bank deposits to pay off the gambling debts of these bankers?[70] Why should Roosevelt promise foreigners that the United States will play the part of a good neighbor, "meeting its obligations"?

Let the Fed meet their own obligations.

Every member of the Fed should be compelled to disgorge, and every acceptance banker and every discount corporation which had made illegal profits by means of public credit unlawfully bootlegged out of the United States Treasury and hired out by the crooks and vultures of the Fed should be compelled to disgorge.

...We know from assertions made here by the Honorable John N. Garner, Vice-President of the United States, that there is a condition in the United States Treasury which would cause American citizens, it they knew what it was, to lose all confidence in their government.

That is a condition that Roosevelt will not have investigated. He has brought with him from Wall Street, James Warburg, the son of Paul M. Warburg. Mister Warburg is the head of the Bank of Manhattan Company. Mister Warburg, alien born, and the son of an alien who did not become naturalized here until several years after this Warburg's birth, is a son of a former partner of Kuhn, Loeb and Company, a grandson of another partner, a nephew of a former partner, and a nephew of a present partner. He holds no office in our Government, but I am told that he is in daily attendance at the Treasury, and that he has private quarters there! In other words, Mister Chairman, Kuhn, Loeb and Company now control and occupy the United States Treasury.

The text of the Executive Order which seems to place an embargo on shipments of gold permits the Secretary of the Treasury, a former director of the Fed of New York, the practices of which have been corrupt, to issue licenses at his discretion for the export of

---

70 Sound familiar? We are still paying off the gambling debts of fat-cat bankers. Remember the "too big to fail" bailouts and stimulus packages that sent billions over billions to the bankers and their friends?

gold coin, or bullion, earmarked or held in trust for a recognized foreign government or foreign central bank for international settlement.

Now, Mister Chairman, if gold held in trust for those foreign institutions may be sent to them, I see no reason why gold held in trust for Americans as evidenced by their gold certificates and other currency issued by the United States Government should not be paid to them.

I think that American citizens should be entitled to treatment at least as good as that which the present administration is extending to foreign governments, foreign central banks, and the bank of International Settlements. I think a veteran of the world war, with a twenty dollar gold certificate, is at least as much entitled to receive his own gold for it, as any international banker in the city of New York or London.

By the terms of this Executive Order, gold may be exported if it is actually required for the fulfillment of any contract entered into prior to the date of this Order by an applicant who, in obedience to the Executive Order of April fifth, nineteen thirty-three, has delivered gold coin, gold bullion, or gold certificates. This means that gold may be exported to pay the obligations abroad of the Fed which were incurred prior to the date of the Order, namely, April twentieth, nineteen thirty-three.

If a European Bank should send one hundred million dollars in Fed currency to a bank in this country for redemption, that bank could easily ship gold to Europe in exchange for that currency. Such Fed currency would represent "contracts" entered into prior to the date of the order. If the Bank of International Settlements or any other foreign bank holding any of the present gambling debt paper of the Fed should draw a draft paper for the settlement of such obligation, gold would be shipped to them because the debt contract would have been entered into prior to the date of order.

Mister Speaker, I rise to a question of constitutional privilege.

Whereas, I charge Eugene Meyer, Roy A. Young, Edmund Platt, Eugene B. Black, Adolph Casper Miller, Charles S. Hamlin, George R. James, Andrew W. Mellon, Ogden L. Mills, William H. Woodin, John W. Poole, J. F. T. O'Connor, members of the Federal Reserve Board; F. H. Curtis, J. H. Chane, R. L. Austin, George De Camp, L. B. Williams, W. W. Hoxton, Oscar Newton, E. M. Stevens, J. S. Wood, J. N. Payton, M. L. McClure, C. C. Walsh, Isaac B. Newton, Federal Reserve Agents, jointly and severally, with violations of the Constitution and laws of the United States, and

Whereas I charge them with having taken funds from the United States Treasury which were not appropriated by the Congress of the United States, and I charge them with having taken over eighty billion dollars from the United States Government in the year nineteen twenty-eight, the said unlawful taking consisting of the unlawful creation of claims against the United States Treasury to the extent of eighty billion dollars in the year nineteen twenty-eight; and I charge them with similar thefts committed in nineteen twenty-nine, nineteen thirty, nineteen thirty-one, nineteen thirty-two, nineteen thirty-three, and in years previous to nineteen twenty-eight, amounting to billions of dollars; and

Whereas, I charge them, jointly and severally with having unlawfully created claims against the United States Treasury by unlawfully placing United States Government credit in specific amounts to the credit of foreign governments and foreign central banks of issue; private interests and commercial and private banks of the United States and foreign countries, and branches of foreign banks doing business in the United States, to the extent of billions of dollars; and with having made unlawful contracts in the name of the United States Government and the United States Treasury; and with having made false entries on books of account; and

Whereas, I charge them jointly and severally, with having taken Fed notes from the United States Treasury and with having issued Fed notes and with having put Fed notes into circulation without obeying the mandatory provision of the Fed Act which requires the Fed Board fix an interest rate on all issues of Fed notes supplied to Fed Banks, the interest resulting therefrom to be paid by the Fed Banks to the Government of the United States for the use of the Fed notes, and I charge them of having defrauded the United States Government and the people of the United States of billions of dollars by the commission of this crime; and

Whereas, I charge them, jointly and severally, with having purchased United States Government securities with United States Government credit unlawfully taken and with having sold the said United States Government securities back to the people of the United States for gold or gold values and with having again purchased United States Government securities with United States Government credit unlawfully taken and with having again sold the said United States Government securities for gold and gold values, and I charge them with having defrauded the United States Government and the people of the United States by this rotary process; and

Whereas, I charge them, jointly and severally, with having unlawfully negotiated United States Government securities, upon which the Government liability was extinguished, as collateral security for Fed notes and with having substituted such securities for gold which was being held as collateral security for Fed notes, and with having by the process defrauded the United States Government and the people of the United States, and I charge them with the theft of all the gold and currency they obtained by this process; and

Whereas, I charge them, jointly and severally, with having unlawfully issued Fed currency on false, worthless and fictitious acceptances and other circulating evidence of debt, and with having made unlawful advances of Fed currency, and with having unlawfully permitted renewals of acceptances and renewals of other circulating evidences of debt, and with having permitted acceptance bankers and discount dealer corporations and other private bankers to violate the banking laws of the United States; and

Whereas, I charge them, jointly and severally, with having conspired to have evidences of debt to the extent of one billion dollars artificially created at the end of February, nineteen thirty-three, and early in March, nineteen thirty-three, and with having made unlawful issues and advances of Fed currency on the security of said artificially created evidences of debt for a sinister purpose, and with having assisted in the execution of said sinister purpose; and

Whereas, I charge them, jointly and severally, with having brought about a repudiation of the currency obligations of the Fed Banks to the people of the United States, and with having conspired to obtain a release for the Fed Board and the Fed Banks from their contractual liability to redeem all Fed currency in gold or lawful money at the Fed Bank and with having defrauded the holders of Fed currency, and with having conspired to have the debts and losses of the Fed Board and the Fed Banks unlawfully transferred to the Government and the people of the United States; and

Whereas, I charge them, jointly and severally, with having unlawfully substituted Fed currency and other irredeemable paper currency for gold in the hands of the people after the decision to repudiate the Fed currency and the national currency was made known to them, and with thus having obtained money under false pretenses; and

Whereas, I charge them, jointly and severally, with having brought about a repudiation of the national currency of the United States in order that the gold value of the said currency might be given to private interests, foreign governments, foreign central banks of issues, and the Bank of International Settlements, and the people... to be left without gold or lawful money, and with no currency other than a paper currency irredeemable in gold, and I charge them with having done this for the benefit of private interests, foreign governments, foreign central banks of issue, and the Bank of International Settlements; and

Whereas I charge them, jointly and severally, with... having unlawfully permitted and made possible "new financing" for foreigners, at the expense of the United States Treasury to the extent of billions of dollars, and with having unlawfully permitted and made possible the bringing into the United States, immense quantities of foreign securities, created in foreign countries for export to the United States, and with having unlawfully permitted the said foreign securities to be imported into the United States instead of gold, which was lawfully due to the United States on trade balances and otherwise, and with having lawfully permitted and facilitated the sale of the said foreign securities in the United States, and

Whereas, I charge them, jointly and severally, with having unlawfully exported United States coins and currency for a sinister purpose, and with having deprived the people of the United States of their lawful circulating medium of exchange; and I charge them with having arbitrarily and unlawfully reducing the amount of money and currency in circulation in the United States to the lowest rate per capita in the history of the Government, so that the great mass of the people have been left without a sufficient medium of exchange...; and

Whereas I charge them, jointly and severally, with having arbitrarily and unlawfully raised and lowered the rates of money and with having arbitrarily increased and diminished the volume of currency in circulation for the benefit of private interests at the expense of the Government and the people of the United States, and with having unlawfully manipulated money rates, wages, salaries and property values both real and personal, in the United States...; and

Whereas I charge them, jointly and severally, with having brought about the decline in prices on the New York Stock Exchange and other exchanges in October, nineteen twenty-nine, by unlawful manipulation of money and currency in circulation: by theft of funds from the United States Treasury;... by service rendered to foreign and domestic speculators and politicians, and by unlawful sale of United States gold reserves abroad; and...

Whereas, no private interest should be permitted to buy United States Government securities with the Government's own credit unlawfully taken; and, whereas currency should not be issued for the benefit of said private interests or any interests on United States Government securities so acquired; and

Whereas I charge them, jointly and severally, with failure to protect and maintain the gold reserves and the gold stock and gold coinage of the United States, and with having sold the gold reserves... to foreign Governments, foreign central banks of issue, foreign commercial and private banks, and other foreign institutions and individuals at a profit to themselves; and I charge them with having sold gold reserves of the United States so that between nineteen twenty-four and nineteen twenty-eight the United States gained no gold on net account, but suffered a decline in its percentage of central gold reserves from forty-five point nine percent in nineteen twenty-four to thirty-seven point five percent in nineteen twenty-eight, notwithstanding the fact that the United States had a favorable balance of trade throughout that period; and

Whereas I charge them, jointly and severally, with having conspired to concentrate United States Government securities and thus the national debt of the United States in the hands of foreigners and international money lenders and with having conspired to transfer to foreigners and international money lenders title to and control of the financial resources of the United States; and

Whereas I charge them, jointly and severally, with having destroyed independent banks in the United States, and with having thereby caused losses amounting to billions of dollars to the depositors of the said banks and to the general public of the United States; and

Whereas I charge them, jointly and severally, with the failure to furnish true reports of the business operations and the true conditions of the Fed to the Congress and the people, and having furnished false and misleading reports to the Congress of the United States; and

Whereas I charge them, jointly and severally, with having published false and misleading propaganda intended to deceive the American people and to cause the United States to lose its independence; and

...Whereas I charge them, jointly and severally, with having robbed the United States Government and the people of the United States by their theft and sale of the gold reserves of the United States and other unlawful transactions, and with having created a deficit in the United States Treasury, which has necessitated to a large extent the destruction of our national defense and the reduction of the United States Army and Navy and other branches of the national defense; and

Whereas I charge them, jointly and severally, of having reduced the United States from a first class power to one that is dependent, and with having reduced the United States from a rich and powerful nation to one that is internationally poor; and

Whereas I charge them, jointly and severally, with the crime of having treasonably conspired and acted against the peace and security of the United States, and with having treasonably conspired to destroy constitutional government in the United States....

*End of McFadden Remarks in Congress

Congressman McFadden's bold attempt to have the Fed investigated and abolished failed, and we therefore suffer today from the evolved evil of the Fed. Nothing has changed, except the Fed has grown stronger and more deeply rooted. Evidence, as is revealed in Congressman McFadden's remarks before Congress, is "easily" found, yet is absent from the "common sense of the community." How is it that the Fed isn't just a bad economic memory today? It's a tribute to the vital part the media and "education" continue to play in keeping people ignorant about politics and *their* money.

Lenin—Keynes—Bernanke—Navellier—Greenspan—DeSilver

Economist John Maynard Keynes, *The Economic Consequences of the Peace:*

Lenin is said to have declared that the best way to destroy the Capitalist System was to debauch the currency. By a continuing process of inflation, governments can confiscate, secretly and unobserved, an important part of the wealth of their citizens. By this method they not only confiscate, but they confiscate arbitrarily; and, while the process impoverishes many, it actually enriches some. The sight of this arbitrary rearrangement of riches strikes not only at security, but at confidence in the equity of the existing distribution of wealth. Those to whom the system brings windfalls, beyond their deserts and even beyond their expectations or desires, become "profiteers," who are the object of the hatred of the bourgeoisie, whom the inflationism has impoverished, not less than of the proletariat. As the inflation proceeds and the real value of the currency fluctuates wildly from month to month, all permanent relations between debtors and creditors, which form the ultimate foundation of capitalism, become so utterly disordered as to be almost meaningless; and the process of wealth-getting degenerates into a gamble and a lottery. Lenin was certainly right. There is no subtler, no surer means of overturning the existing basis of society than to debauch the currency. The process engages all the hidden forces of economic law on the side of destruction, and does it in a manner which not one man in a million is able to diagnose.

Keynes says, in *Essays in Persuasion:*

This progressive deterioration in the value of money through history is not an accident, and has had behind it two great driving forces—the impecuniosities[71] of Governments and the superior political influence of the debtor class.

Ben Bernanke, Federal Reserve Board of Governors member, said in his remarks before the National Economists Club, Washington, DC, November 21, 2003:[72]

The U.S. government has a technology, called a printing press (or, today, its electronic equivalent), that allows it to produce as many U.S. dollars as it wishes at essentially no cost. By increasing the number of U.S. dollars in circulation, or even by credibly threatening to do so, the U.S. government can also reduce the value of a dollar in

---

71 Not having money; hard-up; without funds - Webster's Encyclopedic Dictionary (1942).

72 Bernanke was appointed the club's chairman in 2006.

terms of goods and services, which is equivalent to raising the prices in dollars of those goods and services. We conclude that, under a paper-money system, a determined government can always generate higher spending and hence positive inflation.[73]

Investment counselor Louis Navellier, from his newsletter of February 27, 2009:

Apparently, there's no shortage of money in Washington. President Obama has spent much of his first five weeks in office responding to the financial crisis, and each of his proposed solutions carries with it a hefty price tag.

It all started with Treasury Secretary Geithner's $2 trillion bank bailout, only to be followed up by Obama's $787 billion economic stimulus package. And yesterday, our Commander-in-Chief unveiled his blueprint for a $3.6 trillion budget, which will further expand an already bloated deficit.

Just as I told you in the February issue, the U.S. government's spendthrift ways and jaw-dropping deficits are the perfect recipe for stirring up inflation and driving down the value of the U.S. dollar.

Alan Greenspan, Federal Reserve Chairman (1987–2006), said in *Gold and Economic Freedom* (1966):

In the absence of the gold standard, there is no way to protect savings from confiscation through inflation. There is no safe store of value. If there were, the government would have to make its holding illegal, as was done in the case of gold. If everyone decided, for example, to convert all their bank deposits to silver or copper or any other good and therefore decline to accept checks as payments for goods, bank deposits would lose their purchasing power and government-credited bank credit would be worthless as claims on goods. The financial policy of the welfare state requires that there be no way for the owners of wealth to protect themselves.

This is the shabby secret of the welfare statists' tirades against gold. Deficit spending is simply a scheme for the confiscation of wealth. Gold stands in the way of this insidious process. It stands as a protector of property rights. If one grasps this, one has no difficulty in understanding the statists' antagonism toward the gold standard.[74]

---

73 Bernanke is blaming the ills of the Fed on the government. The printing press does not belong to the government; it belongs to the Fed. The relationship between the Fed and the government is incestuous, but the government is the government, and the Fed is a private banking cartel. The Fed uses the "full faith and credit of the United States" as collateral via bonds, and the government borrows at will, but government does not own the press. The national debt represents principal and interest owed to lenders. Above, replace "government" with "Fed," and the statement is mostly true.)

74 If gold was the great protector, why did the Great Depression happen? The best protection is a dead Fed, no fractional-reserve banking, replaced with United States notes with stringent oversight.

On April 3, 1933, President Roosevelt, by executive order (6102) confiscated Americans' gold. Not until January 1975, nearly forty-two years later, were Americans again allowed to own gold-bullion coins. It is hard to believe—in America, allegedly the land of the free—that Americans were forbidden from protecting the sweat of their brows by owning something with intrinsic value: gold.

We had gold and silver as currency. We had United States notes and then Federal Reserve notes. With a dead Fed, we need the United States Government to issue United States "notes." —yes, fiat money, but paper regulated and protected by strict regulations and oversight by *our* Government.

Drew DeSilver, senior writer at the Pew Research Center, wrote this on October 9, 2013:

> With the Republican-led House engaged in a stare-down with Senate Democrats and President Obama over raising the federal debt ceiling, it seems an opportune time to dig into the actual numbers describing the national debt, the debt limit and interest payments on the nation's credit line:
>
> As of Sept. 30 **the federal government's total debt stood at $16.74 trillion**, according to the Treasury Department's monthly reckoning. Nearly all of it is subject to the statutory debt ceiling, which is currently set at a hair under $16.7 trillion; as a result, at the end of September there was just $25 million in unused debt capacity remaining.
>
> The **debt is about equal to gross domestic product** (GDP), which was $16.661 trillion in the second quarter. The government's first read on GDP for the third quarter, which ended Sept. 30, isn't due till the end of this month, but it likely will be delayed because of the federal shutdown. Debt as a share of GDP has risen steeply since the 2008 financial crisis.

There was approximately $1.29 trillion in circulation as of July 2, 2014, of which $1.24 trillion was in Federal Reserve notes (see FederalReserve.gov). So, how do we pay off $18 trillion in debt if we only have $1.24 trillion in circulation? My superior understanding of math tells me it can't be done. So, what is the solution? You are about to discover a tried-and-true legal method to pay off the national debt within two years, neuter inflation and deflation, and virtually eliminate the risk of depressions. Here we go:

Honorable John R. Rarick (LA) Testimony[75]
House of Representatives—May 11, 1972

> Mr. Speaker, the current effects of our Government to hold down price increases have served to focus the attention of thoughtful students on a little discussed facet of our money

---

75 As part of his testimony, Representative Rarick references and quotes T. David Horton, who then quotes a number of other authorities. A bit hard to follow so watch where you're reading.

system. This system, because of a long process of miseducation and studied silence, is not now understood as it was prior to adoption of the Federal Reserve System more than half a century ago. It is based upon debt, has serious implications for the future of our country, and invites what may be the greatest war in history.

Every debt-dollar demands an interest tribute from our economy for every year that dollar remains in circulation. These interest costs force up the price of every commodity and service and contribute greatly to inflation.

One hundred and ten years ago, on President Lincoln's recommendation, the Congress authorized the issue of interest-free United States notes. Many of these notes are still in circulation and their interest-free status has saved the American economy billions of dollars.

Attempts to fight inflation in the United States by the highest interest rates here in over 100 years are bound to fail for high interest rates drive costs and prices up while holding production down. For this reason, the present administration has succeeded only in bringing about the anomalous situation of a depression in the midst of rising prices. The result has been to engorge financiers with profits at the expense of every other sector of the economy.

Moreover, so long as the manipulators of the money seek to maximize bank profits by high interest rates, prices must continue to skyrocket. Only by forcing these rates down can production be encouraged and costs reduced, which will minimize price increases.

Under the Constitution, the Congress has responsibility of issuing the Nation's money and regulating its value—Article I, section 8, clause 5. In a recent brilliant analysis of our money system by T. David Horton, Chairman of the Executive Council of the Defenders of the American Constitution, able lawyer and keen student of basic history, suggests a proven remedy for our current predicament that will enable the Congress to resume its constitutional responsibility to regulate our Nation's money by liberating our economy from the swindle of the debt-money manipulators, by the issuance of national currency in debt-free form.

Early in the present Congress I introduced legislation (H.R. 351) the main aim of which to accomplish such liberation by authorizing our National government to purchase the Federal Reserve System, and to place it under the control of experienced administrators who recognize the basic soundness of the traditionalist money system, and who can be depended on to act in the interests of the American people and American financial needs.

In order that the indicated analysis and proposal of Mr. Horton may be available to our colleagues, I quote it as part of my remarks.

Monetary Crisis—Its Threat to Liberty and the Remedy (Address of T. David Horton):

In 1797 John Adams wrote to Thomas Jefferson, "All the perplexities, confusion and distress in America arise, not from defects of the Constitution or Confederation; not from any want of honor or virtue, as much as downright ignorance of the nature of coin, credit and circulation."

The power to issue money is the supreme prerogative of government.

The history of contemporary money policies may be traced back to what has been called "the crime of 1666" when Barbara Villers, mistress to Charles II, helped the British East India Company gain a rake-off starting at two pence on the pound of the royal coinage. These corrupt practices were multiplied and by 1694, William Paterson, founder of the privately owned Bank of England would declare, "The Bank hath benefit of the interest on all monies that it creates out of nothing."

With the crime of 1864, the National Bank Act, we find private banks gaining the power to issue money directly and a struggle commenced that has continued to the present day. Our own national heritage, if we are allowed to know it, is full of emphatic statements upon the subject of money.

The great American monetary historian, Alexander Del Mar, declared:

> Money is perhaps the mightiest engine to which man can lend an intelligent guidance. Unheard, unfelt, unseen, it has the power to so distribute the burdens, gratifications and opportunities of life that each individual shall enjoy that share of them to which his merits or good fortune may fairly entitle him, or, contrariwise, to dispense with them so partial a hand as to violate every principle of justice, and perpetuate a succession of…slaveries to the end of time.

What have we done with our money? More than a hundred years ago John C. Calhoun said that we had given the banks the government credit for nothing, only to borrow it back again at interest.

In the 1930s Marriner Eccles, then Chairman of the Board of Governors of the Federal Reserve System, admitted to Congressman Wright Patman that, "What that privately owned central bank used to buy three billion dollars' worth of government bonds was the right" as he called it, "to create credit money."

Congressman Usher L. Burdick confirmed this in an interview published in 1959:

We want to sell four billion dollars' worth of bonds, and we sell it in New York to those who haven't got a dime, and they don't need any money because they simply enter credit to the government on the books! And then, before such money is paid out, they get the currency because they bundle up those bonds and bring them down here to Washington and get an equal amount of currency. Then they've got the money! But they didn't have the money before the government gave it to them.

In the meantime, of course, the government continues to pay interest on those bonds. There is an incredulity regarding money matters that may be due in part to the fact that these gigantic legalized swindles simply boggle the imagination.

G. W. L. Day wrote in his book, *This Leads to War*:

The mystery which has shrouded the subject of banking is every bit as deep as that which obscures the hocus-pocus of witch-doctoring; and with just the same blind respect with which the simple natives of Sumeria once gaped and goggled while their priests muttered their incantations and examined the entrails of chickens. For centuries we have listened with awe to the dictums of finance, believing that its high priesthood is possessed of knowledge superhuman and that its mysteries are sacrosanct and incomprehensible to the common run of man.

Henry Ford put it this way: "If the American people knew the corruption in our money system, there would be a revolution before morning."

What are the reasons for the disparity that we find in the manner in which we tend to accept some things, but refuse and fail to know some of the simplest of truths with regard to our money? One of the reasons may be explained this way:

We have a situation here where—if one of you deposits $100 in a bank account and if you write checks upon that deposit twice—if you do it in my country, I have to come around and put you in jail and lock you up! You have committed a felony. Yet the very same bank in which you deposited that $100 can write checks on that same $100 not once, not twice, but five or ten times, even 20 times and can do so with impunity. This is called the fractional reserve system.

We penalize one man who writes checks on the same money twice and send him to jail. We glorify the banker who writes checks on the same money ten times and send him to Congress. The difference between the banker's activity and the activity of the "paperhanger," as we'll call him, (who writes checks on the same money more than once) is that the banker charges interest for lending the same money ten times!

Dr. Carl F. M. Sandberg said:

> From those not previously familiar with these things, have come expressions of interest and enthusiasm, but also reluctance to accept as truth the fact that our government, without getting anything whatsoever in return, gives the Federal Reserve notes to private bankers for them to loan out at interest, even back to the government itself. To them this seems so senseless as to be unbelievable.
>
> This is one reason why we find a certain incredulity with regard to accepting some of the basic facts of life that relate to our money system. But it is not the enormity of the outrage that is most important. It is not the fact that the swindles of high finance amount to billions of dollars. It is the fact that our present debt money system does not work, that is doing us the greatest injury.

...The importance of controlling the volume of money in any country is absolute master of all industry and commerce.

Added to the fact that all of our money is debt money, we need to consider a second point, and that is our profit system: I remember as a small boy, puzzling myself over a problem that arose when I was reflecting upon the profits that I was making out of shoveling snow, mowing lawns, delivering newspapers, or whatever, saving up for the day when I would go to college. I figured: If I make a profit (and I'm supposed to be working to make a profit) and if everybody else is making a profit, where is the money to come from? I take my quarters and put them in a little bank—I was taking money out of circulation. My profit is what I took out of circulation. If everybody else did the same, a problem might develop.

I didn't come to any conclusions, but it was obvious to me, and it is probably obvious to any other ten-year-old, that there is a problem with regard to our money if we are to operate on a profit system. If every business is run at a profit, then every business is creating a partial vacuum in the money supply, and this can lead and always has led over a period of time to cataclysm. This is the assistance that the free enterprise system affords to the controllers of our money system, when it is decided by those controllers to cause a depression. Unwittingly, so long as we tolerate a debt-money system, we contribute to our own undoing.

Periodically, we get into a depression, as we're not able to distribute to our own people the very necessaries of life. Willing workers are left idle, producing nothing, while products rust and food rots—for want of the money which our debt-money system deprives us. A physician told me recently that the second most common diagnosis made today by the general practitioner is malnutrition. This is America in 1972.

At the same time, we are sending more than one hundred million dollars' worth of wheat to Russia, to feed their workers who make more guns to kill our boys (and more ICBMs to threaten our cities). Our own people are hungry, and the manipulators of our debt-money system decree that we send our food to our enemies. This is insane. But we are not without remedy.

First, we must understand that our debt-money system creates a vacuum in the money supply. Second, we must understand that in order to have a healthy economy with everybody making more and more goods and reflecting more and more profit we must have an expanding money supply.

So, our debt-money system is exactly the wrong kind of money system that we need for a healthy economy. Rather than continually expanding the supply of money to meet the demands of ever-increasing goods and services that are being placed on the market, our debt-money system decrees that the money supply shall contract because every dollar that is in circulation has a little tag on it, called interest, which commands that there must be withdrawn from circulation six cents or nine cents or twelve cents or whatever the interest tag dictates, in order for that dollar to remain in circulation for another year.

The solution to this problem is not new. We can find it in the works of Abraham Lincoln that are now more than one hundred years old. These quotations are from Lincoln's speeches on money reform:

> Money is the creature of law, and the creation of the original issue of money should be maintained as an exclusive monopoly of the national government.

> The wages of men should be recognized in the structure of and in the social order as more important that the wages of money.

> No duty is more imperative on the government than the duty it owes the people to furnish them a sound and uniform currency, and of regulating the circulation of the medium of exchange, so that labor will be protected from a vicious currency, and commerce will be facilitated by cheap safe exchanges.

> The monetary needs of increasing numbers of people advancing toward higher standards of living can and should be met by the government.

> The circulation of a medium of exchange issued and backed by the government can be properly regulated.

Government has the power to regulate the currency and the credit of the nation. Government possessing the power to create and issue currency and credit as money and enjoying the right to withdraw both currency and credit from circulation by taxation and otherwise need not and should not borrow capital at interest as the means of financing government work and public enterprise.

The government should create, issue, and circulate all the currency and credit needed to satisfy the spending power of the government and the buying power of consumers. The privilege of creating and issuing money is not only the supreme prerogative of government, but it is the government's greatest creative opportunity.

What Lincoln was referring to was the issuance of a national currency, sometimes referred to as Lincoln Greenbacks. I don't know how many here have seen or remember seeing what today are the remaining issues of approximately three hundred million dollars that was put into circulation more than one hundred years ago. They are the United States notes, which bear the red seal. Our ordinary Federal Reserve notes bear, appropriately enough, a dour black seal. These black seals are debt money. Before they may circulate, a debt must be created. A United States note with a red seal is spent into circulation and is interest free. There is no interest incurred in the issuance of it. There is no interest incurred in maintaining it in circulation.

The importance of this device that Lincoln initiated during the Civil War, which we need to copy if we are to emancipate our commerce from the thralldom of debt money, is recognized by the bankers themselves. The London *Times* is quoted as being the mouthpiece of high finance in John Howland Snow's book, *Government by Treason*. The *Times* is quoted as follows, referring to the Lincoln Greenbacks:

If that mischievous financial policy, which had its origin in the North American Republic during the late war (Civil War) in that country, should become indurate down to a fixture, then that government will furnish its own money without cost. It will pay off its debts and be without debt. It will have all the money necessary to carry on its commerce. It will be prosperous beyond precedent in the history of civilized governments of the world. The brains and the wealth of all countries will go to North America. *That government must be destroyed...*

If we want to try to remedy the situation where our money system, instead of expanding at a time when we need more money, contracts and thereby forces us into periodic depression, we need to adopt the measures that Lincoln initiated; namely, the issuance of a national currency. If, coupled with this, we require the banks to lend our money not ten or fifteen times, but limit them to three times, this would be enough, and this can be done by setting the reserve requirements at thirty-three and a third percent.[76] If these two things are done, it will not only provide an immense source of tax-free revenue and provide our commerce with a source of money that is interest free, but also, it will keep the banking institutions from taking away the control of the amount of money in circulation, which they now do by their fractional reserve system.

As it stands, by multiplying the number of times that the same dollar is loaned out, the banking fraternity in fact controls much more of the total purchasing power available to bid for goods than the control that is exercised by the original issuing authority. This can be stopped by doing these two things: Issuing United States notes on the one hand, and increasing reserve requirements on the other.

It has been wondered why it is we are drifting slowly, but apparently uncontrollably, toward Socialism. The answer to that perplexing question can found in our debt money system. If we have a situation where there are two things that are drawing money out of circulation, namely the debt issuance of the currency in the first place and the profit motive in the second place, we find that it is necessary, in order to make the economy run at all, for this slack to be taken out.

The manner in which this is characteristically done in modern times is by means of a government deficit. Namely, the government spending more money than it takes in. The theory apparently is, that if the government operates at enough of a loss (and we've lost more than four hundred billion dollars) then this will keep enough money in circulation to make up for the vacuum that the debt-money system on the one hand and the profit motive system on the other creates in the money supply. Yes, we all know it is impossible to borrow our way out of debt. We know that sooner or later in this type of operation there must be an accounting, and with that accounting we find depression.

When we come up to a period of recession or depression we find that the Socialists and the Communists are the only ones around with available remedies. The remedy that they suggest for the problem that is created by a restricted money supply, of having more productivity than you can distribute, is the same remedy that was advocated by the fellow who decided to kill the goose that laid the golden egg. They can take care of the problem—too many golden eggs to distribute—by killing the goose. And there is no doubt it is possible to eliminate these unmarketable surpluses by restricting production. But restricting production is not the answer. It's comparable to killing the goose that laid the golden egg.

---

76 I highly respect Mister Horton's opinion. He may be right, but giving any amount of fractional-reserve privilege to the banks makes me nervous.

The answer is to have sufficient money. Sufficient blood supply in our economy; to have it stay viable and to have it stay prosperous. This can be done only if we get away from our debt-money system which forces us periodically into depression.

Another measure that we may consider in attempting to deal with the problems that we have in a money system that is basically diseased, is to try to establish some means of local control of local purchasing power.

...The original theory behind the Federal Reserve System was that it would provide de-centralized control. With twelve de-centralized Federal Reserve Banks, we were told, we would have an ability to adjust local needs to local demands. We know now that this was merely a pretext. It was a gigantic fraud. It never did and never was intended to do any such thing. It was a European-style central bank subject to the control of money manipulators which would keep us from having any local control of our local purchasing power.

What can we do individually in our States to offset this? One suggestion is to have other States follow the example of North Dakota. North Dakota has a bank.[77] North Dakota is the only State in the Union that does have a bank. The Bank of North Dakota is owned and operated by that State. It allows a certain limited amount of local control of local purchasing power. Local improvements are financed through that bank. Student loans are supported through that bank. You would not find it possible in North Dakota to get the people there to give up the Bank of North Dakota.

We have in other parts of the country, banks that are similarly named, but the Bank of Nevada or the Bank of Oregon or the Bank of California in every instance is a state chartered, privately-owned financial institution.

If we wish to copy the example of the Bank of North Dakota we will find that that bank provided its people with a source of credit that survived even the Great Depression of the nineteen thirties.

[Methods of Local Control of Local Purchasing Power]
Coupled to this we can institute in our local communities a certain amount of local purchasing power issued by the community itself. This can be in either one of two forms.

In one case, the merchants of a particular community can agree to honor each other's checks, payable to bearer and insured against being cleared through the bank, which would cancel them, but intended to circulate as a local currency. Those merchants in that particular community will find that they will have authority to control a certain

---

77 Please Google the Bank of North Dakota to see the power and success of banking outside the Federal Reserve.

amount of their own local purchasing power. They will find that their own people, on whom they depend for livelihood, are less likely to trade elsewhere than they will be in their own local community, as long as the currency that is there is circulating locally.

The other way to obtain local control of local purchasing power is by means of local or county vouchers circulating as currency. These vouchers can be made substantially interest-free under most state statutes. If this is done, local improvements can be made without our local governments going to the lending institutions to borrow back the very tax money that the local communities have with the commercial financial institutions.

In case too many people become alarmed of the consequences of this, it is to be pointed out that we now have a certain amount of non-interest bearing money in circulation. All of our fractional currency; that is to say, the pennies, the nickels, the dimes, the quarters and the halves, all of these are non-interest bearing in their form. They are manufactured in our mints; they are paid into circulation, circulate freely; they do not draw interest, and they provide the government a very valuable source of revenue.

In the fiscal years nineteen sixty-six through nineteen seventy, inclusive, the amount of seigniorage[78] paid into the Treasury by the mints amounted to more than four billion dollars. The profit ratio on this type of currency is something on the order of six-to-one (You end up with six times as much currency as you have cost going into making the fractional coinage). The cost ratio in making the Federal Reserve notes is more on the order of six hundred to one. And during these same four fiscal years, in spite of the fact that more than fifty billion dollars in Federal Reserve notes was manufactured by the Bureau of Printing and Engraving and turned over to the banks—not one cent in seigniorage was paid into the Treasury!

In arresting this swindle and in emancipating our commerce from a debt-money system we will find that the threat that is now posed by the Socialist and the Communists largely disappears. Their remedies for our ills are being accepted gradually for two reasons. One, there are no competing remedies being offered; two, our debt-money system compels the government to spend more than it takes in, because this is the only way we can keep the economy going! And this defect, this use of a debt-money system, is what is forcing us gradually, and sometimes more rapidly than many of us like to think, down the tube to Socialism. By liberating our economy from its debt-money system, we will be safeguarding our own freedoms. Further than this, we will be protecting the world from a threat which seems ominous enough now, but if we usher in the era of prosperity that is available to us and that the bank controllers themselves admit will come to us, we will

---

78 A government revenue from the manufacture of coins calculated as the difference between the face value and the metal value of the coins.

find that the threat of Socialism and Communism, even on the international scale, will largely dwindle and fade away.

Therefore, we must order our priorities. We must decide as individuals whether we are going to address ourselves to the problem of correcting a grave injustice that is perpetrated on our economy and on our government, by getting rid of a debt-money system. We must order our priorities and decide that we are going to spend our money and give of our substance and ourselves to this fight, rather than be distracted by the current basketball game, football game or by any number of other diversions that are continually waved before us.

If we want bread and circuses, then what we're going to get is Socialism. If we want to make our principal pastime, our principal activity, the running of our own affairs and the reinstallation of constitutional control over our currency, then we will find that the support of such organizations as the Oregon Legislative and Research Committee will reward our individual efforts, which will be responsive to a real national and local need.

Therefore, those who have elected to forego the entertainments of the hour to come here to study the question of what to do about our money system are to be commended. It is the people right here in this auditorium upon whom the well-being of our Republic rests.

Those of us who have studied the American Revolution realize that it took a very small percentage of the American people to accomplish that feat. The burden rested upon relatively few shoulders. The fact that we can see about us others who appear to be more interested in other things should not dissuade us. We should be prepared to give of our substance and our time to such organizations as this, that have a positive remedy that is something other than a Socialist remedy; a remedy that has been proven; a remedy that will work; and a remedy for which our posterity will thank us, if we are able to accomplish it.

—End of Horton testimony, as relayed by Rarick

The Honorable John R. Rarick and attorney T. David Horton, quoted above, offered viable solutions. I greatly respect the opinions of these two men. My concern is that issuing United States notes to match the "spending power of the government" would bankrupt us quicker than a politician saying no to a tax cut. I'm with the makers of *The Money Masters* documentary,[79] and others, who say we need and deserve a 100 percent reserve. Please read and print out a copy of the **Monetary Reform Act** at TheMoneyMasters.com (find links at my website, SqueakyWheelPolitics.com).

---

79 *The Money Masters,* a three-hour documentary (YouTube or DVD at TheMoneyMasters.com. It is the most concise and relevant information on the Federal Reserve you will find anywhere. Take a look and ask your friends, family, and elected officials to take a look.

America will be debt-free within two years by, as Judge Rarick notes, paying off United States bonds with debt-free United States notes—debt-free money akin to the Greenbacks President Lincoln issued. In tandem, we will need to prevent banks from creating an avalanche of inflation via their fractional-reserve banking system as they do today. Following is a nifty solution that American economist Professor Milton Friedman[80] (1912–2006) advanced to maintain a stable money supply without inflation and deflation while dissolving the debt: while the Treasury buys United States bonds back on the open market with debt-free United States notes, local bank-reserve requirements will be proportionally raised, keeping the amount of money in circulation constant.

As bondholders are paid off with United States notes, bondholders would deposit the currency, thereby making available the money banks need to increase reserves. Once the United States bonds are completely replaced with United States notes, banks would be at the required 100 percent reserve, thus ending the current used-and-abused fractional-reserve system.

All decisions on the ebb and flow of money for the American economy must be the result of statistical data on population growth and the price-level index. This would ensure steady, stable money growth, stable prices, and no sharp changes in the money supply. A new monetary committee manned by monetary regulators and the Treasury Department would have no discretion in that matter, except in time of war. But then, world conflict will dissipate once the Fed is dead. To assure the process is open and honest, all deliberations will be open to the public—just the opposite of the super-secretive meetings held by the Federal Reserve Board. This will work! It will work because the major causes of economic instability will have been removed—that is, the Federal Reserve banking system, along with fractional-reserve banking. Also, United States membership in the International Monetary Fund (IMF), Bank for International Settlements (BIS), and the World Bank must be abolished. We will therefore have eliminated the danger of severe depression. As noted by Professor Milton Friedman on the single cause of severe economic depression, "I know of no severe depression, in any country or any time, that was not accompanied by a sharp decline in the stock of money and equally of no sharp decline in the stock of money that was not accompanied by a severe depression."

Issuing our own currency is not a radical remedy. On the contrary, it has been advocated by presidents Jefferson, Madison, Jackson, Van Buren, and Lincoln. It has been used at different times throughout Europe as well. For example, Guernsey, one of the small islands in the English Channel, has been using debt-free money to pay for large building projects for nearly two hundred years. Guernsey is one of the most successful examples of just how well a debt-free money system can work. In about 1815, the impoverished island could not afford more new taxes, so it decided to try an innovative idea: issue its own paper money. The money was colorful paper notes backed by nothing, but the people of this tiny island agreed to accept them and trade with them. To ensure wide circulation, the people declared the fiat paper money good for the payment of taxes. This was not a new idea;

---

80 Milton Friedman was an American economist who received the 1976 Nobel Memorial Prize in Economic Sciences for his research on consumption analysis, monetary history and theory, and the complexity of stabilization policy.

it is exactly what America did before the American Revolution, and there have been many other examples throughout the world. It makes no difference whether you're talking about a small island like Guernsey or a large country like the United States; debt-free money is debt-free money whether ten or a hundred notes are issued.

Be assured that the constitutional authority and responsibility to authorize the issuance of debt-free money (United States notes) rest exclusively in the hands of our Congress. Our Congress also has the exclusive power to reform the ill-advised banking laws enacted over a hundred years ago. No ifs, ands, or buts about it, the international banking cartel will scream to the depths of hell that issuing and using debt-free money will cause severe inflation, and it will give many, many other dire predictions. Consider the source and ignore it—and don't allow elected officials to give in to the cartel's tactics. Give them a copy of this book and others, like *None Dare Call It Conspiracy*. Remind them that it has been the Federal Reserve banking system, and particularly fractional-reserve banking, that has been the real cause of over 90 percent of all inflation. Send them to the inflation calculator. Remind them that the Fed and fractional-reserve banking equals recession, depression, boom, and bust—over and over and over again. The Fed and fractional-reserve banking are going, and if your elected officials refuse to support and act, do everything in your power to oust them.

Thomas Edison:

If the United States can issue a dollar bond it can issue a dollar bill. The element that makes the bond good makes the bill good also. The difference between the bond and the bill is that the bond lets the money broker collect twice the amount of the bond and an additional 20%. Whereas the currency, the honest sort provide by the Constitution, pays nobody but those who contribute in some useful way. It is absurd to say our Country can issue bonds and cannot issue currency. Both are promises to pay, but the one fattens the usurer and the other helps the people.

Archibald E. Roberts, from his 1983 testimony before the Idaho Senate Affairs Committee in support of HJ Memorial #3, calls for repeal of the Federal Reserve Act of 1913:

Mister Chairman, the question of course is a very explicit one and that is that it really asks are we able to continue operating the economy without the Federal Reserve. I would point out, Mister Chairman, sir, that the United States of America operated until 1913 without the Federal Reserve through the existing agencies of government which still exist and function today. But the real control has been usurped from these agencies, authorized under the Constitution, and their power has been limited to merely approving what decisions are made by the owners of the Federal Reserve. So to answer your question, of course we'd continue the economy, but without paying the horrendous interest rates to the owners of the Federal Reserve. I would point out further, Mister Chairman, that it would be our objective to repudiate the one trillion dollar national debt[81] because it is not owed to us, it is owed to the Federal Reserve System. Since the Federal Reserve System, Mister Chairman, is a criminal conspiracy, the ill-gotten gains, this trillion dollar debt, a lien against all private property in the United States, obviously is a criminal act against the people of the United States.[82]

We can organize, educate, and legislate. It will likely require "some assembly." We need to be "on fire." I love the movie *Man on Fire*, starring Denzel Washington. We need to band together and neutralize the "professionals" like Denzel's character did—except our "neutralization" must be nonviolent. It is not hard to know how the "professionals" (international banking cartel) will act. Exposure is their worst enemy. At first, the professionals will spare no expense or tactic to discredit me and any and all others working to abolish their happy, big playground. They'll pooh-pooh our challenge, ridicule, and try to laugh it off. When that doesn't work, they will use any and all means to neutralize our efforts. After all, they are the professionals. But they can be brought down hard, just like David felled Goliath. Even though a recession or depression would add fuel to our fire, the arrogance of the professionals dictates that there will be another economic crisis.

I know, it seems overwhelming, since others have tried and failed for a hundred years or so. Why draft and push an Act abolishing the Fed and issuing United States notes when there appears to be little to no chance of enactment? Professor Milton Friedman offered two reasons:

> It is worth discussing radical changes, not in the expectation that they will be adopted promptly but for two other reasons. One is to construct an ideal goal, so that incremental changes can be judged by whether they move the institutional structure toward or away from that ideal. The other reason is very different. It is so that if a crisis requiring or facilitating radical change does arise, alternatives will be available that have been carefully developed and fully explored.

How can we win? We win with determination and faith.

J. A. Riis:[83]

> When nothing seems to help, I go and look at a stonecutter hammering away at his rock, perhaps a hundred times without as much as a crack showing in it. Yet at the hundred and first blow, it will split in two, and I know it was not that blow that did it, but all that had gone before.

---

81   The national debt has grown a bit since these words were spoken in 1983; today it's over 19 trillion.

82   Reprinted in Roberts's *The Most Secret Science* (1984): 56–57.

83   Jacob August *Riis* (1849–1914) was a Danish-American social reformer, "muckraking" journalist, and social-documentary photographer.

If we can deliver to people the cause and solution as given herein, we can succeed. We can be the "hundred-and-first blow."

Milton Friedman on a Proposed Constitutional Amendment

When the Constitution was enacted, the power given to Congress "to coin money, regulate the value thereof and of foreign coin" referred to commodity money: specifying that the dollar shall mean a definite weight in grams of silver or gold. The paper money inflation during the Revolution, as well as earlier in various colonies, led the framers to deny states the power to "coin money; emit bills of credit [i.e., paper money]; make anything but gold and silver coin a tender in payment of debts." The Constitution is silent on Congress's power to authorize the government to issue paper money. It was widely believed that the Tenth Amendment, providing that the powers not delegated to the United States by the Constitution are reserved to the States respectively, or to the people, made the issuance of paper money unconstitutional.

During the Civil War, Congress authorized greenbacks and made them a legal tender for all debts public and private. After the Civil War, in the first of the famous greenback cases, the Supreme Court declared the issuance of greenbacks unconstitutional. One fascinating aspect of this decision is that it was delivered by Chief Justice Salmon P. Chase, who had been Secretary of the Treasury when the first greenbacks were issued. Not only did he not disqualify himself, but in his capacity as Chief Justice convicted himself of having been responsible for an unconstitutional action in his capacity as Secretary of the Treasury.

Subsequently an enlarged and reconstituted Court reversed the first decision by a majority of five to four, affirming that making greenbacks a legal tender was constitutional, with Chief Justice Chase as one of the dissenting justices.

It is neither feasible nor desirable to restore a gold-or-silver coin standard, but we do need a commitment to sound money. The best arrangement currently would be to require the monetary authorities to keep the percentage rate of growth of the monetary base within a fixed range. This is a particularly difficult amendment to draft because it is so closely linked to the particular institutional structure. One version would be:

"Congress shall have the power to authorize non-interest-bearing obligations of the government in the form of currency or book entries, provided that the total dollar amount outstanding increases by no more than 5 percent per year and no less than 3 percent."

It might be desirable to include a provision that two-thirds of each House of Congress, or some similar qualified majority, can waive the requirement in case of a declaration of war, the suspension to terminate annually unless renewed.

A Constitutional Amendment would be the most effective way to establish confidence in the stability of the rule. However, it is clearly not the only way to impose the rule. Congress could equally well legislate it.[84]

We shall make the Federal Reserve banking system and fractional-reserve banking, history. And, so they can never return, we must keep this history and our corrective action eternally in the conscious-ness of every generation via education. Don't count on government to educate your children and grandchildren; you must do it. When they are old enough, take them into your library, start their education, and quiz them on what they've learned. Children's books should be written and games created so that children could start getting this vital information even before they learn to read.

To start, let's get the House and Senate to pass the following Resolution:

---

84 *A Program for Monetary Stability* (1960): 66–76, 100–101.

FEDERAL RESERVE: HOUSE OF REPRESENTATIVES AND SENATE RESOLUTION CREATING INVESTIGATIVE COMMITTEE, LEADING TO CORRECTIVE ACTION

The United States House of Representatives and Senate do hereby resolve to create an investigative committee to gather information, facts, and testimony and then write and pass an Act to accomplish the following:

1. Restore political accountability for monetary policy.
2. Restore confidence in and governmental control over America's money and credit.
3. Stabilize the money supply and price level.
4. Establish full-reserve banking.
5. Prohibit fractional-reserve banking.
6. Retire the national debt by authorizing and directing the Treasury Secretary to print United States notes and use them to purchase, in open-market operations or otherwise, all outstanding federal debt held by the public; thereby the net (public) national debt is to be completely retired and replaced with United States notes; Treasury Deposits are to be created for intra-United States-government debt in quantity sufficient to extinguish the remaining gross national debt.
7. Remove the causes of economic depressions, without additional taxation, inflation, or deflation by, in part, abolishing the Federal Reserve Act of 1913 and the Federal Reserve banking system; replace all interest-bearing Federal Reserve notes and derivatives with non-interest-bearing United States notes.
8. Withdraw from international banks such as the Bank for International Settlements, the International Monetary Fund, the World Bank, and all other international banks, whereas such membership is inconsistent with and in direct conflict with the purposes of the proposed Act of Congress.
9. Repeal all conflicting Acts.

Whereas, for an Act to accomplish all the above, the House of Representatives and Senate shall use the information found in the book, "*Screwed, Blued, Tattooed, and Sold Down the River;*" view *The Money Masters;* review and study the Monetary Reform Act presented at TheMoneyMasters.com; read the testimony of Archibald E. Roberts before the Idaho Senate Affairs Committee in support of HJ Memorial #3 calling for repeal of the Federal Reserve Act of 1913, along with his book *The Most Secret Science;* Gary Allen's *None Dare Call It Conspiracy;* and other such sources (see bibliography) to compose the Act; then, pass it.

Whereas, any portion of this Act deemed unconstitutional shall not render the remaining Act invalid;

Therefore, this Act is hereby passed by the United States House of Representatives with the United States Senate concurring, this _____ day of _____, 20____.

4

Blued

Blue: Colloq., sad, dejected, depressed, dispirited, downhearted.

—*Roget's College Thesaurus*

Few, very few, understood that the single, solitary cause of the Great Depression was the Federal Reserve. As I researched and saw the pain and misery, despair, and hopelessness intentionally imposed on our parents and grandparents, I started to burn, really burn, and that fire will not be extinguished until the Fed is dead.

NOT YOUR LAND FARM BOY

Eight years after passage of the 1913 Federal Reserve Act the Fed intentionally brought about the "Agricultural Panic of 1921." Commodity prices fell 50%; industrial production fell 32%. Farm foreclosures in 1920-21 ran into the thousands. We know the "Panic" was intentionally produced by the Fed because of the Senate Silver Hearings held in 1939. Senator Robert L. Owen, Chairman of the Senate Banking and Currency Committee (allegedly, a regretful co-author of the Federal Reserve Act) testified as follows:

> In the early part of nineteen-twenty, the farmers were extremely prosperous. They were paying off their mortgages and buying a lot of new land, at the insistence of the government—had borrowed money to do it—and then they were bankrupted by a sudden contraction of credit and currency which took place in 1920. The Federal Reserve Board met in a meeting which was not disclosed to the public. They met on the eighteenth of May, nineteen-twenty and it was a secret meeting. Only the big bankers were there, and their work of that day resulted in a contraction of credit (by ordering banks to call in outstanding loans) which had the effect the next year of reducing the national income fifteen billion dollars, throwing millions of people out of employment and reducing the values of lands and ranches by twenty billion dollars.

Philip David Swing (1884–1963) - Republican Congressman from Imperial County, California. The Honorable Congressman Swing was first elected to the House of Representatives in 1920. He made the following speech in the House of Representatives, May, 23, 1922:

> I was present at a meeting of the bankers of Southern California held in my district in the middle of November, nineteen-twenty, when W. A. Day, then Deputy Governor of the Federal Reserve Bank of San Francisco, spoke for the Federal Reserve Bank and delivered the message which he said he had been sent there to deliver. He told the bankers there assembled that they were not to loan any farmers any money for the purpose of enabling the farmer to hold any of his crop beyond harvest time. If they did, he said, the Federal Reserve Bank would refuse to discount a single piece of paper taken in such a transaction. He declared that all the farmers should sell their crops at the harvest time. No one could be in any doubt for one minute as to what the natural, logical, and necessary consequences of such a policy would be. If the entire crop of the

country is thrown on the market at the time of harvest, of course the market would be depressed. The Federal Reserve Board deliberately set out to bear the market.

Over five thousand smaller banks went killed off and the Fed vultures swooped in with pennies on the dollar to feast on their entrails. Simultaneously, the Fed vultures feasted on the entrails of a good number of other businesses they had bankrupted

I'M GREATLY DEPRESSED ALL OVER AGAIN (1929-39)

It started on Thursday, October 24, 1929. Sell! Sell! Sell! The following Tuesday, October 29, 1929 Wall Street came tumbling down. My father was 22 years old. A migrant labor camp was his home and an empty boxcar was his transportation for the next ten years or so. A hard life made harder for him and so many by so few. By March of 1930 more than 3.2 million people were unemployed, but half of those were unemployed before the crash.

The Fed vultures were now ready for the grand feast we refer to as 'The Great Depression." After working overtime cranking out mass quantities of its "money" the Fed slammed on the brakes. The Fed and Euro bank boys shut off the easy money and raised the discount rate. Some say when Wall Street tumbled, stocks fell 90%. Between 1929 and 1933 the Fed cut the money supply by one-third and a herd of commercial banks disappeared. Writing in "The United States' *Unresolved Monetary and Political Problems*," William Bryan described what happened:

> When everything was ready, the New York financiers started calling 24 hour broker call loans. This meant that the stock brokers and the customers had to dump their stock on the market in order to pay the loans. This naturally collapsed the stock market and brought a banking collapse all over the country because banks not owned by the oligarchy were heavily involved in broker call loans at this time, and bank runs soon exhausted their coin and currency and they had to close. The Federal Reserve System would not come to their aid.

And the feast to top all feasts continued as the Fed vultures gorged themselves on independent, small town banks. The Federal Reserve Act had worked beyond their wildest plans. Enter stage-left, the Fed's butler, little Frankie Roosevelt. And what was the butler to do? With an Executive Order, dated April 5, 1933 little Frankie Roosevelt delivered America's gold bullion, gold coins, and gold-backed notes over to the Fed banks on silver platters. And, little Frankie left the bank with the Fed's intrinsically-worthless fiat paper currency for the American people to use.

IT'S MINE! ALL MINE!

So said the Fed. With America's gold in its left pocket, and an iron hand over the money supply the Fed really went to work. Hey, the Fed still had one empty pocket to fill. January 31, 1934, little Frankie reduced the gold content of the dollar by almost 41%. Had you been allowed to buy it, an ounce of gold would now cost you $35. Yesterday you could have actually bought that same ounce of gold for just under $21. Overnight, the value of America's gold in the Fed's left pocket increased almost $3 billion dollars!

I've heard that a drowning person will desperately snatch at a matchstick thrown their way. In the midst of the Great Depression, our being "tattooed" (the imposition of Social Security) was a matchstick thrown to a desperate, destitute people. The chapter, "Screwed" (particularly the information on the Federal Reserve), puts you well on your way to seeing how we were screwed blue. Now, for that matchstick.

5

Tattooed

Tattoo: To prick the skin and stain the punctured spots with a coloring substance, forming lines and figures upon the body.

—*Webster's Encyclopedic Dictionary* (1942)

Social Security number: A "tattoo" the government requires that might as well be etched on your buttocks at birth. From the cradle to the grave, without this tattoo, you cannot go to school, get a job, apply for loans, acquire medical insurance, recoup Social Security money fraudulently confiscated from your paychecks, or file tax returns to get back a dime on the dollar of the illegal taxes you were forced to pay.

—D.H. Mason (2014)

SOCIAL SECURITY (SS) AND THE NUMBER (TATTOO)

Having an overwhelming desire to be free and to control my future without interference and duress turned me against the involuntary compliance and suppression of the Social Security system many, many years ago. Figuring out the shameful, immoral nature of Social Security took me some time. Something my father told me came to mind: "If you can't figure it out, it's likely a scam."

People *must* save for retirement, but requiring people to put their futures into the hands of a specific body (the government) and then depend on fellow slaves to fund their retirements is cruel and evil. Only a fool or a slave would put his or her economic future into the hands of a body admittedly $18 trillion in debt. I'm no fool. How is it possible that here in America, a so-called free country, I am required to put my economic future into the hands of a bankrupt, corrupt government?

The Social Security trust funds are two funds holding government debt obligations (IOUs) related to what are traditionally thought of as Social Security benefits. The larger fund is the Old-Age and Survivors Insurance (OASI) Trust Fund, holding interest-bearing IOUs bought with surplus OASI payroll-tax revenues. The second, smaller fund is the Disability Insurance (DI) Trust Fund, which also holds in trust more interest-bearing IOUs, bought with surplus DI payroll-tax revenues.

In 1960, a landmark United States Supreme Court ruling[85] gave Congress the power to amend and revise the schedule of Social Security benefits. The Court also ruled that recipients have no contractual right to receive benefits. As noted repeatedly from a variety of sources: "The trust funds do not represent a legal obligation to Social Security program recipients, and Congress could cut or raise taxes on such benefits if it chooses." On November 25, 1998, Michael D. Tanner,[86] in a commentary entitled "Is There a Right to Social Security?" wrote the following:

> You worked hard your whole life and paid thousands of dollars in Social Security taxes. Now it's time to retire. You're legally entitled to Social Security benefits, right? Wrong. There is no legal right to Social Security, and that is one of the considerations that may decide the coming debate over Social Security reform.

> Many people believe that Social Security is an "earned right." That is, they think that because they have paid Social Security taxes, they are entitled to receive Social Security benefits. The government encourages that belief by referring to Social Security taxes as "contributions," as in the Federal Insurance Contribution Act. However, in the 1960 case of Fleming v. Nestor, the U.S. Supreme Court ruled that workers have no legally binding contractual rights to their Social Security benefits, and that those benefits can be cut or even eliminated at any time.

---

85 Fleming v. Nester 363 U.S. 603 [1960].

86 Michael D. Tanner is a senior fellow at the Cato Institute specializing in health care reform, social welfare policy, and Social Security. He coauthored two books on the issue: *A New Deal for Social Security* and *Common Cents, Common Dreams*. His latest book is *Leviathan on the Right: How Big-Government Conservatism Brought Down the Republican Revolution*.

Ephram Nestor was a Bulgarian immigrant who came to the United States in 1918 and paid Social Security taxes from 1936, the year the system began operating, until he retired in 1955. A year after he retired, Nestor was deported for having been a member of the Communist Party in the 1930s. In 1954 Congress had passed a law saying that any person deported from the United States should lose his Social Security benefits. Accordingly, Nestor's $55.60 per month Social Security checks were stopped. Nestor sued, claiming that because he had paid Social Security taxes, he had a right to Social Security benefits.

The Supreme Court disagreed, saying "To engraft upon the Social Security system a concept of 'accrued property rights' would deprive it of the flexibility and boldness in adjustment to ever changing conditions which it demands." The Court went on to say, "It is apparent that the non-contractual interest of an employee covered by the [Social Security] Act cannot be soundly analogized to that of the holder of an annuity, whose right to benefits is bottomed on his contractual premium payments."

Isn't that…precious.

So, all the monies you and your employers (all by you, if self-employed) paid into the Social Security (SS) system via Social Security taxes "do not represent a legal obligation" to you. It gets worse: the money you pay into Social Security today is not being set aside for your retirement days; it's being paid out to current SS recipients. It's referred to as a "pay-as-you-go" system. Any leftover funds (the surplus) the government replaces with interest-bearing IOUs, and, of course, it spends the proceeds as it sees fit. Social-security recipients therefore live under a constant shadow of doubt, wondering whether SS bankruptcy is around the corner.

So it came to pass, while we were being screwed blue during the Great Depression, big-banker bud Roosevelt, and a Congress of mostly Democrats, gave the Federal Government control over the future economic security of every American—tattooing and enslaving all and all to come, until we amend the current Social Security Act and abolish mandatory contributions. Given the amendments proposed herein, the Social Security retirement program will be tempting, yet it will not be mandatory; there are also tempting alternatives available for all.

Here's how it went down:

It was January 17, 1935. The Seventy-Fourth Congress had barely convened when President Roosevelt sent over his Economic Security Bill. The Bill was introduced that day in the Senate by Senator Robert Wagner (D-NY) and in the House by Congressmen Robert Doughton (D-NC) and David Lewis (D-MD). During a Ways and Means Committee meeting on March 1, 1935, Congressman Frank Buck (D-CA) made a motion to change the name of the Bill to the "Social Security Act of 1935." The motion was carried by a voice vote of the committee. The Social Security Act was only thirty-five pages originally. Go to my website to read the original Economic Security Bill—I mean, the original Social Security Act of 1935.

I don't know where it came from, but over the years, I had the thought that the Social Security Act gave us the numbers (tattoos) to identify the individual accounts that the Act had also created. Wrong. The Act did not give us the numbers or individual accounts. There never were individual accounts, ever. And, three bureaucrats (the Social Security board created by the Act), all on their own, allegedly (after consulting with other agency bureaucrats) came up with the number scheme a few months after passage of the Act. On December 17, 1935, the board approved the nine-digit option.[87] Even though the 1935 Act notes at Section 1104 (42 U.S.C. 1304) that the right to alter, amend, or repeal any provision of the Act was reserved to Congress, it was the three bureaucrats who imposed the number scheme on America. The legally needed congressional action to alter the Act appropriately, to approve the scheme, was never taken.

As noted on the Social Security Administration's website (SSA.gov), "At its inception, the SSN's only purpose was to uniquely identify U.S. workers, enabling employers to submit accurate reports of covered earnings for use in administering benefits under the new Social Security program. That is still the primary purpose for the SSN." Well, yes, it certainly was created to "uniquely identify U.S. workers," but so the government could track and ensure individual compliance in payment of imposed taxes. *That* is the primary purpose of the SSN. The number should be keyed to a private, personal account, like a bank-account number, not keyed to the person, like the SSN (tattoo) is today.

All federal employees (the president and members of Congress included) were exempt from Social Security until 1983. The 1983 SS Amendments captured Congress, the president, vice-president, federal judges, and certain executive-level political appointees, as well as all federal employees hired in any capacity on or after January 1, 1984. This does not mean that the federal employees referenced above lost their lucrative retirement systems, but they now are paying into Social Security, too. Many state and local government workers are exempt from Social Security because they have alternative retirement systems set up by their employers. Well, any of us can, and many do, have additional retirement systems established, but such arrangements are not "alternative" retirement plans and do not supersede the mandatory compliance of SS withholding. How is it that federal (until 1983), state, and local "servants" are not participants in the SS scam and have "alternative retirement systems," but the "masters" (we, the citizens/taxpayers) are not allowed the option? When most federal folks were brought into the SS, my thought was, "No, no, don't bring them in; let us out!" I worked twenty-three years for Southern Pacific railroad, so I paid into railroad retirement, not Social Security (SS) during those years. However, I did pay into Social Security before and after my railroad years. I recently received a letter from SS (June 15, 2015) informing me that I could draw SS in the amount of "about $487 a month at the present time." In the letter was this section:

---

87 Charles McKinley and Robert W. Frase, *Launching Social Security: A Capture-and-Record Account, 1935–1937* (1970), 323.

Windfall Elimination Provision (WEP)—In the future, if you receive a pension from employment in which you do not pay Social Security taxes, such as some federal, state or local government work, some nonprofit organizations or foreign employment, and you also qualify for your own Social Security retirement or disability benefit, your Social Security benefit may be reduced, but not eliminated, by WEP. The amount of the reduction, if any, depends on your earnings and number of years in jobs in which you paid Social Security taxes and the year you turn 62 or become disabled. For more information, please see Windfall Elimination Provision (Publication No. 05-10045) at www.socialsecurity.gov/WEP.

So, a person pays fully into both, but cannot draw fully from both. There is an additional section explaining that the less you make/pay in, the higher percentage your retirement return will be. Does that sound a little…what's it called…oh, yeah—socialist?

My goal is to have an Act passed by Congress to amend the current SS Act *and* allow Americans the option of opting out of the SS system in lieu of alternative retirement systems. Some—no, many—people will oppose anyone opting out of Social Security. I understand their fear. But how is it moral or ethical that I can be compelled to pay for another person's retirement and have no guarantee whatsoever for my own? But it has been adjudicated so! Wrongly, in my opinion. Therefore, the only option is to change the law, and that is what the Social Security Reconstruction and Freedom Act will do.

Social Security funding for current recipients and those who do not want to opt out can be easily accomplished. First, individual accounts will be established; all monies paid in by individuals and/or their employers on the individual's behalf will be deposited into their *personal* accounts; all existing accounts will be converted to individual accounts. The "tattoo" will identify the account, not the individual. Any shortfalls for payments to current recipients and/or future recipients will be paid from the taxation of those individuals and/or corporations that were the class-A stockholders of the Federal Reserve banking system, and by other means and methods deemed necessary, to fulfill those payments; proper investment by the right people will diminish the need for such alternatives.

Also, upon retirement, account holders will have the option of drawing monthly payments from their individual accounts, or take a lump-sum payment that must be reinvested into an interest-bearing private retirement account, from which monthly payments can be extracted, and/or an annuity account. The account holder will also have the option of taking a partial lump-sum payment. The news article that follows here in a few pages shows how Chile took social security private; the article is titled, "Chile's Privatized Social Security Program is 30 Years Old and Prospering." No matter the account holder's choice of options, any monies remaining at death will go to the account holder's heirs or estate.

The powers that be, think we are too stupid to plan and invest for retirement on our own. Not stupid, ignorant. There is a monumental difference between "stupid" and "ignorant." Ignorant is simply a lack of knowledge. Stupid is stupid, and there is no cure. There are many safe, secure ways of investing that are far less risky than turning over your economic future to a body that is $18 trillion in debt—and climbing—that gives you no right of ownership, no guarantee of return, and no right of inheritance.

Setting aside monies for retirement must be mandatory. As for survivors' insurance, it's called… oh, yeah…life insurance. And disability insurance is easily purchased from private sources and supplemented by things like workers' compensation programs. Life insurance may be needed as additional economic security for spouses and dependents. However, upon death, a private retirement fund would pass to a person's heirs/estate, thereby reducing the need for survivors' insurance (life insurance). Even if a person mirrored government investment strategies, the private fund would be private property passable to heirs upon death. There are economic geniuses who will create private retirement accounts that will never lose money and thereby be sound and safe and assure a comfortable retirement life. So, whom do you trust more with your retirement? A government with debt increasing $2 million every few minutes that admits it has no legal obligation to you concerning your retirement, or masters of investment who work for you?

Social Security (SS) is eighty years old. The July/August 2015 *AARP Bulletin* had a big spread entitled "Happy Birthday, Social Security, Celebrating 80 Years of Better Lives." The writer, Robert Dallek (author of books on John Kennedy and Lyndon Johnson and of an upcoming biography of Franklin Roosevelt[88]), assures the reader that SS will always be with us and will never collapse. Hey, Bob, tell it to the Greeks! Not to say that Social Security has not skimmed the top of helping people, but you can see what "help" could or should be in the alternatives given herein.

From the *AARP Bulletin* article:

Eighty years after its birth in the depths of the Great Depression, Social Security is deeply woven into the nation's fabric. But Americans were initially skeptical of a program that seemed contrary to their faith in rugged individualism. "It is difficult now to understand fully the doubts and confusions in which we were planning this great new enterprise," FDR's Secretary of Labor Frances Perkins wrote later. In a conversation with Supreme Court Justice Harlan Stone, Perkins, whom Roosevelt had tasked with designing what seemed like a radical departure from traditional ideas about the role of government in American life,[89] confided her uncertainty about how to make this work within constitutional bounds. Stone in reply whispered, "The taxing power of the Federal Government, my dear; the taxing power is sufficient for everything you want and need."

Harlan Fiske Stone (1872–1946) was a Republican, a lawyer, and jurist. A native of New Hampshire, Stone served as Dean of Columbia Law School (his alma mater) in the early twentieth century. He was appointed the fifty-second Attorney General before becoming an Associate Justice of the Supreme

---

88 Do you think he might be a socialist (a Democrat of today) who never saw a social program he didn't love?
89 Ya think?

Court in 1925. In 1941, Stone became the twelfth Chief Justice of the United States, serving a relatively short term, until his death in 1946. He was the first Chief Justice not to have served in elected office. His most famous dictum was, "Courts are not the only agency of government that must be assumed to have capacity to govern."

Judge Stone—Really? "The taxing power is sufficient for everything you want and need." The court can govern? Where is that in the Constitution? What about freedom? What about liberty? I see Judge Stone's attitude as condescending arrogance. Raise your right hand if you agree.

SOCIAL SECURITY ALTERNATIVES

Home-Grown Pension Alternative to Social Security
By David Cay Johnston, *New York Times*, March 21, 1997

OXFORD, Ohio—For 28 years Bill McKinstry taught economics at Miami University here, including a course on Social Security in which he warned that the system faced an inevitable crisis. Now retired, Professor McKinstry considers himself fortunate that most of his pension money comes from the Ohio Teachers' Retirement System, one of the few pension plans in the country that operate apart from Social Security.

You don't have to go as far away as Chile to find alternatives to Social Security. Nearly two million state and local government employees are exempt from paying Social Security taxes. Along with several hundred thousand retirees, they are eligible for benefits that—while more costly—almost always provide a better deal than the federal system.

"There is a general conception that everyone in the United States pays Social Security taxes," said Richard Thau, executive director of Third Millennium, a nonprofit advocacy organization for people under 35 that is about to release a study extolling plans that exempt employees from Social Security. "But several million people have managed to escape the Social Security tax. They are all government employees and we think their experience is an interesting model for considering alternatives to Social Security."

The Advisory Council on Social Security, which issued three separate proposals early this year to overcome the retirement system's financing problems, agreed on at least one thing: All 1.9 million workers currently in exempt plans should be brought into Social Security, providing a shot-in-the-arm to Social Security revenues.

But Mr. Thau disagrees. "Folding these plans into Social Security," he said, "is akin to chopping down a rain forest without determining first the prospects that within the forest is the cure for cancer." The study, which looked at seven plans outside Social Security covering 1.3 million government employees, was conducted by William Even, an economist at Miami University, and David A. MacPherson, an economist at Florida State University. It concluded that the vast majority of people now paying Social Security taxes would receive less in retirement benefits than they and their employer paid, while those outside it could expect to earn annual returns, after inflation, of 1.6 to 3 percent.

Only one-income couples who make less than $40,000 will receive more from Social Security than was paid in, the study says. But supporters of Social Security, which is tilted to help low-wage workers more than those with higher incomes, say that is exactly why it is so important to preserve the system.

Karen C. Burke, a legal scholar at the University of Minnesota, said that redistributing income "is an explicit and important goal" of Social Security[90], while in contrast, private pension plans "are distinctly skewed in favor of high earners."

Professor Even agreed that providing a more generous payoff to lower-wage workers made sense, but complained that Social Security's rules, largely written when the vast majority of wage earners were men, created all kinds of anomalies. "Two-earner couples subsidize one-earner couples with the same income," he said. "Now what sense is there in that?"

Even for those with modest earnings, the government pensions are often a better deal. The study looked at what would happen to people who start their careers at age 25, retire at 62, and enjoy real wage gains averaging 1 percent a year better than the inflation rate. A worker who retired with an income of $20,000 would get $7,468 from Social Security, but the average benefit from the seven alternative systems would be $18,951, or 2.5 times as much. But they are even better for more affluent workers. Those earning $100,000 under an exempt system would retire with 7.5 times more than Social Security alone would pay.

The most significant difference is in how the systems are funded. Social Security is primarily a pay-as-you-go system, in which today's workers pay the benefits for today's retirees. Only a small portion of Social Security revenues are invested—in Treasury bonds; the plans rely largely on money set aside by the workers earlier in their careers. The state and local government pension systems invest a large portion ...in the stock market.

Still, the local alternatives, since they are intended to serve as a full pension, cost more. Compared with the combined 10.5 percent of wages, up to $64,500 this year, that are designated for retirement benefits under Social Security, the plans range from 18.6 percent of payroll for one covering Colorado State workers, to 24 percent for civil servants in Los Angeles. Taxpayers pick up all or most of those costs. Government workers in Los Angeles, for example, paid only 4.7 percent of their paycheck directly.

Mr. McKinstry, the retired professor, likes his pension just fine, but is worried that those citing arrangements like his as a justification for abandoning Social Security are going too far in

---

90 Really! Can it be made any clearer than that? The money you pay into SS is not for your retirement; the government can give it to whomever it pleases.

advocating a system where workers would mostly rely on their own retirement accounts. "I certainly hope we are not going to turn people loose with their retirement savings," he said, "so they can lose it with some broker who has a hot stock tip."[91]

Chile's Privatized Social Security Program is 30 Years Old, and Prospering
By Bob Adelmann, *The New American* May 3, 2011[92]

As a quiet example of how privatizing Social Security works in the real world, Chile's 30-year experiment is succeeding beyond expectations. Instead of running huge deficits to fund the old "PayGo" system, private savings now exceed 50 percent of the country's Gross Domestic Product.

Prior to May 1, 1981, the Chilean system required contributions from workers and was clearly in grave financial trouble. Instead of nibbling around the edges to shore up the program for another few years, José Piñera, Secretary of Labor and Pensions under Augusto Pinochet, decided to do a major overhaul of the system:

> We knew that cosmetic changes—increasing the retirement age, increasing taxes—would not be enough. We understood that the pay-as-you-go system had a fundamental flaw, one rooted in a false conception of how human beings behave. That flaw was lack of a link between what people put into their pension program and what they take out. So we decided to go in the other direction, to link benefits to contributions. The money that a worker pays into the system goes into an account that is owned by the worker.

The system still required contributions of 10 percent of salary, but the money was deposited in any one of an array of private investment companies. Upon retirement, the worker had a number of options, including purchasing an annuity for life. Along the way he could track the performance of his account, and increase his contribution (up to 20 percent) if he wanted to retire earlier, or increase his payout at retirement.

How well has the system performed? John Tierney, a writer for the *New York Times*, went to visit Pablo Serra, a former classmate and friend in Santiago a few years ago, and they compared notes on how well their respective retirement programs were doing. Tierney brought along his latest statement from Social Security, while his friend brought up his retirement plan on his computer. It turned out that they both had been contributing about the same amount of money, so the comparison was apt, and startling, said Tierney:

---

91 Oh, it's all right for Professor McKinstry to opt out of Social Security, but not the common person? It seems the Professor thinks most people are too ignorant to be "turn[ed]…loose with their retirement savings." He may be right. There certainly should be education, training (in school from kindergarten through college), guardrails, stockbroker limitations, and oversight, but let's give people the freedom to manage their own retirement funds.

92 www.thenewamerican.com

Pablo could retire in 10 years, at age 62, with an annual pension of $55,000. That would be more than triple the $18,000 I can expect from Social Security at that age.

OR

Pablo could retire at age 65 with an annual pension of $70,000. That would almost triple the $25,000 pension promised [to me] by Social Security starting a year later, at age 66.

OR

Pablo could retire at age 65 with an annual pension of $53,000 and [in addition receive] a one-time cash payment of $223,000.

Tierney wrote that Pablo said "I'm very happy with my account." Tierney suggested that, upon retirement, Pablo could not only retire nicely, but be able to buy himself a vacation home at the shore or in the country. Pablo laughed it off, and Tierney wrote: "I'm trying to look on the bright side. Maybe my Social Security check will cover the airfare to visit him."

According to *Investor's Business Daily*, the average annual rate of return for Chilean workers over the last 30 years has exceeded 9% annually, *after inflation*, whereas "U. S. Social Security pays a 1% to 2% (theoretical) rate of return, and even less for new workers."

As expected, the capital accumulated in these privatized accounts has generated substantial growth in Chile's economy. As noted by Wikipedia, "Chile is one of South America's most stable and *prosperous* nations, leading Latin American nations in human development, competitiveness, *income per capita*, globalization, *economic freedom*, and low perception of corruption." [Emphases added.]

High domestic savings and investment rates helped propel Chile's economy to average growth rates of 8% during the 1990s. The privatized national pension plan (AFP) has encouraged domestic investment and contributed to an estimated total domestic savings rate of approximately 21% of GDP.

This was anticipated by Piñera when the plan was originally designed and implemented in 1981. In reviewing the success of the plan after just 15 years, Piñera said, "The Chilean worker is an owner, a capitalist. There is no more powerful way to stabilize a free-market economy and to get the support of the workers than to link them directly to the benefits of the market system. When Chile grows at 7 percent or when the stock market doubles…Chilean workers benefit directly, not only through high wages, not only through more employment, but through additional capital in their individual pension accounts."

All of which should resonate with American workers who have been forced to contribute to a failing Social Security system for years. And yet when given the opportunity to support any sort of privatization, as during the Clinton and Bush administrations, the idea gained little traction. And now that Rep. Paul Ryan's "Road Map" offers the chance for those same workers to contribute just one-third of their Social Security taxes to similar private accounts, the idea continues to fall on deaf ears.

However, according to Rasmussen Reports, that may be changing. Nearly half of those polled now correctly understand "that making major long-term cuts in government spending will require big changes" in Social Security, Medicare, and Defense. That figure, adds Rasmussen, "suggests a growing awareness of budgetary realities among the American people."

To privatize Social Security makes nothing but sense, as in dollars and cents. The ownership of private property has always propelled economic prosperity, higher wages and improved standards of living. Only those whose goals are to impoverish the American worker and reduce his ability to manage his own affairs and control his own future would resist such an attractive alternative.

As noted by Piñera,

> "This is a brief story of a dream that has come true. The ultimate lesson is that the only revolutions that are successful are those that trust the individual, and the wonders that individuals can do when they are free."

SOCIAL SECURITY RECONSTRUCTION AND FREEDOM ACT

An Act to amend the Social Security Act so as to reconstruct the social security retirement system, abolish mandatory compliance, and in lieu thereof, require and allow private retirement investment, and other changes.

Be it enacted by the House of Representatives and Senate of the United States of America in Congress assembled, that:

Whereas this Act shall be cited as the Social Security Reconstruction and Freedom Act, hereinafter referred to as the Act, and

Whereas, so Americans may better prepare for retirement with increased retirement income, they may voluntarily stay in the current social security retirement system (SSRS) but are no longer required to do so; that is, not required to pay into the Social Security system.

Whereas, whether it is SSRS or a private retirement program (PRP):

1. Privately-owned individual numbered retirement accounts must be established; like a brokerage or bank account, all numbers are tied to the account, not the individual.
2. Individual retirement accounts are the private property of the individual payee with right of inheritance.

3. Every individual, whether employee or self-employed, shall contribute a minimum of ten percent (10%) into their privately-owned retirement account. Individuals may contribute any amount over ten percent (10%) that they choose.

4. Retirement contributions shall be made on all wages, salaries, and compensation for services by individuals until age sixty (60), even though an individual can draw on their retirement account after age forty-five (45).

5. Employers may voluntarily contribute as much as they choose to an employee's retirement account.

6. Any shortfalls for payments to current recipients and/or future recipients of Social Security for the next twenty-seven years from date of passage of this Act will be paid from the taxation of those individuals and/or corporations that were the Class-A stockholders of the Federal Reserve banking system and other means deemed necessary to achieve this goal.

7. The United States Government will not replace incoming Social Security funds with bonds or any other type of IOUs; all incoming funds will be controlled and invested by a consortium of private investment consultants. The money shall be invested in any one of an array of private investment companies chosen by the individual contributor. Interested companies shall post resumes; a private consortium of consultants chosen by Congress shall determine the best nine, and individuals are free to choose any of the nine. The number of such companies can be increased if Congress deems it appropriate. Government and/or banking personnel can not simultaneously serve as a member of the consortium of consultants.

8. Individuals may retire any time after age forty-five (45); individuals may draw retirement and continue working with no penalties. Upon retirement, retirees have options including:

    a. Purchasing an annuity.
    b. Drawing a higher yearly pension or splitting retirement—that is, drawing a yearly pension and, in addition, receiving a one-time cash payment. The one-time cash payment shall not exceed thirty percent (30%) of the total amount of the account. Yearly pension amount shall be based on reasonable life expectancy calculations via competent sources Congress shall approve.
    c. The ability to track the performance of their personal accounts.

9. All retirement account contributions and withdrawals are exempt from any and all means of taxation.

10. All public and private educational systems are hereby required to educate and train students (from kindergarten through college) regarding retirement needs, requirements, methods, and sources of investing.

11. To avoid losses from poor investing, Social Security's private consortium of investors and all other persons investing retirement funds shall be licensed, certified, bonded, and insured against loss of customers' retirement monies (the principal amount invested) and shall act as a partner and advisor to their customers.

12. All retirement funds shall be invested and insured so as to earn an average minimum per annum interest of five percent (5%). Any group or individual investment consultant failing to

earn such amount for two consecutive years shall be removed from the list of qualified investment consultants. The SSRP private consortium of investors and all other person's investing any person's retirement funds shall be paid 2%) of the total interest earned over 5%.

Whereas, individual disability insurance shall no longer be the responsibility of the Federal Government and shall be addressed by the states and their residents.

Whereas, any portion of this Act deemed unconstitutional shall not render the remaining Act invalid;

Therefore, this Act is hereby passed by the United States House of Representatives with the United States Senate concurring, this _____ day of _____, 20____.

6

Sold Down the River

SOLD DOWN THE RIVER[93]

A term coined by slaves as a response when asked what happened to friends and family members.

---

93   http://www.npr.org/sections/codeswitch/2014/01/27/265421504/what-does-sold-down-the-river-really-mean-the-answer-isnt-pretty.

REGIONAL GOVERNMENT

Regional government is a socialist form of government. Let me be a little clearer here. Regional Government is a Socialist dictatorship. Regional governance usurps city, county, state and federal jurisdiction with its methodical and stealth consolidation of political authority into the Executive Branch of the Federal Government. The implementation of Regional Government has meant the piecemeal transfer of political authority from elected representatives to appointed agents and bureaucrats. Though practically distilled of jurisdiction and only used by socialist bureaucrats for tax collection, geographical identification, and illusionary effect, traditional units of self-governance (city, county, state, and federal) do still exist.

The Illinois Report (February, 1979)) defines the terms "regionalism" and regionalization" appropriately:

The term "regionalism" generally refers to the existing regional agencies, regional units or structures which have been established by the Federal Government, the States and local government, quasi-government, area-wide planning agencies, or administrative units of the federal and state governments. In addition to this practical description of what "regionalism" is, as used in this report, "regionalism" may also refer to the concept of "regionalizing" or "regionalization." When used in this manner, "regionalism" pertains to the ideal or body of thought, developed and promoted by the Federal Government, which is concerned with the consolidation, merger or establishment of multi-state, multi-county and multi-local governmental units; i.e., "regional governance."

Regional governance is the necessary prerequisite to the establishment of a one-world government. Like ivy growing on a wall, regional governance came upon us slowly, but today, it has our wall completely covered.

We will have world government whether or not we like it. The only question is whether world government will be achieved by conquest or consent.

—Paul Warburg (1868–1932), quoted in the film *Wake Up Call*[94]

Throughout the 1980s and 1990s, I researched and wrote in support of my political activities. Those activities included challenging the illegal taxation of labor as profit, and I held positions in several active groups: I was president of the Solano County Chapter of the Committee to Restore the Constitution, a founding board member of Benicians Against Redevelopment, president of the Community Rights Association (CRA), and a CRA representative to the Benicia Housing Element Advisory Committee. Along the way, I filed a few citizen complaints (without success) with the Solano County Grand Jury involving loss of jurisdiction and rights, the result of city compliance to regional regulations and requirements. Read them in full at my website.

---

94 Paul Warburg was chief architect of the Federal Reserve banking system. The film *Wake Up Call* can be found on YouTube.

I became politically active because of what I began to learn in the early 1980s. In late summer of 1982, I attended a freedom rally in Sacramento, California. I was looking for new sources of information on the income-versus-wages issue. There, I found literature and lectures from various groups and individuals. A retired United States Army Major wearing a side arm lectured and passed out information on Posse Comitatus. An elderly college professor lectured on jury nullification. Then there was Bernadine Smith, a petite, soft-spoken woman who lectured on regional government.

Bernadine's lecture was intense, complex, and not easy to follow. But I was following enough to know I didn't like what I was hearing. The fifty sovereign states merged into ten federal regions by executive order, and governed by appointed bureaucrats; city and county jurisdictions "voluntarily" merged into subregions overseen by a regional council of government, with authority centered in the president's office. I bought Archibald E. Roberts's *Emerging Struggle for State Sovereignty*, a book that started me on an extraordinary course of study and political action.

After reading that book, I wanted to know if regional government had made its way to my small town of Benicia, California. At the time, Benicia's population was around twelve thousand and growing rapidly. I called John Cody, a fellow railroader who had served several terms on the Benicia City Council. John said, "You want to know about regional government, call Olivia O'Grady." I was surprised there was someone in little Benicia that I could talk to. After a long phone conversation, Mrs. O'Grady invited me to her home. It was the winter of 1982, a rainy Saturday afternoon; she made strong coffee, and before I realized it, four hours had passed. Mrs. O'Grady was an elderly widow who had spent a long life documenting and challenging regional government. That meeting began our friendship and my studentship, which lasted until her death in 1994.

Within a week of our first meeting, Mrs. O'Grady introduced me to Lillian Wilt, another elderly widow who lived nearby. Mrs. Wilt was an expert on world government, education, and world banking systems. She was a Daughter of the American Revolution, a retired librarian, and a classical pianist. Mrs. Wilt had lived and worked in Washington, DC, for a number of years, while her husband had worked for the Department of Health, Education, and Welfare. When we met, Mrs. Wilt was still doing occasional lectures at Bay Area colleges and for private organizations. She had spent a long life researching, documenting, and challenging world government, the socialization of our educational system, and the Federal Reserve banking system. The Wilt files were as detailed and extensive as the O'Grady files. Mrs. Wilt was very proud that Gary Allen had done research in her files for his book *None Dare Call It Conspiracy*. Like Mrs. O'Grady, Mrs. Wilt opened her mind and her extensive files to me. We became fast friends, and she, too, became my personal teacher. Mrs. Wilt died in 1996.

I love research and writing. I love having the knowledge of a paralegal—that is, being able to research, dissect, and write about my discoveries. Having twelve-plus years of mentorship by Mrs. Wilt and Mrs. O'Grady and access to their extensive files and inheriting the O'Grady files, along with extensive research and writing from the Wilt files, has been—well, it feels as if I was divinely led to them. What were the odds that these two great ladies could be neighbors in the small town where my wife and I had settled and lived for twenty-five years? And it was as if they were waiting for me to show up, waiting for the time when I would find them and treasure their life's work and knowledge. Very few had taken an interest in their files, their life's work, for many years. Yet, they continued to document and speak out against America's slide toward a socialist government and the New World Order. When I met them, they were excited, eager, and thankful that someone like me had found them. I was just as excited, eager, and thankful.

Mrs. O'Grady and Mrs. Wilt were both habitual researchers and documentarians. They witnessed, documented, and challenged the advance of one-world government, and the construction and implementation of its prerequisite, regional government—their files include a historical, blow-by-blow description of it all. The O'Grady files were left to me, including over three thousand pounds of documents, meticulously filed in World War II, army-surplus file cabinets. It's been a few years, but the last time I saw the Wilt files, they were rotting away in a dark, dank basement. I often wonder how many like Bernadine Smith, Mrs. O'Grady, and Mrs. Wilt are out there, and what is the condition of their life's work, their files. Every searcher, researcher, and writer dreams of finding such treasure. Sometimes, after a long session of research and study amid their books and documents stacked high, I'd take a long look around and utter the words, "It's all here."

Yes, *all* there. As my research continued I discovered the "treasure" contained some fool's gold. It has to do with the originators and origins of our trek from freedom to slavery. I found biased opinions and misinterpretations persuasively presented as factual evidence. This "fool's gold" is not exclusive to the O'Grady and Wilt files; it's everywhere. Who gets the blame? The Jews, of course! This charge stands out in *The Beasts of the Apocalypse,* a book that Mrs. O'Grady published in 1949. She confirmed shortly before her death that she did not write it; California State Senator Jack B. Tenney did. When it was published, Senator Tenney was serving as Chairman of the Senate Fact-Finding Committee on Un-American Activities in California (1941–1949). Senator Tenney later published under his own name such books as *Zion's Trojan Horse.*

Senator Tenney tweaked the truth for emphasis (maybe it was simple ignorance on his part). For example, in the 1949 book, chapter 4 starts with, "Money has been said to be the root of all evil." I always offer a correction for this common mistake. It is the *love* of money that is the root of all evil.

> *For the love of money is the root of all evil; which while some coveted after, they have erred from the faith, and pierced themselves through with many sorrows.*
>
> —I TIMOTHY 6:10 (SAINT JAMES BIBLE)

The 1949 Tenney book gives an impressive timeline of significant historical events. The author "knew" the Jews were to blame, and then gathered the "evidence" to prove it. Evil this, that, and the other happened, and there were Jews in the vicinity; I rest my case.

Evil works in mysterious ways. I learned in my paralegal training that everything must be confirmed by at least two additional sources. Information I have via the O'Grady and Wilt files, I have confirmed in triplicate—except the "evidence" that the drive for world dominance is a "Jewish conspiracy." Throughout history, the Jews have been evil's biggest scapegoat. When all else fails, blame the Jews! Our condition (screwed, blued, tattooed, and sold down the river) can be traced to the deeds of mortals. Some acted with motive, some acted with ignorance. Evil is not bound by race, color, avowed creed, gender, or place of national origin; such distinctions have no weight in this matter. Like goodness and wisdom, evil, ignorance, and stupidity do not discriminate. Our condition is the result of a conspiracy to establish a specific type of one-world government. This conspiracy came to America over a hundred years ago and is now bearing needed fruit: regional (socialist) governance of the United States of America. But it is not a Jewish conspiracy; it is an evil conspiracy of wealthy, egotistical fools. So what?

If you're awakened in the middle of the night, and your home is ablaze, your first priority is not finding out how the fire started. It may have been arson, it may have been an electrical short, or it may have been heathens in the basement rubbing sticks together, but it doesn't matter in the middle of the night when your home is ablaze. Our condition deserves a similar response. There will be plenty of time to assess blame once you and your family are safe, when the fire is out, and the smoke clears.[95]

The first question I asked Mrs. O'Grady was, "How does regional government come into the city?

She answered, "Regional government comes into the city through the General Plan." She quickly retrieved the city's current General Plan from one of the old army-surplus file cabinets lining the wall. I'd never seen a general plan. I'd never been to a city council meeting. I'd never been to city hall. That was about to change.

Mrs. O'Grady never missed a city council meeting. In recognition, the city council had a small plaque bearing her name mounted on the back of the seat where she regularly sat—second row from the front on the right, third seat in—the second Tuesday of every month, for some forty years. Mrs. O'Grady battled blindness the last five years of her life, but she managed. She used a machine that made the letters on documents about an inch tall. Someone was always there to take her to Mass and to city council meetings. She opposed any action that brought Benicia into the regional fold, putting her in conflict with "educated" mayors and council members on a regular basis. Mrs. O'Grady was not discouraged by their opposition. She would say, "It was important to get my objections in the public record." My paralegal studies, but more so Mrs. O'Grady, taught me that not objecting to an issue at the appropriate time can hinder a legal challenge later (silence equals acceptance).

Before one particular city council meeting, I helped Mrs. O'Grady pass out background information on an issue coming before the council that evening. I overheard one man (a housing developer)

---

95   I volunteered, trained, and served as a fireman/emergency medical first responder for five years (2001–2006) with the Crockett-Carquinez Fire Department (Engine 77, Port Costa). I joined in October 2001, one month after 9/11. Most of our calls were medical, but we did on occasion breach burning buildings to save lives and property.

say, as he crumpled the handout and walked inside, "This is all water under the bridge!" When I spoke on the issue, I remarked on overhearing the man's "water under the bridge" comment. I held up the handout and added, "That's true, but if you'll take a look at this 'water under the bridge,' you'll see how we all got sold down the river. And maybe, we could keep that from happening again here tonight."

My first major work with Mrs. O'Grady started in 1986. Over substantial community opposition, the Benicia City Council established a redevelopment agency (a major regional governance conduit) and council members appointed themselves as the agents. I spoke at one of the public hearings, noting that establishing a redevelopment agency (RA) gave increased power of eminent domain to appointed agents. A council member responded that the council members would be the agents, and we had elected them. I responded, "Yes, but when you take off your elected city council hat and put on the appointed agent's hat, you have increased powers of eminent domain that can be used to take private property. What good is kicking you out of office after you have taken my property?" Generally, creating an RA transfers people's authority to govern over their city through their elected officials to appointed bureaucrats over which they have no authority. An RA can declare an area in the city "blighted," divert the tax revenue generated by that area to its use, and demolish the area and rebuild as it sees fit.

The method used by the Benicia City Council to establish the redevelopment agency is one used over and over again across America to erase local jurisdiction in a piecemeal manner. It's called a "public hearing." I've heard the process referred to as "using the law to destroy the law." The council held the public hearing, heard most citizens say no, and over those objections, established the RA with a three-to-two vote. And the battle was on.

I was working full time and going to school full time (paralegal courses at Saint Mary's College in Moraga). I took a herder[96] job for the railroad. At the semester break, I cut back from a full course load to half. It would take me an additional six months to earn my paralegal certification, but this battle against a RA in my own backyard was more important. I helped Mrs. O'Grady and others get the issue on the ballot. We believed an informed electorate would not allow an RA in its city. We formed Benicians Against Redevelopment (BAR). We walked precincts, stood in front of supermarkets, talked and wrote, and gathered enough signatures to get the issue on the April 1986 ballot. Thanks to an honorable man, John Silva, editor of the *Benicia Herald* at the time, a "pro" and "con" redevelopment article was included in the local paper each week.

I wrote several of the "con" articles and did a substantial amount of research and writing for the group (mostly from Mrs. O'Grady's files). I also wrote the argument against redevelopment for the voter pamphlet. We informed the community, and it voted to abolish the RA the city council had

---

96 A herder manually lines switches for trains to enter or exit mainline tracks onto or from a branch line. The job was on the graveyard shift (11:00 p.m.–7:00 a.m.) in Suisun, California. I usually had two trains to tend during my shift, leaving me some time to read and write.

created. Two of the three pro-redevelopment council members were also replaced. I suspect that by now, Benicia has joined the fold and has a redevelopment agency.

Likely the most important project I worked on was Mrs. O'Grady's Solano County grand jury complaint against regional government. I wrote and helped compile supporting documents from her files. Mrs. O'Grady knew her files like the back of her hand—a good thing, considering her near blindness. She filed the complaint with the Solano County grand jury on June 6, 1991. When we were compiling the complaint, I knew it was monumentally too broad for a county grand jury, but Mrs. O'Grady insisted. I'm eternally grateful for her insistence. This complaint, hereinafter referred to as "the O'Grady Complaint," represents the essence of the O'Grady files on regional government, revealing the origins, objectives, goals, methods, and evolution of regional governance. To follow are highlights of the O'Grady Complaint. The Complaint is extensive, accompanied with thirty-one sections of supporting documents (called the exhibit book [EB]) in one binder and another thick binder referred to as the general folder (GF). In the following O'Grady Complaint excerpt, you will see references to the supporting documents in the EB and the GF. The entire complaint and supporting evidence will eventually be found at my website.

O'Grady Complaint

THE PROBLEM IS THE LOSS OF REPRESENTATIVE GOVERNMENT.

When I say "Representative Government" I mean political authority "We, the people" have through ELECTED Representatives within our Federal, State, County and City units of government. The loss of the people's ability to govern government is the direct result of the construction, promotion and implementation of the Regional Governmental Structure, i.e., Regionalism, Regionalization, Regional Governance, Regional Government.

The Illinois Report (Report of the Joint Committee on Regional Government, submitted to the Illinois General Assembly and Governor Thompson (February, 1979)) defines the terms "regionalism" and regionalization" appropriately for this Complaint:

The term "regionalism" generally refers to the existing regional agencies, regional units or structures which have been established by the federal government, the states and local government, quasi-government, area-wide planning agencies, or administrative units of the federal and state governments. In addition to this practical description of what "regionalism" is, as used in this report, "regionalism" may also refer to the concept of "regionalizing" or "regionalization." When used in this manner, "regionalism" pertains to the ideal or body of thought, developed and promoted by the Federal Government, which is concerned with the consolidation, merger or establishment of multi-state, multi-county and multi-local governmental units; i.e., "regional governance."

The idea of "Regionalism" was first publicly aired during the New Deal era. In its 1935 Report, the National Resources Committee recommended a division of the United States into twelve administrative districts, with all districts reporting to a national coordinating agency responsible to the President. On April 21, 1935 an article appeared in the *New York Times* magazine entitled "Nine Groups instead of the 48 States" with the subheading, "States Rights Would be Abolished and the Country would be divided into Nine Departments."

Under the Roosevelt administration the 78th Congress passed the "Reorganization Act of 1939." The Act included a provision whereby Presidents would have continuing authority to initiate reorganization plans in the future.

President Truman appointed the First Hoover Commission (1947–48). This body's recommendations resulted in the passage of the Reorganization Act of 1949.

In 1953, President Eisenhower appointed the Kestnbaum Commission which issued "the most comprehensive review of intergovernmental relations since the adoption of the Constitution." Garni, *The New Federalism*, Exhibit Book (EB), Section 24, p. 4.

The Advisory Commission on Intergovernmental Relations (ACIR)[97] was formed by Congress in 1959 (a recommendation of the Kestnbaum Commission). **The ACIR has been a major force in the regionalization of America.** The ACIR (a quasi-federal agency) enjoys the unique authority of "counseling" local, state and national levels of government. Many ACIR recommendations are paralleled by policies of the National League of Cities, U.S. Conference of Mayors, and the National Association of Counties, three of twenty-six private organizations within the Public Administrative Clearinghouse. Roberts, *Emerging Struggle for State Sovereignty* 24–26, 42, 44–47, 72–74, 83, 246.

The Public Administrative Clearinghouse (1313), formed in 1929, has grown into a conglomerate of twenty-six entirely independent private organizations. Since 1938 these organizations have had their offices at 1313 E. 60th Street, Chicago, Illinois, thus the title "1313." Besides being a center for the formulation and distribution of regional policy, 1313 is designed to train and place a new "administrative class" at every level of government. EB Sections 12–14, 24; Roberts, *Emerging Struggle for State Sovereignty* 24, 26, 39, 47, 72–73, 161.[98]

The ACIR digests input from 1313 and formulates regional legislation for rubber stamp passage by state and local governments. A substantial number of ACIR legislative proposals (mail-order legislation) are disseminated by the Council of State Governments in its annual volume entitled "Suggested State Legislation." The National Governor's

---

97 The ACIR operated until 1996.

98 It's easy to gloss over what you are reading here, but what you are being told is most important.

Conference Report (67th annual meeting) carried thirty-eight ACIR legislative proposals under the title, "Model Legislation to Local Governments: Model Legislation from the Advisory Commission on Intergovernmental Relations." Additionally, a ten-volume ACIR State Legislative Program offered model statutes in the following categories for adoption by respective state legislators: (1) State Government Structure and Process; (2) Local Government Modernization; (3) State and Local Revenues; (4) Fiscal and Personnel Management; (5) Environment, Land Use and Growth Policy; (6) Housing and Community Development; (7) Transportation; (8) Health; (9) Education; (10) Criminal Justice. Roberts, *Emerging Struggle for State Sovereignty* 26.

Working together, the ACIR and 1313 have helped formulate and distribute information and legislation necessary to construct, promote and implement the Regional Governmental Structure.

On March 27, 1969 President Nixon entered into the Federal Register, White House Directive titled "Restructuring of Government Service Systems" and therewith merged the fifty sovereign States into eight (later ten) federal regions in violation of United States Constitution, Article IV.

I need to break from the O'Grady Complaint here for correction and clarification. The White House (President Nixon) Directive dated March 27, 1969, establishing eight federal regions, was not titled "Restructuring of Government Service Systems" but "Statement on Establishing Common Regional Boundaries for Agencies Providing Social and Economic Services." Wikipedia notes, "The ten standard federal regions were established by OMB (Office of Management and Budget) Circular A-105, 'Standard Federal Regions' in April, 1974." You will find the text of the circular at my website (a PDF titled "OMB 10 regions"). As noted therein, "This Circular formally establishes ten standard federal regions, uniform regional boundaries, and common regional office head-quarters locations." Note that the circular "formally" establishes ten regions. That's because the ten regions had already been created in 1969, which the circular goes on to note. In reference to President Nixon's March 27, 1969 directive, the OMB circular notes, "The original directive was amended on May 21, 1969, to upgrade planned sub-regional offices in Seattle and Kansas City to full regional status. This provided two additional federal regions, with minor adjustments in the original boundaries."

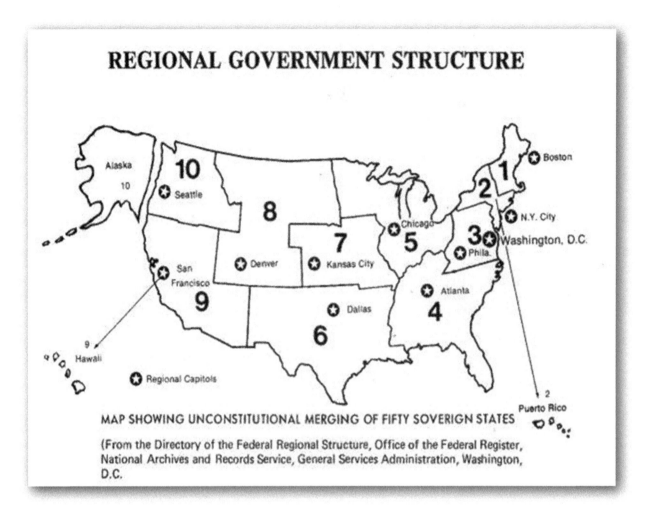

REGIONAL GOVERNMENT STRUCTURE

MAP SHOWING UNCONSTITUTIONAL MERGING OF FIFTY SOVERIGN STATES

(From the Directory of the Federal Regional Structure, Office of the Federal Register, National Archives and Records Service, General Services Administration, Washington, D.C.

1. Connecticut, Maine, Massachusetts, New Hampshire, Rhode Island, Vermont
2: New Jersey, New York, Puerto Rico, Virgin Islands
3: Delaware, District of Columbia, Maryland, Pennsylvania, Virginia, West Virginia
4: Alabama, Florida, Georgia, Kentucky, Mississippi, North and South Carolina, Tennessee
5: Illinois, Indiana, Michigan, Minnesota, Ohio, Wisconsin
6: Arkansas, Louisiana, New Mexico, Oklahoma, Texas
7: Iowa, Kansas, Missouri, Nebraska
8: Colorado, Montana, North Dakota, South Dakota, Utah, Wyoming
9: Arizona, California, Hawaii, Nevada (American Samoa, Guam, Northern Mariana Islands, Trust Territory of the Pacific Islands)
10: Alaska, Idaho, Oregon, Washington

On February 10, 1972 with Executive Order 11647 President Nixon established regional councils for each of the ten federal regions. Each council was staffed with appointed administrators from the nine grant-making agencies. The councils served as conduits for regional policy and as clearinghouses for grant money applications under the A-95 review system. In 1973 President Nixon added two more agency administrators to the Councils. President Carter added five more agency administrators to each of the ten councils.

On July 22, 1981 President Reagan restructured the ten federal councils (Executive Order 12314). On February 24, 1983 "in order to eliminate a mechanism for inter-agency and intergovernmental coordination which is [was] no longer needed" President Reagan abolished the ten federal councils (Executive Order 12407); no longer needed because October 1, 1983 (Executive Order 12372) "marked the end of the old A-95 review and the onset of the new intergovernmental review process." EB Section 17, p. 13, 17.

The new intergovernmental review process "requires federal agencies to use state and local processes of intergovernmental coordination for review of proposed federal financial assistance, state plans, direct development activities and environmental documents." "State and local processes of intergovernmental coordination" are now carried out through the Governor's Office of Planning and Research (OPR) and the State Clearinghouse (Division of OPR). EB Section 17, p. 19–25.

The Office of Management & Budget (OMB) is the Overseer of the Regional Governmental Structure. Next in the chain of command is the Under Secretaries Group for Regional Operations. EB Section 3.

Over the years the composition of the Group has changed. Housing, Education & Welfare and the Office of Economic Opportunity no longer exist. Added to the Under Secretaries Group are the Deputy Directors of Housing & Urban Development, Health & Human Services, Education and Energy. The Law Enforcement Assistance Administration is now the Federal Emergency Management Administration (FEMA). EB Section 7.

Federal Executive Boards (FEBS). "Federal Executive Boards serve as a means for disseminating information within the Federal Government and for promoting discussion of federal policies and activities of importance to all federal executives in the field." FEBS "exist in 26 metropolitan areas that are important centers of federal activity."[99] GF Section 4, p. 2.

The California Council on Intergovernmental Relations (CCIR): Predecessor to the Governor's Office of Planning and Research (EB Section 17, p. 32); very influential and successful in the regionalization of California;[100] responsibilities included:

1. review all intergovernmental problems and engage in long range planning in these areas;
2. produce direction to the local planning assistance function and to act as the central point of contact for those bodies which deal with specific intergovernmental problems;

---

99 "Metropolitan areas that are important centers of Federal activity." Really? What are the Feds doing here? Oh, yeah, destroying the Constitution and seizing jurisdiction.

100 I'm using California as the example; every State has gone through this process.

3. review the allocation of governmental services and resources between state and local governments and to make recommendations for changes where necessary;

4. serve as a sounding board for new ideas and new programs and recommendations for implementation at state and local levels. EB Section 17, p. 6.

To improve state-local coordination, it should be provided by inserting a provision in the State Administrative Manual that all state agencies will, when establishing or changing boundaries for the administration of state functions, to the greatest extent possible, establish those boundaries on the basis of locally defined regional boundaries. To assist them in this work, the Council on Intergovernmental Relations should be identified as the state-local intergovernmental coordinating agency. EB Section 17, p. 5.

The same year (1969) President Nixon divided the United States into eight [then ten] federal regions the CCIR divided California into nine regions (EB Section 17, p. 11). Attempted legislation (AB 4242) and newly proposed legislation (AB 3) would "establish 7 geographic regions encompassing the state and would establish a regional development and infrastructure agency in each region." EB Section 3, p. 2, General Folder (GF), Section 27.

The Office of Planning and Research (OPR): The OPR and the area-wide clearinghouses such as the Association of Bay Area Governments (ABAG), "are the entities responsible for implementing Presidential Executive Order 12372 (Intergovernmental Review of Federal Programs) in California." The OPR is the Single Point of Contact responsible for transmitting state and local comments developed under California's procedures for intergovernmental review of federal financial assistance and direct development activities to the appropriate federal agencies. EB Section 17, pp. 13, 17, 19-31. Sub-state regional councils, agencies and clearinghouses include regional planning commissions, economic development districts and councils of government.

In 1958, the Metropolitan Municipal Bill of Rights, as adopted by the League of California Cities, stressed home rule, cooperation and Metropolitan Councils to be established under the Joint Powers Law. In 1959, 120 delegates from 56 cities formed the Bay Area Metropolitan Council. In 1960, 135 delegates representing nine counties and 52 cities approved by-laws and recommended that each Board of Supervisors and City Council authorize execution of a Joint Powers Agreement and become members of the Association of Bay Area Governments (ABAG).

On February 24, 1961, ABAG's first official General Assembly was held with a charter membership of six counties and 54 cities. *The Emergence of a Regional Concept*, EB

Section 19, pp. 2–9. ABAG includes San Francisco, Marin, Sonoma, Napa and Solano counties and a great number of cities. ABAG is an area-wide clearinghouse for federal assistance applications. ABAG's clearinghouse responsibilities, EB Section 17, pp. 23–25. Approximately 102 jurisdictions (1986) "voluntarily" joined ABAG:

> This Committee (Illinois Joint Committee on Regional Government) found that the Federal Government has used the "carrot and stick" approach to promote the formulation of the sub-state regional districts in Illinois and other States. By offering to finance local projects through federal assistance programs, the Federal Government has induced many units of government to establish the required regional structure to apply for and review grant applications for federal funds. Thus, in many cases, for units of local government to receive federal money, they must belong to a regional commission, all federal guidelines must be met in order to receive the federal funds, and it is the planning commissions who determine if the guidelines have been met. In a short time, the units of local government become dependent upon the federal funds and are under pressure to meet all federal requirements continually, or else have the funding cut off. *Illinois Report*, EB Section 1, pp. 20–21.

Local Agency Formation Commissions (LAFC) have contributed to the construction, promotion and implementation of the Regional Governmental Structure. "The Intergovernmental Council on Urban Growth and Local Agency Formation Commissions came into being at the same time in 1963; both were part of a related package of urban affairs legislation." LAFC, General Folder (GF) p. 3. LAFC has "country-wide jurisdiction, without distinction between city and county territory." LAFC. GF Section 13, part 5.

"There is a substantial body of evidence which indicates that by promoting regional planning agencies, the Federal Government has and is encroaching upon the traditional rights, powers and duties of the State of Illinois and its units of local government." *Illinois Report*, EB Section 1, p. 19.

Illinois is not alone. It has been happening in California, its counties and cities and across the Nation.

> This intrusion of the Federal Government into state and local affairs has not been accidental, but has been carried out as part of a deliberate policy to increase federal power at the expense of the states and local units of government. This conclusion is no subjective judgment, but is well-documented. *Illinois Report*, EB Section 1, p. 23.

Completion of the Regional Governmental Structure requires increased usurpation of the governing authority of city and county elected representatives. This is being attempted in California by various means and groups.

Assembly Member Willie Brown introduced two Bills in 1990 (AB 4242 and AB 3 [Son of AB4242]):

> This Bill would create, in state government, the State Growth Management Commission consisting of 19 persons appointed, in specified numbers, from lists submitted by various specified organizations representing different interests. The commission would succeed to the powers, duties, and responsibilities of the Office of Planning and Research and the Office of Planning and Research would serve as staff to the commission. The commission would be required to, among other things, review the plans of state agencies and regional agencies for consistency with the State Conservation and Development Plan, which would be prepared by the commission, and to resolve, as specified, any inconsistencies.
>
> The Bill would establish 7 geographic regions encompassing the state and would establish a regional development and infrastructure agency in each region. By requiring the participation of cities, counties, and special districts in the regional agency, this bill would impose a state-mandated local program.
>
> The Bill would state the findings of the Legislature that growth problems including traffic congestion, inadequate waste disposal and sewage capacity, lack of affordable housing, and deteriorating water and air quality, transcend existing local government boundaries. This bill would state the declaration of the Legislature of the need to reorganize local government to create a means for regional action on regional problems. AB 3, pp. 2–3 GF. Section 27.[101]

ABAG and the "blue-ribbon" committee Bay Vision 20/20 have formulated their own regional governance plans. Bay Vision 20/20 is a private commission of business executives, environmentalists and other community activists. Despite the affiliations, the members say they act as Bay Area citizens.

Since the beginning, the people have been brought in for "validation," to give Regionalism the "color of law." Commissions and "blue-ribbon" committees are always given plenty of guidance. The "approved solution" is always regional government.

In September of 1974, the El Dorado Board of Supervisors stated (Resolution 447-74):

---

101 Well, I have AB 4242, but AB 3 is missing from my folders. It's buried here somewhere.

"WHEREAS, it has been brought to the attention of this Board that a report has been issued by the Institute for Local Self-Government, asserting the authority of the Governor's Office, the Office of Intergovernmental Management, and the Council on Intergovernmental Relations, which presents prima facie evidence of a deliberate, calculated attempt to mislead, coerce, and inhibit the rights of citizens to determine the need for, the desirability of, and the method to bring about changes in the structure of their local governments; and

WHEREAS, the "Summary of Conclusions" in this report states:

"There must be a CLIMATE OF CHANGE in order for the restructuring of local government to occur, whether this restructuring involves drastic reform, reorganization, modernization, or a minor administrative realignment. While the following does not represent an exclusive list, the factors mentioned here are those which most often create such a climate:

- COLLAPSE of government's ability to provide such needed services;
- CRISIS of major magnitude;
- CATASTROPHE that has a physical effect on the community;
- CORRUPTION of local officials;
- high COST of government and the desire for higher levels of services." (emphasis in the original); and

WHEREAS, this document is entitled "The Politics of Change in Local Government Reform"; and

WHEREAS, the techniques described in this report have apparently been used; and

WHEREAS, the cited report actually states that LOCAL GOVERNMENT IS MEETING THE PROBLEMS OF TODAY, and that no pressure is building up to cause the citizens to wish the desired reforms and then recommends the use of "change agents" to develop a climate for change, using diversionary tactics to confuse and disorient the citizens, and to deceive them about the need for reform. EB Section 25, p. 8.

Although not recognized as a threat to representative government or challenged by the general public or their elected officials, regionalization has not been without opposition and setbacks:

On June 21, 1960, Assemblyman Sheridan Heglund (D. San Diego County) wrote a guest column for Capital News Service. He voiced his opposition to what he called "a well-organized, concerted effort to destroy traditional county government." He stated, "A key plank is to scuttle elected officials and replace them with 'professionally-trained' appointees, over whom the electorate would have little if any control." EB Section 14, p. 1.

Governor Reagan's 1973 task-force report on local government was a black eye for Regional Government:

"The $270,000 study concluded that the existence of so many units of local government in California is an asset rather than a liability. Reagan's preference—that local government be streamlined, perhaps through a merger of counties—was rejected." Conclusions of the Report included:

1. The issue of too many governments has been exaggerated.
2. The public has chosen this type of government and likes it.
3. Citizen participation (and satisfaction with government) decreases as the size of the governmental unit increases.
4. No alternative set of county boundaries would, over the long run, necessarily be any better than the present ones.

The Report consistently took the view that the lower the level of government the better. EB Section 23.

Numerous California counties have stated their opposition to the regionalization of California and requested inquiry into the constitutionality of Regional Government. For example, El Dorado County Board of Supervisors passed Resolution No. 487-73 on October 16, 1973. EB Section 25, p. 6:

> Whereas, El Dorado County, through the use of existing methods and structures of government, has demonstrated that cooperation with neighboring counties and cities can solve mutual problems, and
>
> Whereas, there is increasing evidence of a determined effort toward regional redistricting as a substitute for such cooperation, which effort does not originate at the local level, and appears to be developing into a direct attack on the autonomy of city and county government; and
>
> Whereas, under the direction of the California Council on Intergovernmental Relations (an appointed body), the state has been divided into arbitrary multi-county regions (sub-state regions), presumably with appointed regional councils replacing authority previously and properly reserved to elected municipal and county officials; and

Whereas, these sub-state regions are intended to become local agencies for the administration of state and federal programs, and will not represent the citizens in the local areas; and

Whereas, this movement is not confined to the State of California, but is taking place in other states as well, and all such sub-state regionals interlock with the division of the United States into Ten Standard Federal Regions, as mandated by the President in an Executive Order (EO 11647, 12 February 1972)[102] which place California with Nevada, Arizona and Hawaii in "Region Nine" without the knowledge or consent of the citizens; and

Whereas, it would appear that EO #11647 is in direct violation of Article IV, Section 3 and 4 of the Constitution of the United States and of the Tenth Amendment, as well as Article 1, Sections 2, 22, 23, and Article 3, Section 1 of the California Constitution.

Consider the testimony of T. David Horton (Pioche, Nevada, member District of Columbia, Virginia and Nevada bar; member United States 9th Circuit Court of Appeals for the District of Columbia; Chairman, Executive Council, Defenders of the American Constitution, Inc.; Publisher, Square Dollar Series; professional witness before numerous Congressional Committees in matters pertaining to constitutional inquiries; graduate Ohio State University, American University, Washington, DC, Catholic University, Washington, DC, and Hamilton College, Clinton, New York; Legal Council, Committee to Restore the Constitution. On April 11, 1978, before the Joint Committee on Regionalism, Illinois Legislature, Mr. Horton states:

To ignore the original intent of the Constitution is to ignore its only lawful meaning. Therefore, it is not just constitutional heresy to depart from the original meaning of the Constitution, it is unlawful. And that is the key to the examination of the regionalism concept. For example, figure one shows ten regions where state boundaries are deleted, but government functions are to be carried on and performed within these regions. This is a basic violation of the intent and of the express language of the Constitutional Agreement. Damage is already being done to our local representative institutions through efforts of intimidation and bribery to take over governmental functions. The stated plan is to intensify the process and to establish contact directly with local officials, by-passing state and county governments. And in the process using tax funds—public funds—for the basic purpose of defeating one of the principal objects of the law.

---

102 EO 11647 (1972) did not establish the ten Federal regions; it established a Federal regional council for each of the ten Federal regions, which were established in 1969, as noted earlier. This does not invalidate the constitutional violations of the establishment and implementation of regional governance.

The purpose of the law can be summarized this way: "to prevent coercion, whether by bribery or by force." And what is the effect being made by the federal agencies when they say to legislators: "You must do what we say, or you won't get this money?" That is a form of bribery. And it is using the very processes of the law—not the law itself, but the processes of the law—to subvert our basic institutions.

That is one reason why the problem of defending our local governments requires us to return to basics. We need to understand that in the last analysis we are dealing with what had been described as a sedition, which is an attempt by indirect means—the quiet means (we might say "the quiet revolution")—to basically change our form of government.

The reason local control of local affairs works best is the same reason that the free-enterprise system works best—namely, that our county commissioners when they make decisions, and make mistakes, have to look eyeball to eyeball at the people who are adversely affected by those mistakes. And if they find a solution, they are much more likely to be responsive, and put that solution into effect. True, even local officials, if they make a mistake, tend to have a vested interest in their error. But they're much more likely to correct an error if (1) they are local, and (2) they are periodically accountable by election. This is the principle that needs to be reincorporated into our structure of government if we are to be protected from attacks against it.

The wisdom and success of the principle of local control of local affairs by elected officials, state and local, who are periodically accountable to their constituents, is well known. But the tentacles of self-aggrandizing centralized power are spreading themselves by means of regional governance throughout the social and political structure of our institutions. City councils are bribed, legislators are intimidated and citizens are taxed for purposes that not only lack their consent, but call forth their sincere and steadfast opposition.

The grouping of the states of the United States into "regions" for the purpose of exercising governmental powers (multi-state regionalism) and the intimidation of the legislature of each state to divide the state into regions for the purpose of exercising governmental power (sub-state regionalism) constructs a system of government by appointed bureaucrats that by-passes and undermines the lawful government of each state by its elected state and local office-holders. The by-passing of our lawfully elected officials in the exercise of governmental power is sedition.

The so-called "Executive Order No. 11647," is purporting to group the several States into ten "regions" is void.[103] This is the conclusion that was arrived at by the Joint Interim Study Committee of our sister state, your neighbor, Indiana, in its report which gives the following reasons for its conclusions:

First, "it (the so-called Executive Order) was legislative in nature and thus invalid under Article 1 of the Constitution of the United States, which vests 'all legislative power herein granted' in the Congress of the United States."

And second, "neither the states nor the Congress have ever granted authority to any branch of the Federal Government to exercise regional control over the states."

Federally imposed regionalism is further void because it violates yet another express provision of the U.S. Constitution—Article IV, Section 3: "nor (shall) any State be formed by the Junction of two or more States, or parts of States, without the consent of the Legislatures of the States concerned as well as of the Congress." The exercise in multi-state regions of governmental powers combines to that extent, the states that have a right under the Constitution to remain free and independent. It is precisely to that extent that multi-state regionalism also violates Article IV, Section 3.

Americans have long wondered what redress they have against politicians promising their way into office, swearing on their oath to "support this Constitution" and thereafter proceeding to violate every Constitutional limitation at the earliest opportunity. The use of the state's legislative power can enforce observance of constitutional requirements. The measure recommended by the Indiana Committee is one way to "support this Constitution," by enforcing it.

A few words to those who tell us if we enforce our Constitution, and violate the Divine Right not of Kings but of Bureaucrats, we shall forfeit the spoonful of pottage the usurpers threaten to take from us. We supplied that pottage. By the resourceful and resolute use of the state's legislative power, even the funds being misused as pottage can be taken from those who would substitute their will for the requirements of the Constitution and the judgment of our elected representatives.

In correctly analyzing the problem, we are halfway to the solution. The problem is usurpation. The solution is to enforce the Constitution. The sky will not fall

---

103 Please see previous footnote.

if we enforce the Constitution. We can however be engulfed, just as the Roman Republic was engulfed, by the "constant encroachments of irresponsible centralism." EB Section 2.

Also consider, California Constitution (CC), Article XI, 1(a) states:

The State is divided into counties which are legal subdivisions of the State. The Legislature shall prescribe uniform procedures for county formation, consolidation, and boundary change. Formation or consolidation requires approval by a majority of electors voting on the question in each affected county. A boundary change requires approval by the governing body of each affected county.

California Constitution, Article XI, 2 states:

(a) The Legislature shall prescribe uniform procedures for city formation and provide for city powers.
(b) Except with approval by a majority of its electors voting on the question, a city may not be annexed to or consolidated into another.

The proposed legislation (AB 3) and other regional legislation, regional plans and proposals of ABAG, Bay Vision 20/20, and other private organizations, represent a major attack on the political authority of California counties and cities. In my opinion, AB 3 not only violates California Constitution, Article XI, but also violates the purpose of having a Constitution (Law) and ELECTED REPRESENTATIVES, that is, to have a government governed by the governed.

...Certainly we will have problems that transcend local government boundaries, that's why we have a state and federal government. ELECTED OFFICIALS of these LAWFUL units of government can most effectually deal with *any* problem. However, the cost (paid for at the expense of every American taxpayer) and effect of the construction, promotion, and implementation of the Regional Governmental Structure has economically and politically undermined our ELECTED representatives' ability to act at federal, state, county and city levels.

O'Grady Complaint Continued

When Did You First Learn Of or Discover the Problem?

I first discovered "the problem" in the late forties, a threat to the Constitution/s I had taken an oath to uphold only a few years before. On November 13, 1942, I was given the honor of becoming a citizen of the United States of America. With great joy and thanksgiving, I took an oath to protect, preserve, and defend the Constitution of the United States of America and the constitution of the State of California. And so, you have my motive for devoting over forty years studying, documenting, and seeking a solution to "the problem" I have presented to you.

My first encounter was at the local level, through a copy of the policies, beliefs, and purposes of the United World Federalist, Inc. that were being taught in the Benicia High School. What was being taught was very alarming:[104]

> We call for the United States immediately to declare that it is a fundamental objective of United States foreign policy to support and strengthen the United Nations and to develop it into a World Federal Government, with limited powers adequate to make, enforce and interpret world laws to maintain peace and prevent aggression.

Also, changes were necessary in the United Nations:

> A revised STRUCTURE to administer the NEW power…would involve transfer of some authority from the United States…to the United Nations.

Then early in 1949 the California Legislature passed Assembly Joint Resolution #26 [read AJR 26 at my website], a Resolution requesting "[t]he Congress of the United States…call a convention for the sole purpose of proposing amendment of the Constitution to expedite and insure the participation of the United States in a World Federal Government.

These were the policies and beliefs of the United World Federalist! We were amazingly close to having a convention called. Then, early in 1950, the California legislature passed Senate Joint Resolution #1 (relative to withdrawing the application to Congress made by AJR #26). It was withdrawn because the state legislature learned that a world federal government would require "[t]he surrender of national sovereignty, (and) nullify our Constitution," giving "such government the power of taxation," and would "require the creation of a world army to maintain peace, and such army would be composed in a large part of soldiers from other nations, and would be subject to the control of a world legislature, with the result that the American people would be in danger of losing their liberties, their free institutions, and their freedom of action." Senate Joint Resolution # 1

Thanks to the courageous and loyal California senators, the "California Plan" calling for a world federal government was rescinded. The rescinding action was authored by

---

104 See EB Section 31, "The Policy of the United World Federalist, Inc."

Senators Donnelly, Tenney, Kraft, W. P. Rich, Desmond, Sutton, Hulse, Crittenden, and Gibson. Other states rescinded their adopted resolutions. For the moment, national sovereignty and our Constitution were safe. It wasn't long before I saw that what could not be accomplished (a world federal government) by legal means (the legislative process) was being attempted by other means: a quiet revolution.

What "influences, powers and motives" caused California and other states to propose and adapt AJR #26? Were they not aware that their actions subverted their oath to protect, preserve, and defend the United States Constitution and their respective State? Finding answers to these questions led me to the grassroots level—local government, the government closest to the people.

A 1941 pamphlet (which I will make available on request) entitled "Urban Redevelopment and Housing," by the National Resources Planning Board in Washington, DC, states:

> Replanning and rebuilding of towns and cities should be approached first from the National point of view and should be undertaken as an integral part of National policy. This is carried out with the maximum possible coordination with all the developments and changes that the future may require. Something in the nature of a general supervisory organization is called for, separate and apart from the actual work of planning. The proper agency for such supervision would appear to be the National Resources Planning Board.... ...This central agency of the Executive Office of the President should indicate the broad framework, both National and Regional within which the urban planning would be done. In all probability it will be necessary and desirable to work out some sort of regional organization for the better coordination of urban planning with the planning for larger areas. Possibly this might be done jointly by the National Resources Planning Board and the Consolidated Federal Agencies... Moreover, the number of technicians in the country capable of doing the job (urban planning) is limited. Consequently, the federal agency in Washington and probably through regional offices, would, in the outset, have to provide guidance on an executive scale.

> Federal aid...consideration should be given to singling out one urban community for immediate demonstration, initiation of a training program for city planning, setting up institutions and principles of in-service training in regions and collaborating closely with established universities.

The pamphlet provided a clue as to how restructuring of local government (cities and counties) would be accomplished....

"CALIFORNIA PLAN" WOULD HAVE ABOLISHED THE UNITED STATES

WE ARE GRATEFUL TO THE SENATORS LISTED BELOW WHO IN A SECOND TRY FINLLY GOT THE CALL FOR A CONSTITUTIONAL CONVENTION AND A WORLD GOVERNMENT TAKEOVER OF THE UNITED STATES STOPPED.

Senate Joint Resolution No. 1

CHAPTER 23

Senate Joint Resolution No. 1—Relative to withdrawing the application to Congress made by Assembly Joint Resolution No. 26 of the 1949 Regular Session, to propose a constitutional amendment for American participation in a World Federal Government.

[Filed with Secretary of State April 4, 1950.]

WHEREAS, Assembly Joint Resolution No. 26 was passed at the 1949 Regular Session of the Legislature of the State of California; and

WHEREAS, That Assembly Joint Resolution urged an amendment to the Constitution of the United States permitting this Country's participation in a World Federal Government; and

WHEREAS, It has come to the attention of certain Members of the Legislature that not all the pertinent facts relating to that subject were available and presented when this resolution was passed; and

WHEREAS, Said resolution was not a mere memorialization of the Congress but an application by the Legislature of this State, pursuant to Article V of the Constitution of the United States, that the Congress of the United States call a convention for the sole purpose of proposing amendment of the United States Constitution to expedite and insure the participation of the United States in a World Federal Government; and

WHEREAS, If similar application to the Congress is made by the legislatures of two-thirds of the states, the Congress shall have no choice but to call a convention for such purpose; and

WHEREAS, Said resolution, if acted upon and ratified by the Government of the United States would entail the surrender of our national sovereignty, nullify our Constitution, bring into being a form of law whereby American citizens could be tried by citizens of other countries and imprisoned in foreign jails; and

WHEREAS, In order to provide financial support for this world government, it would be necessary to give such government the power of taxation or to require contributions from member nations, and in either event the principal source of funds required for the support of such government would of necessity be the United States, with a resulting heavy burden on the American taxpayer and the lowering of the American standard of living; and

WHEREAS, The establishment of such World Federal Government would require the creation of a world army to maintain peace, and such world army would be composed in a large part of soldiers from other nations, and would be subject to the control of a world legislature, with the result that the American people would be in danger of losing their liberties, their free institutions, and their freedom of action; and

WHEREAS, The creation of such a world army would result in the abolition of the independent military establishment of the United States and the surrender of the Panama Canal, with consequent imminent peril to our national safety; now, therefore, be it

Resolved by the Senate and the Assembly of the State of California, jointly, That the proposal in said Assembly Joint Resolution No. 26 be withdrawn; and be it further

Resolved, That the Secretary of the Senate is hereby requested to transmit copies of this resolution to the members of the Senate and House of Representatives from this State, and to the presiding officer of each of the legislatures of the several states.

The above resolution rescinded the "California Plan" for world government. The above resolution was known as Senate Bill No. 1, and dated April 4, 1950. This rescinding action was authored by Luther Gibson, Jack Tenney, Fred Kraft, %.P. Rich, Earl Desmond, Louis Sutton, Ben Hulse, and Bradford Crittendon. (All were senators.) It passed by a narrow vote, but it did not remove culprits from office howe

As California became regionalized, a pattern emerged. I'll use my hometown, Benicia, as an example. It began with housing. The Benicia Housing Authority was established to provide housing during World War II. In the early fifties, the Housing Authority, with the aid of the City of Benicia, applied for a federal loan to study the need for low-rent housing. Seventy-five units were built; however, this issue was very controversial, since the public was denied the right to vote, even though state law (in the California Constitution, Article 34) mandated the people's right to vote BEFORE low-rent housing could be constructed in a community. The Housing Authority continues to be an arm of the Federal Government in Benicia (and throughout the United States).

On October 13, 1959, the first general plan was adopted in the City of Benicia. Quote from the Benicia Citizens Planning Committee: "A community must demonstrate to the satisfaction of the Housing and Home Finance Agency that it has a feasible method for carrying out a WORKABLE PROGRAM OF URBAN RENEWAL before it can qualify for loan and grant funds."

Besides advocating urban renewal, redevelopment, and so on, the general plan also accentuated metropolitan (regional) government in Benicia. The general plan was prepared by Sydney Williams of Pacific Planning, a firm that was very active at the time in preparing reports for the State of California on metropolitan (regional) government and other related issues.

As a result of the general plan's adoption, a redevelopment agency was established but was shortly thereafter abolished. On January 5, 1971, the City of Benicia became a member of ABAG (Association of Bay Area Governments); however, in a very short time, because of ABAG's objectives, the Benicia City Council rescinded its membership in ABAG. On October 7, 1986, Benicia again joined ABAG, allegedly to obtain cheaper insurance; however, concerned citizens felt that the so-called benefits of ABAG membership would cause Benicia to lose its local autonomy. A petition of 1949 signatures to overrule Resolution No. 86-186 was presented to the city council, which was received without comment. Thus, public participation was totally ignored.

Benicia's and Solano County's membership in ABAG, the coordination and cooperation with other regional government agencies such as the Governor's Office of Planning and Research, the Department of Housing and Community Development, Department of Commerce, Department of Housing and Urban Development, BCDC (Bay Conservation and Development Commission), Coastal Conservancy, and so on has resulted in a piecemeal transfer of city and county political authority to agencies and appointed administrators within the regional governmental structure.

The "bait" for submission to ABAG and other regional government agencies is GRANT MONEY AND LOANS available from revenue sharing and from community development block grants—in other words, GRANT MONEY AND LOANS for all phases of economic development and rehabilitation, loans to developers and businesses, job training, and programs of all sorts. However, to be eligible for grant money, local governments, including that of Benicia, must comply with guidelines and mandates of the regional government agencies. Compliance with the regional guidelines and mandates of regional government agencies and the legislature, plus specially trained, nonelected professionals operating in every level of government, has resulted in the loss of local government's jurisdiction over all land use in its community; and, without the knowledge of the general public, replaced our constitutional, representative form of government with a new form of government: regional government.

In 1949, when the California legislature adopted AJR No. 26, a question was asked—what "influences, powers and motives" caused state legislators to adopt legislation that subverted the oath they had sworn to uphold? The question is applicable to local government officials, including Benicia's, who have implemented and continue to aggressively implement the guidelines and mandates of the regional government....

The following editorials demonstrate a gradual awakening of Americans:

1. One World No 50 States (EB Section 31, p. 9). Rescission of U.N. Charter, its changes, etc. *Vallejo Times Herald* editorial, August 7, 1971.
2. One World Government (EB Section 31, p. 14) *Vallejo Times Herald* editorial, November 30, 1973:

> "Can the U.S. Government, such as we know it, as a union of 50 states be obliterated and America then become just a member state in a World Government?" Robert S. Allen, in his nationally syndicated column Inside Washington said recently "this is where we are heading" and he quoted a powerful authority for this prediction—Richard Gardner, professor of law, Columbia University, and former Deputy Assistant Secretary of State for International Organizations during the Kennedy and Johnson Administrations:

> The new house of world order will be built from the bottom rather than from the top...an end-run around National Sovereignty, eroding it piece by piece, is likely to get us world order faster than the old-fashion frontal assault...He added "That even as Nations resist appeals for world government and the surrender of national sovereignty, economic

and political interests are forcing them to establish more far ranging institutions to manage their mutual interdependence." Gardner then reminded his readers that, "In his first press conference as Secretary of State, Kissinger said the U.S. was entering a new phase of foreign policy and this would involve the building of new international structures for world order and peace—and that Kissinger will begin looking for new solutions through more effective international institutions at the global and regional levels."

3. Push for One-World Flag (EB Section 31, p. 10)—*Vallejo Times Herald* editorial, March 21, 1973:

> World Federalists ridiculed "as a pipe dream" a move to bring the United States into a One-World government under one flag—but a news account concerning the Model United Actions Club held recently at UC Berkeley by high school students indicates the movement has all but succeeded toward this end—"a highly determined effort is being made, to convince the students of our high schools that world peace will come only when all the nations of the world are obliterated and are put under one flag." In reporting on this event in Berkeley— each student was given the final text of the Universal Declaration of Human Rights as promulgated by the UN and forms to fill out to RENOUNCE THEIR CITIZENSHIP OF THE UNITED STATES and become PLANETARY CITIZENS. The students received a planetary passport and a Citizen's ID card.

4. It's Your Freedom, Keep It. (EB Section 31, p. 11)—*Vallejo Times Herald* editorial, July 4, 1973:

> Know that there is a force in existence which is determined to change "Independence" to "Interdependence." It is the force pushing for a One-World government and Planetary Citizenship to replace our United States Citizenship.

... "Restructuring" continued, a reorganization of state and local governments; revisions of the state constitutions; revisions of the Federal Constitution via treaties; revisions of city and county charters; revision and centralization of judicial and school systems, etc., resulting in a piecemeal transfer of governmental authority to APPOINTED managers and administrators.

The United States was not alone.

The United Nations Organization (UNO) has been busy implementing its assigned task of regionalizing the world. Not satisfied with existing government boundaries and forms of government, it has meddled into the internal affairs of member nations.... A member nation of the UNO, England is now feeling the full effect of the need of regionalism.... The Town and Country Planning Act of 1947 set the stage for England.

To lock in this appendage and make it an integral part of the body politic, the Town and Country Planning Act of 1968 was passed by Parliament. Further inroads were made on traditional "home rule" of the 140 County and County Borough Councils through the formation of forty-four Planning Authorities to supersede and replace "local" planning.

—NEW HAMPSHIRE REPRESENTATIVE NELSON A. PRYER, *DON BELL REPORTS*,
11/22/74. EB SECTION 31, PP. 15–16.

I have tried, as briefly as possible, to outline the "influences, powers and motives" that caused so many of our elected representatives to participate in the construction, promotion, and implementation of a new form of government without the knowledge and consent of the American people.

Our constitutional, representative form of government continues to be "restructured," replaced by regional governance. The United States Government continues its push for regional world governments, with participation in the creation of the Western Hemisphere Free Trade Zones, beginning with Mexico, Canada, and the United States. Later, these regional world governments (common markets) will, in turn, merge through a regional government system—into a one-world government—a NEW WORLD ORDER.

End of O'Grady Complaint.

Regional Government: Conclusion
The O'Grady Complaint chronicles the establishment and implementation of regional governance over what we know as the United States of America. Along with the power to tax, city, county, state, and federal jurisdictions are left with the authority to decide the where and how of regional policies. The people's ability to govern within those respective jurisdictions via their elected officials is today little more than an illusion. In a methodical, piecemeal manner, regionalism has been centralizing jurisdiction into the executive branch of the Federal Government for well over sixty years, as is chronicled herein.

To see how regional government has taken over and how you, the citizen, no longer governs, you need only travel to city hall. Ask the planning director how many federal grants your city or county has received or has pending. Does your city or county have a redevelopment agency? Ask to see a copy of your locality's general plan, where you can see how city and county jurisdiction (your control) has been contracted away. The regional division of your state is also part of your state's constitution, wherein you will find how your state legislators have passed the necessary legislation to make it "legal."

Decades of coercion and economic blackmail have made regional boundaries and governance a reality, leaving your control and rights no place to dwell. The people we elect (city, county, state, federal) have about as much sway as gnats have over a bull elephant's digestive system. Notwithstanding some very impressive challenges, our progressive slide into serfdom has been completed.

The Solution Is Legislative

Let's see... where do we start... oh yeah, abolish most federal agencies and rescind the grant-making power of every remaining federal agency. Specify that remaining federal agencies are "for information purposes only." They shall exist only to research and report their findings to Congress. It will be left to Congress whether any action should be taken. I know, I know, some people think the earth is going to spin off its axis if the EPA is abolished and mass quantities of people will go homeless and die without HUD and HHS. Nay, nay! They will not. Although, some will work to make those things come to pass so as to show the need for their dictatorial existence. So what do you want? Do you want an army of diverse jurisdictions not easily corrupted, thereby creating representative government? Or do you want to be governed by a dictator and a socialist army of appointed bureaucrats?

As for the inquiries suggested herein, as much as possible, try not to ask a question to which you do not know the answer. Such a method gives you insight into the knowledge and truthfulness of the person being questioned. Remember, showing respect and a little humility go a long way. Answers to most of the following questions can be found in your locality's general plan.

Questions for Your County and City Elected Officials:

1. Has our county/city signed a joint-powers agreement with a regional council of government? If so, where can I obtain a copy?

    a. What is that regional council of government called?
    b. How many counties/cities are members of that private corporation?
    c. Doesn't the joint-powers agreement allow the regional council of government to have power over our zoning, housing, and land use?

2. Does our county/city receive a so-called fair-share number for housing?

    a. From where does that number come and what is it based on?
    b. Has or will the county/city rezoned private property based on that quota of housing?

3. How many grants has our county/city received from the Federal Government?

   a. From which agencies or departments?
   b. What are the requirements of those grants?

4. Has our county/city created a redevelopment agency?

   a. Who are the agency officials?
   b. Has/will that agency use its increased power of eminent domain to take private property?
   c. Would you agree to reassert the authority the people have given each of you, our elected representatives and then work to abolish regional governance over our County/City?

At this point, there are four objectives:

1. INSPIRE public hearings on regionalism and land-control edicts before the county commission.
2. ENCOURGE adoption of a county/city resolution rejecting the federal regional concept and land-control regulations.
3. DEMAND formation of a joint state legislative committee to investigate all aspects of federal regionalism and land-control edicts, examine their effect upon local government, and determine their constitutionality.
4. SUPPORT passage of state laws that enforce the United States Constitution within the borders of the state, protect the freedoms of person and property guaranteed to the people by the United States Constitution, and provide criminal sanctions for violators.

In January 2016, an armed occupation of the Malheur National Wildlife Refuge in Harney County, Oregon, by Ammon Bundy and others, demonstrated that some are challenging the federal usurpation of local jurisdictions. Yes, whoever controls the land controls the people. Ryan Bundy, one of the seven defendants noted their county — nearly 10 times the size of Rhode Island — had gone from a jewel to "the biggest weed patch in the country," because the Federal Government controlled most of the land and restricted logging and ranching.

Had the Bundy crew gone unarmed with informational handouts (including corrective legislative acts as enclosed herein), sat down, and refused to leave, forcing the Feds to oust them by force, perhaps hundreds, maybe even thousands of people would have joined them; they could then have gone from one federally occupied "stronghold" to another across the nation and thereby educated and gained public support for their legitimate position. I believe that every new location they came to would bring more and more people to sit in with them.

The chart below shows the amount of land held by the Federal Government in western states (not including Indian reservations).

Arizona	45%	New Mexico	35%
California	45%	Oregon	52%
Colorado	36%	Utah	66%
Idaho	64%	Washington	30%
Montana	30%	Wyoming	50%
Nevada	87%		

What the...? When Alaska was admitted to the union in 1959, the people were allowed to occupy approximately 4 percent of "their" state.

The Federal Government should have exclusive jurisdiction over those lands acquired for purposes listed in the Constitution, no more, no less. It is obvious that the Federal Government is currently occupying millions of acres within allegedly "sovereign" states, without the concurrence of those states. Having the power of private property firmly in mind, the Founders clearly set constitutional limitations to prevent the Federal Government from accumulating property. Few reasons are noted for the Federal Government to own property: for a seat of government, for military uses, and for needful buildings; this is the very limited power given to Congress in the United States Constitution, Article I, Section 8, Clause 17:

> To exercise exclusive legislation in all cases whatsoever, over such district (not exceeding ten miles square) as may, by cession of particular states, and the acceptance of Congress, become the seat of the government of the United States, and to exercise like authority over all places purchased by the consent of the legislature of the state in which the same shall be for the erection of forts, magazines, arsenals, dockyards, and other needful buildings.

During the Constitutional Convention in 1787, an early draft read, "To exercise like authority over all places purchased for forts, etc." Madison noted that "Eldridge Gerry contended that this power might be made use of to enslave any particular state by buying up its territory and that the strongholds proposed would be a means of awing the state into an undue obedience to the General Government." Madison said that Rufus King[105] moved "to insert after the word 'purchased' the words 'by the consent of the Legislature of the State.' This would certainly make the power safe." Even as limited as the Founders could make it, this clause allowing the Federal Government to own and control property within a state continued to bother some. They thought mischief would develop.

The Federal Executive Branch and its multitude of appointed agents and bureaucrats didn't need to buy the land; they just took control via regional governance. They awed every City, every County, and every State, into undue obedience. Yes, a bit of mischief developed.

---

105 Rufus King (1755–1827) was an American lawyer, politician, and diplomat; Massachusetts delegate to the Continental Congress; attended the Constitutional Convention; one of the signers of the United States Constitution; represented New York in the Senate, served as minister to Britain; Federalist candidate for both vice-president (1804 and 1808) and president (1816).

The objective of the current economic, social, and political convulsion is the establishment of regional governance throughout the land. "Regionalism" seeks to dissolve county governments, transfer state powers to a central authority in Washington, administer the affairs of U.S. citizens through a network of appointed planners and programmers in federal regions and state sub-divisions, seize control of the land and production facilities, change the form of government, reduce Americans to the status of economic serfs on the land which once was theirs, and erect a dictatorship of the financial "elite" upon the ruins of the Republic.

—ARCHIBALD E. ROBERTS, *EMERGING STRUGGLE FOR STATE SOVEREIGNTY*

What Now?

Emerging Struggle for State Sovereignty by Archibald E. Roberts is a must-have reference book. Since it was first published in 1979, regional governance has advanced and improved its ability to usurp and rule. Still, obtain a copy as a learning foundation (find it at Amazon.com). We've got a long, hard road ahead to overthrow regional governance. Roberts's "Committee to Restore the Constitution" county chapters were a great tool for organizing, educating, and legislating, but for all their good work, regional governance is bigger and stronger than ever.

What I have relayed to you here on regional governance is only a starting point; the acts, petitions, and resolutions to follow can be a catalyst. But getting rid of the Federal Reserve would likely do the most damage to regional governance, as it is the fuel that feeds that monster of usurpation and socialist dictatorship. You can not afford to take no for an answer from your elected representatives. They want regional governance? Show 'em the door. Some may be disrespectful, condescending and vindictive. Be kind. Be respectful. Stand your ground. Your freedom and your children's freedom are at stake here. Remember, we can't lose. Freedom has always and will forevermore win over slavery. But that does not mean you can sit back and wait for it to happen. We fight—we must fight—and there are enough of us willing never to give in. We will win.

For now, my website, SqueakyWheelPolitics.com, will have to be our place of "assembly." I am available to travel and speak and help organize, but I'm just one. We really need fresh men and women, both old and young, who can quickly "catch fire" in this battle. We need an army willing to *never give in*. What we want, we shall achieve: a Republican form of government along with limited government, low taxation, a free-market economy, individual liberty, a strong national defense, and constitutional sovereignty. We can restore control of government to the people and end the dictatorship.

Some supporters will want to add issues outside the subject boundaries set herein. Forget about it! The issues I list are the only issues I'm addressing and challenging, at this time—no additions, no subtractions; no racist, anti-Semitic, or other rants and rages allowed. You want to challenge and rectify important problems of our day, as defined herein? Join me. If not, go in peace.

As for doing away with regional government, Chapter 7 to follow has the model acts, petitions and resolutions that need to be passed by our federal, state, county, and city elected officials. None of that happens until there is a ho'bunch of organizin' and educatin'. Go to **SqueakyWheelPolitics.com**, where you will find these acts, petitions, and resolutions for downloading and editing, so as to tailor them to your specific jurisdictions and elected officials.

7

Needed Acts, Petitions, Resolutions - Federal, State, County, City

(Please note: All acts, petitions, and resolutions given herein may be updated as I receive input and feedback. All suggestions will be considered. Go to my website (squeakywheelpolitics.com) to offer suggestions and for updates.)

FEDERAL

CONSTITUTIONAL RESTORATION ACT

An ACT

to abolish regional governance and restore constitutional governance within the United States and within every State of the Union.

Whereas, this Act shall be cited as the Constitutional Restoration Act, hereinafter referred to as the Act; and

Whereas this Act shall be implemented over a three-year transition period, beginning thirty days after the date of enactment of this Act; and

Whereas, responsible authorities on constitutional law declare the establishment and implementation of Regional Government a violation of United States Constitution, Article IV, Sections 3 and 4 (in part), and the 10th Amendment:

Article IV

Section 3. New States may be admitted by the Congress into this union; but no new states shall be formed or erected within the Jurisdiction of any other State; nor any State be formed by the Junction of two or more States, or parts of States, without the Consent of the Legislatures of the States concerned as well as of the Congress.

Section 4. The United States shall guarantee to every State in this Union a Republican Form of Government....

Amendment X (1791)

The powers not delegated to the United States by the Constitution, nor prohibited by it to the states, are reserved to the states respectively, or to the people; and

Whereas, the intent of the framers of the United States Constitution was to guarantee to each state sovereignty/jurisdiction over all matters within its boundaries except for those powers granted to the United States as agent of the state; and

Whereas, two *ultra vires* acts by President Richard M. Nixon, establishing regional governance over the United States, does violate United States Constitution, Article IV, Sections 3 and 4 (in part), and the 10th Amendment. The first illegal presidential act is titled Statement on Establishing

Common Regional Boundaries for Agencies Providing Social and Economic Services dated March 27, 1969. The second illegal presidential act is Executive Order No. 11647, The Federal Regional Councils, dated February 12, 1972; and

Whereas, it is obvious that the Federal Government is currently occupying millions of acres within sovereign states without the required consent of those states. With the power of private property firmly in mind, the Founders clearly set forth constitutional limitations to prevent the Federal Government from owning much property itself. There are therefore few reasons noted to have the Federal Government own property: for a seat of government, for military uses, and for needful buildings. This is the very limited power given to Congress in the United States Constitution, Article I, Section 8, Clause 17:

> To exercise exclusive legislation in all cases whatsoever, over such district (not exceeding ten miles square) as may, by cession of particular states, and the acceptance of Congress, become the seat of the government of the United States, and to exercise like authority over all places purchased by the consent of the legislature of the state in which the same shall be for the erection of forts, magazines, arsenals, dockyards, and other needful buildings.

Whereas, federal and state land-use regulations, which seek to transfer control of private property to federal agencies and agents, are in violation of the United States Constitution, the 5th (in part) and the 14th Amendment (Section 1):

Amendment V (1791)

No person shall be... deprived of life, liberty, or property, without due process of law; nor shall private property be taken for public use, without just compensation.

Amendment XIV (1868)

Section 1

All persons born or naturalized in the United States, and subject to the jurisdiction thereof, are citizens of the United States and of the State wherein they reside. No State shall make or enforce any law which shall abridge the privileges or immunities of citizens of the United States; nor shall any State deprive any person of life, liberty, or property, without due process of law; nor deny to any person within its jurisdiction the equal protection of the laws; and

Whereas, law repugnant to the Constitution is void. Maybury v. Madison 5 U.S. 137 (1803); where rights secured by the Constitution are involved, there can be no rule-making or legislation which would abrogate them. Miranda v. Arizona 86 U.S. 1602 (1966); an unconstitutional statute though having the form and name of law is in reality no law, but wholly null and void and ineffective for any purpose. It imposes no duty, confers no rights, creates no office, bestows no power or authority on acts performed under it. No one is bound to obey an unconstitutional statute, and no courts are bound to enforce it. 16 Am. Jur. § 2 at 177; and

Whereas, correcting federal usurpation of constitutional powers is a lawful responsibility of every state legislature and the United States Congress acting in their highest sovereign capacities. Each state is required by constitutional compact to enforce the "Supreme Law of the Land" within its borders, and to declare null and void any *ultra vires* acts of its agents in Washington; and

Whereas, by erecting regional governance, federal agents have acted beyond their delegated powers and thereby erected a new kind of government, a corporate state, upon the ruins of the Republic without the knowledge or consent of the states or their citizens; and

Whereas, federal regionalism has dissolved city, county, state and United States jurisdictions in violation of state and federal constitutions. Regional governance has disfranchised the electorate by usurping the authority of elected officials of every city, county, state, and the United States and replacing it with the governance of appointed regional planners and bureaucrats. Thereby, the Regional Government has seized control of all private property, overthrown state and federal constitutions, and reduced American citizens to the status of economic serfs on the land that once was theirs.

Therefore, to start:

1. There may be others to come, but at this time, the following agencies are hereby abolished, (1) Agriculture, (2) Commerce, (3) Education, (4) Energy, (5) Environmental Protection Agency, (6) Health and Human Services, (7) Housing and Urban Development, (8) Interior, (9) United States Agency for International Development, (10) Transportation, (11) Bureau of Land Management, (12) Advisory Commission on Intergovernmental Relations. The grant-making power of all remaining Federal agencies/departments is hereby abolished. Upon passage of this Act, all former grant-making Federal agencies/departments remaining are for information purposes only; they shall investigate, research and report their findings to Congress and applicable state legislatures and governors, but shall not make or recommend actions to be taken. The number of employees within these agencies/departments shall be reduced to the number of employees needed to adequately investigate, research, and report; Congress shall determine the minimum and maximum number of employees needed.

2. The ten Federal regions are hereby abolished as well as all regional confederations within every state and within the United States are hereby null and void. All sub-regions within states and their governing regional councils of government, along with all joint-powers agreements are hereby null and void. Any and all agreements transferring powers and authority to regional authorities by cities, counties, and states are hereby null and void. Cities, counties, and states can and shall continue to coordinate and cooperate to address issues that overlap their boundaries. But no agreements are to be made that diminish or

transfer authority held directly by the citizenry or their respective elected representatives within their respective jurisdictions; and

3. The functions of the defunct Federal agencies/departments and subregion councils of government are hereby, once again, the jurisdictional duty and responsibility of the elected officials of the city, county, state and United States.

4. There is no constitutional provision or statute that explicitly permits executive orders; therefore, Presidents shall no longer issue executive orders. Any and all future orders deemed needed by Presidents shall be submitted to Congress for review, approval, and passage.

Be it understood, if any provision of this Act, an amendment made by this Act, or the application of such provision or amendment to any person or circumstance shall be held to be unconstitutional, the remainder of this Act, the amendments made by this Act, and the application of the provisions of such to any person or circumstance shall not be affected thereby.

This Act is hereby enacted by the Senate and House of Representatives of the United States of America assembled.

STATE

A Petition to the _____State Legislature requesting public hearings on the constitutionality of regional governance, including but not limited to land control edits—leading to corrective State legislation, specifically, the attached Bill to Abolish Regional Governance and Enforce the United States Constitution Within the State of _____.

Whereas, it is the opinion of the undersigned that continued membership of the State of _____ in regional government, under whatever name, is a real and present danger to the freedom of person and property guaranteed to the people by the United States Constitution, and to the sovereignty and proper interest of the people, State of _____; and

Whereas, many responsible authorities on constitutional law declare the establishment and implementation of Regional Government a direct violation of United States Constitution, Article IV, Sections 3 and 4 (in part), and the 10th Amendment:

Article IV

Section 3. New States may be admitted by the Congress into this Union; but no new State shall be formed or erected within the Jurisdiction of any other State; nor any State be formed by the Junction of two or more States, or Parts of States, without the Consent of the Legislatures of the States concerned as well as of the Congress.

Section 4. The United States shall guarantee to every State in this Union a Republican Form of Government....

Amendment X (1791)

The powers not delegated to the United States by the Constitution, nor prohibited by it to the States, are reserved to the States respectively, or to the people; and

Whereas, State Legislators and other elected officials, have taken an oath to uphold the Constitution and must hold as sacred trust their responsibility to protect the personal freedom and liberty of the citizens.

THEREFORE: We, the undersigned residents of the State of _____, do hereby petition the _____ State Legislature to hold public hearings on the constitutionality of the establishment and implementation of regional government, to hear evidence and testimony by witnesses and to take whatever action is necessary to defend the freedoms of person and property guaranteed to the residents of the State of _____;

PRINT NAME   SIGNED

_____

ADDRESS_____

_____

_____

_____

_____

_____

_____

_____

_____

_____

_____

_____

_____

Upon completion please return to _____

(Address)_____

Download the petition from my web site and make copies as needed.

STATE

A Bill to Abolish Regional Governance and Enforce the United States Constitution Within the State of _____

Whereas, by Agreement with her sister States, the State of _____ is duty bound to enforce the Constitution of the United States within her borders; and

Whereas, the Legislature of this State has determined no authority was granted under the terms of the United States Constitution, to either group our State with several other sovereign states into one "region" or to coerce the division of any State into sub-state "regions;" and

Whereas, two *ultra vires* acts by President Nixon, establishing regional governance over the United States, does violate United States Constitution, Article IV, § 3 and § 4 (in part), and the 10th Amendment. The first illegal presidential act is titled Statement on Establishing Common Regional Boundaries for Agencies Providing Social and Economic Services dated March 27, 1969. The second illegal presidential act is Executive Order No. 11647, *The Federal Regional Councils*, dated February 12, 1972. With these two executive orders, sovereign states, Parties to the Constitutional Compact, were merged into regions ruled by appointed regional agents, commissions and councils, and

Whereas, these *ultra vires* acts are null and void because (1) they are legislative in nature: Article I, Section 1 of the United States Constitution notes, "All legislative Powers herein granted shall be vested in a Congress of the United States...," and (2) no authority was granted by the states or by the United States Congress to exercise any such "regional" control over any one or any group of the Parties to the Constitutional Compact, therefore:

BE IT ENACTED BY THE _____ STATE LEGISLATURE, in conformity with the duty of the State of _____ to her People and to her sister states, and in further conformity with the oath of office taken by each of us to support and defend the Constitution of the United States:

1. Any purported act by any person, office-holder, and/or agency claiming to group any State or group of States into a so-called region is beyond the authority granted under the Constitution of the United States and is therefore, null, void, and of no effect within the jurisdiction of this State, and any attempt to enforce such provisions within this State is unlawful, and

2. Any and all regional configurations, agreements and authority is null, void, and of no effect within the jurisdiction of this State, and any attempt to enforce such provisions within this State is unlawful. Appropriate penalties shall be considered and assessed.

COUNTY/CITY

Resolution of _____ County Commission/City Council, State of _____, in support of proposed Federal and State legislation to abolish regional governance and enforce the Federal and State Constitutions.

Whereas, specific legislation has been or soon will be introduced at the Federal and State levels of government. For our United States Congress, the Constitutional Restoration Act, an Act to abolish regional governance and restore constitutional governance within the United States and within every State of the Union. For our State Legislature, a Bill to abolish Regional Governance and enforce the United States Constitution within the State of _____.

Whereas, the Governor's Office and/or the Legislature have divided the State of _____ into multi-county planning districts or sub-regions in which appointed regional councils and agents thereof have seized control. This control, this authority to govern, previously and properly reserved to elected municipal and county officials has been transferred to regional authorities, including authority over land use, zoning and housing, business, private property and thus the people. This control, this authority to govern, has been transferred without the knowledgeable consent of the people of _____ County/City; and

Whereas, the illegal grouping of the State of _____ into Federal region _____ with other sovereign states and subsequent division of the State into sub-regions, governed by regional councils of government, corresponds in function and regulation with the illegal division of the United States into Federal Regions by President Richard M. Nixon. The first illegal presidential act is titled "Statement on Establishing Common Regional Boundaries for Agencies Providing Social and Economic Services" dated March 27, 1969; the second illegal presidential act is Executive Order No. 11647, The Federal Regional Councils, dated February 12, 1972; and

Whereas, many responsible authorities on constitutional law declare the establishment and implementation of Regional Government a violation of United States Constitution, Article IV, Sections 3 and 4 (in part), and the 10th Amendment:

Article IV

Section 3. New States may be admitted by the Congress into this Union; but no new State shall be formed or erected within the Jurisdiction of any other State; nor any State be formed by the Junction of two or more States, or Parts of States, without the Consent of the Legislatures of the States concerned as well as of the Congress.

Section 4. The United States shall guarantee to every State in this Union a Republican Form of Government.

Amendment X (1791)

The powers not delegated to the United States by the Constitution, nor prohibited by it to the states, are reserved to the states respectively, or to the people; and

Whereas, regional governance bypasses our traditional and constitutional government bodies, and usurps the rights and freedoms of individual citizens; rights and freedoms guaranteed by the Constitution of the State of _____ and the Constitution of the United States of America.

THEREFORE, BE IT RESOLVED BY THE _____ COUNTY COMMISSION/CITY COUNCIL THAT:

SECTION 1: The above recitals are adopted.

SECTION 2: The State Legislature shall create a bi-partisan committee to investigate regional governance, particularly as it usurps the power, jurisdiction, and authority of local governmental bodies, leading to corrective legislation, including but not limited to the State Bill referenced herein.

SECTION 3: A copy of this resolution be forwarded to our State legislature and brought to the attention of every member, also, the legislatures of the other sovereign states in so-called federal region _____, our two United States Senators, and all United States Representatives from our State, requesting support, resolution and/or legislative action.

This resolution, introduced by _____, seconded by _____ and lawfully approved, is declared duly passed and adopted this _____ day of _____, 20____.

By:_____, Chairman

APPROVED AS TO FORM AND LEGAL SUFFICIENCY:

_____, Council

IT'S LIKELY GONNA BE A KNOCK-DOWN, DRAG-OUT FIGHT—NEVER GIVE IN

Regaining our lawful authority over government will likely be a knock-down, drag-out fight. Okay. More than likely. Most city, county, state, and federal elected officials like regional government. Regional government has made their jobs easy. Actually, it has made their jobs obsolete, and turned our once grand representative form of government into a socialist dictatorship of the Executive.

Lt. Col. Archibald E. Roberts and constitutional authority T. David Horton did amazing work battling regionalism, but they failed.[106] But without them, and people like Bernadine Smith, Mrs. Wilt and Mrs. O'Grady you would not be reading these words. It appears no one has stepped up to take their places on the regional battlefield. Unfortunately, it appears I may be the only remaining source of information and challenge to regional government. There may be other challengers that have not yet made an appearance. I hope and pray so. But for now, it appears the regional battlefield is left to me... and you.

In order of importance for us to address: Federal Reserve, Regional Government, Social Security, Sixteenth Amendment and then the Seventeenth Amendment. I'm not saying we address these one at a time, but it does us no good to kill off the Seventeenth Amendment if the Federal Reserve is left alive. It is possible the American Free Labor Act could ignite a firestorm of support and challenge, thereby creating the exposure and momentum we need.

For information and updates, come to my website/blog **SqueakyWheelPolitics.com**. You will find links to other important sources of information there. With your help, I want to have built the state-of-the-art, interactive website/blog needed for the challenging trek upon which we are about to embark. The site will freely offer mass quantities of supporting documentation on the issues presented herein. That is not near enough. I want you to be able to go to the site, click on your State, County or City and there, monitor and discover contacts and ways to help with any "squeaky wheel/grease" activity in your jurisdictions. We need "Squeaky Wheels" to report their State, County and City activities to the site, so the needed data-base can be created. Information coming in will need to be confirmed before posting. Your suggestions and support are greatly appreciated.

WE WILL SUCCEED

We succeed where so many other good and competent people failed, because... I say so! Yeah, I wish. No. We don't succeed because of me. We succeed because of you. Start now by buying mass quantities of this book. Give it to friends and family. Send it to your elected officials at all levels. United States

---

106 Again I quote Jacob Riis: "When nothing seems to help, I go and look at a stonecutter hammering away at his rock, perhaps a hundred times without as much as a crack showing in it. Yet at the hundred and first blow, it will split in two, and I know it was not that blow that did it, but all that had gone before."

Congress? We want Congress tripping over it in the halls. We shall succeed because the squeaky wheel always gets the grease. I leave you for now with (again) the advice Sir Winston Churchill gave to the boys at Harrow in 1941:

> *Never give in, never give in, never, never, never, never, in nothing, great or small, large or petty; never give in except to convictions of honor and good sense.*

Laus Deo

Declaration of Independence

When in the Course of human events it becomes necessary for one people to dissolve the political bands which have connected them with another and to assume among the powers of the earth, the separate and equal station to which the Laws of Nature and of Nature's God entitle them, a decent respect to the opinions of mankind requires that they should declare the causes which impel them to the separation.

We hold these truths to be self-evident, that all men are created equal, that they are endowed by their Creator with certain unalienable Rights, that among these are Life, Liberty and the pursuit of Happiness. —That to secure these rights, Governments are instituted among Men, deriving their just powers from the consent of the governed, —That whenever any Form of Government becomes destructive of these ends, it is the Right of the People to alter or to abolish it, and to institute new Government, laying its foundation on such principles and organizing its powers in such form, as to them shall seem most likely to effect their Safety and Happiness. Prudence, indeed, will dictate that Governments long established should not be changed for light and transient causes; and accordingly all experience hath shown that mankind are more disposed to suffer, while evils are sufferable than to right themselves by abolishing the forms to which they are accustomed. But when a long train of abuses and usurpations, pursuing invariably the same Object evinces a design to reduce them under absolute Despotism, it is their right, it is their duty, to throw off such Government, and to provide new Guards for their future security. —Such has been the patient sufferance of these Colonies; and such is now the necessity which constrains them to alter their former Systems of Government. The history of the present King of Great Britain is a history of repeated injuries and usurpations, all having in direct object the establishment of an absolute Tyranny over these States. To prove this, let Facts be submitted to a candid world.

He has refused his Assent to Laws, the most wholesome and necessary for the public good.

He has forbidden his Governors to pass Laws of immediate and pressing importance, unless suspended in their operation till his Assent should be obtained; and when so suspended, he has utterly neglected to attend to them.

He has refused to pass other Laws for the accommodation of large districts of people, unless those people would relinquish the right of Representation in the Legislature, a right inestimable to them and formidable to tyrants only.

He has called together legislative bodies at places unusual, uncomfortable, and distant from the depository of their Public Records, for the sole purpose of fatiguing them into compliance with his measures.

He has dissolved Representative Houses repeatedly, for opposing with manly firmness his invasions on the rights of the people.

He has refused for a long time, after such dissolutions, to cause others to be elected, whereby the Legislative Powers, incapable of Annihilation, have returned to the People at large for their exercise; the State remaining in the mean time exposed to all the dangers of invasion from without, and convulsions within.

He has endeavored to prevent the population of these States; for that purpose obstructing the Laws for Naturalization of Foreigners; refusing to pass others to encourage their migrations hither, and raising the conditions of new Appropriations of Lands.

He has obstructed the Administration of Justice by refusing his Assent to Laws for establishing Judiciary Powers.

He has made Judges dependent on his Will alone for the tenure of their offices, and the amount and payment of their salaries.

He has erected a multitude of New Offices, and sent hither swarms of Officers to harass our people and eat out their substance.

He has kept among us, in times of peace, Standing Armies without the Consent of our legislatures.

He has affected to render the Military independent of and superior to the Civil Power.

He has combined with others to subject us to a jurisdiction foreign to our constitution, and unacknowledged by our laws; giving his Assent to their Acts of pretended Legislation:

For quartering large bodies of armed troops among us:

For protecting them, by a mock Trial from punishment for any Murders which they should commit on the Inhabitants of these States:

For cutting off our Trade with all parts of the world:

For imposing Taxes on us without our Consent:

For depriving us in many cases, of the benefit of Trial by Jury:

For transporting us beyond Seas to be tried for pretended offences:

For abolishing the free System of English Laws in a neighboring Province, establishing therein an Arbitrary government, and enlarging its Boundaries so as to render it at once an example and fit instrument for introducing the same absolute rule into these Colonies.

For taking away our Charters, abolishing our most valuable Laws and altering fundamentally the Forms of our Governments:

For suspending our own Legislatures, and declaring themselves invested with power to legislate for us in all cases whatsoever.

He has abdicated Government here, by declaring us out of his Protection and waging War against us.

He has plundered our seas, ravaged our coasts, burnt our towns, and destroyed the lives of our people.

He is at this time transporting large Armies of foreign Mercenaries to complete the works of death, desolation, and tyranny, already begun with circumstances of Cruelty & perfidy scarcely paralleled in the most barbarous ages, and totally unworthy the Head of a civilized nation.

He has constrained our fellow Citizens taken Captive on the high Seas to bear Arms against their Country, to become the executioners of their friends and Brethren, or to fall themselves by their Hands.

He has excited domestic insurrections amongst us, and has endeavored to bring on the inhabitants of our frontiers, the merciless Indian Savages whose known rule of warfare, is an undistinguished destruction of all ages, sexes and conditions.

In every stage of these Oppressions We have Petitioned for Redress in the most humble terms: Our repeated Petitions have been answered only by repeated injury. A Prince, whose character is thus marked by every act which may define a Tyrant, is unfit to be the ruler of a free people.

Nor have We been wanting in attentions to our British brethren. We have warned them from time to time of attempts by their legislature to extend an unwarrantable jurisdiction over us. We have reminded them of the circumstances of our emigration and settlement here. We have appealed to their native justice and magnanimity, and we have conjured them by the ties of our common kindred to disavow these usurpations, which would inevitably interrupt our connections and correspondence. They too have been deaf to the voice of justice and of consanguinity. We must, therefore, acquiesce in the necessity, which denounces our Separation, and hold them, as we hold the rest of mankind, Enemies in War, in Peace Friends.

We, therefore, the Representatives of the united States of America, in General Congress, Assembled, appealing to the Supreme Judge of the world for the rectitude of our intentions, do, in the Name, and by Authority of the good People of these Colonies, solemnly publish and declare, That these united Colonies are, and of Right ought to be Free and Independent States, that they are Absolved from all Allegiance to the British Crown, and that all political connection between them and the State of Great Britain, is and ought to be totally dissolved; and that as Free and Independent States, they have full Power to levy War, conclude Peace, contract Alliances, establish Commerce, and to do all other Acts and Things which Independent States may of right do. —And for the support of this Declaration, with a firm reliance on the protection of Divine Providence, we mutually pledge to each other our Lives, our Fortunes, and our sacred Honor.

Signers of the Declaration of Independence

Georgia:
Button Gwinnett
Lyman Hall
George Walton

North Carolina:
William Hooper
Joseph Hewes
John Penn

South Carolina:
Edward Rutledge
Thomas Heyward, Jr.
Thomas Lynch, Jr.
Arthur Middleton

Massachusetts:
John Hancock

Maryland:
Samuel Chase
William Paca
Thomas Stone
Charles Carroll of Carrollton

Virginia:
George Wythe
Richard Henry Lee

Delaware:
Caesar Rodney
George Read
Thomas McKean

New York:
William Floyd
Philip Livingston
Lewis Morris

New Jersey:
Richard Stockton
John Witherspoon
Francis Hopkinson
John Hart
Abraham Clark

New Hampshire:
Josiah Bartlett
William Whipple

Massachusetts:
Samuel Adams
John Adams
Robert Treat Paine
Elbridge Gerry

Rhode Island:

Thomas Jefferson
Benjamin Harrison
Thomas Nelson, Jr.
Francis Lightfoot Lee
Carter Braxton

Pennsylvania:
Robert Morris
Benjamin Rush
Benjamin Franklin
John Morton
George Clymer
James Smith
George Taylor
James Wilson
George Ross

Stephen Hopkins
William Ellery

Connecticut:
Roger Sherman
Samuel Huntington
William Williams
Oliver Wolcott

New Hampshire:
Mathew Thornton

United States Constitution

We the People of the United States, in Order to form a more perfect Union, establish Justice, insure domestic Tranquility, provide for the common defense, promote the general Welfare, and secure the Blessings of Liberty to ourselves and our Posterity, do ordain and establish this Constitution for the United States of America.

Article I

Section 1. All legislative Powers herein granted shall be vested in a Congress of the United States, which shall consist of a Senate and House of Representatives.

Section 2. The House of Representatives shall be composed of Members chosen every second Year by the People of the several States, and the Electors in each State shall have the Qualifications requisite for Electors of the most numerous Branch of the State Legislature.

No Person shall be a Representative who shall not have attained to the Age of twenty-five Years, and been seven Years a Citizen of the United States, and who shall not, when elected, be an Inhabitant of that State in which he shall be chosen.

Representatives and direct Taxes shall be apportioned among the several States which may be included within this Union, according to their respective Numbers, which shall be determined by adding to the whole Number of free Persons, including those bound to Service for a Term of Years, and excluding Indians not taxed, three fifths of all other Persons. The actual Enumeration shall be made within three Years after the first Meeting of the Congress of the United States, and within every subsequent Term of ten Years, in such Manner as they shall by Law direct. The Number of Representatives shall not exceed one for every thirty Thousand, but each State shall have at Least one Representative; and until such enumeration shall be made, the State of New Hampshire shall be entitled to chose three, Massachusetts eight, Rhode Island and Providence Plantations one, Connecticut five, New York six, New Jersey four, Pennsylvania eight, Delaware one, Maryland six, Virginia ten, North Carolina five, South Carolina five, and Georgia three.

When vacancies happen in the Representation from any State, the Executive Authority thereof shall issue Writs of Election to fill such Vacancies.

The House of Representatives shall choose their Speaker and other Officers; and shall have the sole Power of Impeachment.

Section 3. The Senate of the United States shall be composed of two Senators from each State, chosen by the Legislature thereof, for six Years; and each Senator shall have one Vote.

Immediately after they shall be assembled in Consequence of the first Election, they shall be divided as equally as may be into three Classes. The Seats of the Senators of the first Class shall be vacated at the Expiration of the second Year, of the second Class at the Expiration of the fourth Year, and the third Class at the Expiration of the sixth Year, so that one-third may be chosen every second Year; and if Vacancies happen by Resignation, or otherwise, during the Recess of the Legislature of any State, the Executive thereof may make temporary Appointments until the next Meeting of the Legislature, which shall then fill such Vacancies.

No Person shall be a Senator who shall not have attained to the Age of thirty Years, and been nine Years a Citizen of the United States and who shall not, when elected, be an Inhabitant of that State for which he shall be chosen.

The Vice President of the United States shall be President of the Senate, but shall have no Vote, unless they be equally divided.

The Senate shall choose their other Officers, and also a President pro tempore, in the Absence of the Vice President, or when he shall exercise the Office of President of the United States.

The Senate shall have the sole Power to try all Impeachments. When sitting for that Purpose, they shall be on Oath or Affirmation. When the President of the United States is tried, the Chief Justice shall preside: And no Person shall be convicted without the Concurrence of two thirds of the Members present.

Judgment in Cases of Impeachment shall not extend further than to removal from Office, and disqualification to hold and enjoy any Office of honor, Trust or Profit under the United States: but the Party convicted shall nevertheless be liable and subject to Indictment, Trial, Judgment and Punishment, according to Law.

Section 4. The Times, Places and manner of holding Elections for Senators and Representatives, shall be prescribed in each State by the Legislature thereof; but the Congress may at any time by Law make or alter such Regulations, except as to the Places of choosing Senators.

The Congress shall assemble at least once in every Year, and such Meeting shall be on the first Monday in December, unless they shall by Law appoint a different Day.

Section 5. Each House shall be the Judge of the Elections, Returns and Qualifications of its own Members, and a Majority of each shall constitute a Quorum to do Business; but a smaller Number may adjourn from day to day, and may be authorized to compel the Attendance of absent Members, in such Manner, and under such Penalties as each House may provide.

Each House may determine the Rules of its Proceedings, punish its Members for disorderly Behavior, and, with the Concurrence of two thirds, expel a Member.

Each House shall keep a Journal of its Proceedings, and from time to time publish the same, excepting such Parts as may in their Judgment require Secrecy; and the Yeas and Nays of the Members of either House on any question shall, at the Desire of one fifth of those Present, be entered on the Journal.

Neither House, during the Session of Congress, shall, without the Consent of the other, adjourn for more than three days, nor to any other Place than that in which the two Houses shall be sitting.

Section 6. The Senators and Representatives shall receive a Compensation for their Services, to be ascertained by Law, and paid out of the Treasury of the United States. They shall in all Cases, except Treason, Felony and Breach of the Peace, be privileged from Arrest during their Attendance at the Session of their respective Houses, and in going to and returning from the same; and for any Speech or Debate in either House, they shall not be questioned in any other Place.

No Senator or Representative shall, during the Time for which he was elected, be appointed to any civil Office under the Authority of the United States, which shall have been created, or the Emoluments whereof shall have been increased during such time: and no Person holding any Office under the United States, shall be a Member of either House during his Continuance in Office.

Section 7. All Bills for raising Revenue shall originate in the House of Representatives; but the Senate may propose or concur with Amendments as on other Bills.

Every Bill which shall have passed the House of Representatives and the Senate, shall, before it become a Law, be presented to the President of the United States; if he approve he shall sign it, but if not he shall return it, with his Objections to that House in which it shall have originated, who shall enter the Objections at large on their Journal, and proceed to reconsider it. If after such Reconsideration two thirds of that House shall agree to pass the Bill, it shall be sent, together with the Objections, to the other House, by which it shall likewise be reconsidered, and if approved by two thirds of that House, it shall become a Law. But in all such Cases the Votes of both Houses shall be determined by yeas and Nays, and the Names of the Persons voting for and against the Bill shall be entered on the Journal of each House respectively. If any Bill shall not be returned by the

President within ten Days (Sundays excepted) after it shall have been presented to him, the Same shall be a Law, in like Manner as if he had signed it, unless the Congress by their Adjournment prevent its Return, in which Case it shall not be a Law.

Every Order, Resolution, or Vote to which the Concurrence of the Senate and House of Representatives may be necessary (except on a question of Adjournment) shall be presented to the President of the United States; and before the Same shall take Effect, shall be approved by him, or being disapproved by him, shall be repassed by two thirds of the Senate and House of Representatives, according to the Rules and Limitations prescribed in the Case of a Bill.

Section 8. The Congress shall have Power To lay and collect Taxes, Duties, Imposts and Excises, to pay the Debts and provide for the common Defense and general Welfare of the United States; but all Duties, Imposts and Excises shall be uniform throughout the United States;

To borrow Money on the credit of the United States;

To regulate Commerce with foreign Nations, and among the several States, and with the Indian Tribes;

To establish a uniform Rule of Naturalization, and uniform Laws on the subject of Bankruptcies throughout the United States;

To coin Money, regulate the Value thereof, and of foreign Coin, and fix the Standard of Weights and Measures;

To provide for the Punishment of counterfeiting the Securities and current Coin of the United States;

To establish Post Offices and post Roads;

To promote the Progress of Science and useful Arts, by securing for limited Times to Authors and Inventors the exclusive Right to their respective Writings and Discoveries;

To constitute Tribunals inferior to the Supreme Court;

To define and punish Piracies and Felonies committed on the high Seas, and Offences against the Law of Nations;

To declare War, grant Letters of Marque and Reprisal, and make Rules concerning Captures on Land and Water;

To raise and support Armies, but no Appropriation of Money to that Use shall be for a longer Term than two Years;

To provide and maintain a Navy;

To make Rules for the Government and Regulation of the land and naval Forces;

To provide for calling forth the Militia to execute the Laws of the Union, suppress Insurrections and repel Invasions;

To provide for organizing, arming, and disciplining, the Militia, and for governing such Part of them as may be employed in the Service of the United States, reserving to the States respectively, the Appointment of the Officers, and the Authority of training the Militia according to the discipline prescribed by Congress;

To exercise exclusive Legislation in all Cases whatsoever, over such District (not exceeding ten Miles square) as may, by Cession of particular States, and the Acceptance of Congress, become the Seat of the Government of the United States, and to exercise like Authority over all Places purchased by the Consent of the Legislature of the State in which the Same shall be, for the Erection of Forts, Magazines, Arsenals, dock-Yards, and other needful Buildings;–And

To make all Laws which shall be necessary and proper for carrying into Execution the foregoing Powers, and all other Powers vested by this Constitution in the Government of the United States, or in any Department or Officer thereof.

Section 9. The Migration or Importation of such Persons as any of the States now existing shall think proper to admit, shall not be prohibited by the Congress prior to the Year one thousand eight hundred and eight, but a Tax or duty may be imposed on such Importation, not exceeding ten dollars for each Person.

The Privilege of the Writ of Habeas Corpus shall not be suspended, unless when in Cases of Rebellion or Invasion the public Safety may require it.

No Bill of Attainder or ex post facto Law shall be passed.

No Capitation, or other direct, Tax shall be laid, unless in Proportion to the Census or enumeration herein before directed to be taken.

No Tax or Duty shall be laid on Articles exported from any State.

No Preference shall be given by any Regulation of Commerce or Revenue to the Ports of one State over those of another: nor shall Vessels bound to, or from, one State, be obliged to enter, clear or pay Duties in another.

No Money shall be drawn from the Treasury, but in Consequence of Appropriations made by Law; and a regular Statement and Account of Receipts and Expenditures of all public Money shall be published from time to time.

No Title of Nobility shall be granted by the United States: and no Person holding any Office of Profit or Trust under them, shall, without the Consent of the Congress, accept of any present, Emolument, Office, or Title, of any kind whatever, from any King, Prince, or foreign State.

Section 10. No State shall enter into any Treaty, Alliance, or Confederation; grant Letters of Marque and Reprisal; coin Money; emit Bills of Credit; make any Thing but gold and silver Coin a Tender in Payment of Debts; pass any Bill of Attainder, ex post facto Law, or Law impairing the Obligation of Contracts, or grant any Title of Nobility.

No State shall, without the Consent of the Congress, lay any Imposts or Duties on Imports or Exports, except what may be absolutely necessary for executing it's inspection Laws: and the net Produce of all Duties and Imposts, laid by any State on Imports or Exports, shall be for the Use of the Treasury of the United States; and all such Laws shall be subject to the Revision and Control of the Congress.

No State shall, without the Consent of Congress, lay any Duty of Tonnage, keep Troops, or Ships of War in time of Peace, enter into any Agreement or Compact with another State, or with a foreign Power, or engage in War, unless actually invaded, or in such imminent Danger as will not admit of delay.

Article II

Section 1. The executive Power shall be vested in a President of the United States of America. He shall hold his Office during the Term of four Years, and, together with the Vice President, chosen for the same Term, be elected, as follows:

Each State shall appoint, in such Manner as the Legislature thereof may direct, a Number of Electors, equal to the whole Number of Senators and Representatives to which the State may be entitled in the Congress: but no Senator or Representative, or Person holding an Office of Trust or Profit under the United States, shall be appointed an Elector.

The Electors shall meet in their respective States, and vote by Ballot for two Persons, of whom one at least shall not be an Inhabitant of the same State with themselves. And they shall make a

List of all the Persons voted for, and of the Number of Votes for each; which List they shall sign and certify, and transmit sealed to the Seat of the Government of the United States, directed to the President of the Senate. The President of the Senate shall, in the Presence of the Senate and House of Representatives, open all the Certificates, and the Votes shall then be counted. The Person having the greatest Number of Votes shall be the President, if such Number be a Majority of the whole Number of Electors appointed; and if there be more than one who have such Majority, and have an equal Number of Votes, then the House of Representatives shall immediately choose by Ballot one of them for President; and if no Person have a Majority, then from the five highest on the List the said House shall in like Manner choose the President. But in choosing the President, the Votes shall be taken by States, the Representation from each State having one Vote; A quorum for this Purpose shall consist of a Member or Members from two thirds of the States, and a Majority of all the States shall be necessary to a Choice. In every Case, after the Choice of the President, the Person having the greatest Number of Votes of the Electors shall be the Vice President. But if there should remain two or more who have equal Votes, the Senate shall choose from them by Ballot the Vice President.

The Congress may determine the Time of choosing the Electors, and the Day on which they shall give their Votes; which Day shall be the same throughout the United States.

No Person except a natural born Citizen, or a Citizen of the United States, at the time of the Adoption of this Constitution, shall be eligible to the Office of President; neither shall any Person be eligible to that office who shall not have attained to the Age of thirty-five years, and been fourteen Years a Resident within the United States.

In Case of the Removal of the President from office, or of his Death, Resignation, or Inability to discharge the Powers and Duties of the said Office, the Same shall devolve on the Vice President, and the Congress may by Law provide for the Case of Removal, Death, Resignation or Inability, both of the President and Vice President, declaring what Officer shall then act as President, and such Officer shall act accordingly, until the disability be Removed, or a President shall be elected.

The President shall, at stated Times, receive for his Services, a Compensation, which shall neither be increased nor diminished during the Period for which he shall have been elected, and he shall not receive within that Period any other Emolument from the United States, or any of them.

Before he enter on the Execution of his Office, he shall take the following Oath or Affirmation:—
"I do solemnly swear (or affirm) that I will faithfully execute the Office of President of the United States, and will to the best of my Ability, preserve, protect and defend the Constitution of the United States."

Section 2. The President shall be Commander in Chief of the Army and Navy of the United States, and of the Militia of the several States, when called into the actual Service of the United States; he may require the Opinion, in writing, of the principal Officer in each of the executive Departments, upon any Subject relating to the Duties of their respective Offices, and he shall have Power to grant Reprieves and Pardons for Offences against the United States, except in Cases of Impeachment.

He shall have Power, by and with the Advice and Consent of the Senate, to make Treaties, provided two thirds of the Senators present concur; and he shall nominate, and by and with the Advice and Consent of the Senate, shall appoint Ambassadors, other public Ministers and Consuls, Judges of the supreme Court, and all other Officers of the United States, whose Appointments are not herein otherwise provided for, and which shall be established by Law: but the Congress may by Law vest the Appointment of such inferior Officers, as they think proper, in the President alone, in the Courts of Law, or in the Heads of Departments.

The President shall have Power to fill up all Vacancies that may happen during the Recess of the Senate, by granting Commissions which shall expire at the End of their next Session.

Section 3. He shall from time to time give to the Congress Information of the State of the Union, and recommend to their Consideration such Measures as he shall judge necessary and expedient; he may, on extraordinary Occasions, convene both Houses, or either of them, and in Case of Disagreement between them, with Respect to the Time of Adjournment, he may adjourn them to such Time as he shall think proper; he shall receive Ambassadors and other public Ministers; he shall take Care that the Laws be faithfully executed, and shall Commission all the Officers of the United States.

Section 4. The President, Vice President and all civil Officers of the United States, shall be removed from Office on Impeachment for, and Conviction of, Treason, Bribery, or other high Crimes and Misdemeanors.

Article III

Section 1. The judicial Power of the United States shall be vested in one Supreme Court, and in such inferior Courts as the Congress may from time to time ordain and establish. The Judges, both of the supreme and inferior Courts, shall hold their Offices during good Behavior, and shall, at stated Times, receive for their Services, a Compensation, which shall not be diminished during their Continuance in Office.

Section 2. The judicial Power shall extend to all Cases, in Law and Equity, arising under this Constitution, the Laws of the United States, and Treaties made, or which shall be made, under their Authority;—to all Cases affecting Ambassadors, other public Ministers and Consuls;—to all Cases of admiralty and maritime Jurisdiction;—to Controversies to which the United States shall be a Party;—to Controversies between two or more States;—between a State and Citizens of another State;—between Citizens of different States;—between Citizens of the same State claiming Lands under Grants of different States, and between a State, or the Citizens thereof, and foreign States, Citizens or Subjects.

In all Cases affecting Ambassadors, other public Ministers and Consuls, and those in which a State shall be Party, the Supreme Court shall have original Jurisdiction. In all the other Cases before mentioned, the Supreme Court shall have appellate Jurisdiction, both as to Law and Fact, with such Exceptions, and under such Regulations as the Congress shall make.

The Trial of all Crimes, except in Cases of Impeachment, shall be by Jury; and such Trial shall be held in the State where the said Crimes shall have been committed; but when not committed within any State, the Trial shall be at such Place or Places as the Congress may by Law have directed.

Section 3. Treason against the United States shall consist only in levying War against them, or in adhering to their Enemies, giving them Aid and Comfort. No Person shall be convicted of Treason unless on the Testimony of two Witnesses to the same overt Act, or on Confession in open Court.

The Congress shall have Power to declare the Punishment of Treason, but no Attainder of Treason shall work Corruption of Blood, or Forfeiture except during the Life of the Person attainted.

Article IV

Section 1. Full Faith and Credit shall be given in each State to the public Acts, Records, and judicial Proceedings of every other State. And the Congress may by general Laws prescribe the Manner in which such Acts, Records, and Proceedings shall be proved, and the Effect thereof.

Section. 2. The Citizens of each State shall be entitled to all Privileges and Immunities of Citizens in the several States.

A Person charged in any State with Treason, Felony, or other Crime, who shall flee from Justice, and be found in another State, shall on Demand of the executive Authority of the State from which he fled, be delivered up, to be removed to the State having Jurisdiction of the Crime.

No Person held to Service or Labor in one State, under the Laws thereof, escaping into another, shall, in Consequence of any Law or Regulation therein, be discharged from such Service or Labor, but shall be delivered up on Claim of the Party to whom such Service or Labor may be due.

Section 3. New States may be admitted by the Congress into this Union; but no new States shall be formed or erected within the Jurisdiction of any other State; nor any State be formed by the Junction of two or more States, or Parts of States, without the Consent of the Legislatures of the States concerned as well as of the Congress.

The Congress shall have Power to dispose of and make all needful Rules and Regulations respecting the Territory or other Property belonging to the United States; and nothing in this Constitution shall be so construed as to Prejudice any Claims of the United States, or of any particular State.

Section 4. The United States shall guarantee to every State in this Union a Republican Form of Government, and shall protect each of them against Invasion; and on Application of the Legislature, or of the Executive (when the Legislature cannot be convened) against domestic Violence.

Article. V

The Congress, whenever two thirds of both Houses shall deem it necessary, shall propose Amendments to this Constitution, or, on the Application of the Legislatures of two thirds of the several States, shall call a Convention for proposing Amendments, which, in either Case, shall be valid to all Intents and Purposes, as Part of this Constitution, when ratified by the Legislatures of three fourths of the several States, or by Conventions in three fourths thereof, as the one or the other Mode of Ratification may be proposed by the Congress; Provided that no Amendment which may be made prior to the Year One thousand eight hundred and eight shall in any Manner affect the first and fourth Clauses in the Ninth Section of the first Article; and that no State, without its consent, shall be deprived of its equal Suffrage in the Senate.

Article. VI

All Debts contracted and Engagements entered into, before the Adoption of this Constitution, shall be as valid against the United States under this Constitution, as under the Confederation.

This Constitution, and the Laws of the United States which shall be made in Pursuance thereof; and all Treaties made, or which shall be made, under the Authority of the United States, shall be the supreme Law of the Land; and the Judges in every State shall be bound thereby, any Thing in the Constitution or Laws of any State to the Contrary notwithstanding.

The Senators and Representatives before mentioned, and the Members of the several State Legislatures, and all executive and judicial Officers, both of the United States and of the several States, shall be bound by Oath or Affirmation, to support this Constitution; but no religious Test shall ever be required as a Qualification to any Office or public Trust under the United States.

Article. VII

The Ratification of the Conventions of nine States shall be sufficient for the Establishment of this Constitution between the States so ratifying the Same.

Done in Convention by the Unanimous Consent of the States present the Seventeenth Day of September in the Year of our Lord one thousand seven hundred and Eighty seven and of the Independence of the United States of America the Twelfth In witness whereof We have hereunto subscribed our Names,

G. Washington
President and deputy from Virginia

New Hampshire:
John Langdon
Nicholas Gilman

Massachusetts:
Nathaniel Gorman
Rufus King

Connecticut:
Wm. Saml. Johnson
Roger Sherman

New York:
Alexander Hamilton

New Jersey:
Wil. Livingston
David Brearley
Wm. Paterson
John Dayton

Pennsylvania:
B. Franklin
Thomas Miffin
Robt. Morris
Geo. Clymer
Thos. FitzSimons
Jared Ingersoll
James Wilson
Gouv Morris

Delaware:
Geo. Read
Gunning Bedford Jun
John Dickinson
Richard Bassett
Jaco. Broom

Maryland:
James McHenry
Dan of St Thos. Jenifer
Danl. Carroll

Virginia:
John Blair
James Madison Jr.

North Carolina:
Wm. Blount
Richd. Dobbs Spaight
Hu Williamson

South Carolina:
J. Rutledge
Charles Cotesworth Pinckney
Charles Pinckney
Pierce Butler

Georgia:
William Few
Abr. Baldwin

Attest William Jackson Secretary

United States Constitution Amendments

The first ten amendments are referred to as the "Bill of Rights."

AMENDMENT I (1791)

Congress shall make no law respecting an establishment of religion, or prohibiting the free exercise thereof; or abridging the freedom of speech, or of the press; or the right of the people peaceably to assemble, and to petition the Government for a redress of grievances.

AMENDMENT II (1791)

A well regulated Militia, being necessary to the security of a free State, the right of the people to keep and bear Arms, shall not be infringed.

AMENDMENT III (1791)

No Soldier shall, in time of peace be quartered in any house, without the consent of the Owner, nor in time of war, but in a manner to be prescribed by law.

AMENDMENT IV (1791)

The right of the people to be secure in their persons, houses, papers, and effects, against unreasonable searches and seizures, shall not be violated, and no Warrants shall issue, but upon probable cause, supported by Oath or affirmation, and particularly describing the place to be searched, and the persons or things to be seized.

AMENDMENT V (1791)

No person shall be held to answer for a capital, or otherwise infamous crime, unless on a presentment or indictment of a Grand Jury, except in cases arising in the land or naval forces, or in the Militia, when in actual service in time of War or public danger; nor shall any person be subject for the same offense to be twice put in jeopardy of life or limb; nor shall be compelled in any criminal case to be a witness against himself, nor be deprived of life, liberty, or property, without due process of law; nor shall private property be taken for public use, without just compensation.

AMENDMENT VI (1791)

In all criminal prosecutions, the accused shall enjoy the right to a speedy and public trial, by an impartial jury of the State and district wherein the crime shall have been committed, which district shall have been previously ascertained by law, and to be informed of the nature and cause of the accusation; to be confronted with the witnesses against him; to have compulsory process for obtaining witnesses in his favor, and to have the Assistance of Counsel for his defense.

AMENDMENT VII (1791)

In Suits at common law, where the value in controversy shall exceed twenty dollars, the right of trial by jury shall be preserved, and no fact tried by a jury, shall be otherwise reexamined in any Court of the United States, than according to the rules of the common law.

AMENDMENT VIII (1791)

Excessive bail shall not be required, nor excessive fines imposed, nor cruel and unusual punishments inflicted.

AMENDMENT IX (1791)

The enumeration in the Constitution, of certain rights, shall not be construed to deny or disparage others retained by the people.

AMENDMENT X (1791)

The powers not delegated to the United States by the Constitution, nor prohibited by it to the States, are reserved to the States respectively, or to the people.

AMENDMENT XI (1795)

The Judicial power of the United States shall not be construed to extend to any suit in law or equity, commenced or prosecuted against one of the United States by Citizens of another State, or by Citizens or Subjects of any foreign State.

AMENDMENT XII (1804)

The Electors shall meet in their respective states and vote by ballot for President and Vice President, one of whom, at least, shall not be an inhabitant of the same State with themselves; they shall name in their ballots the person voted for as President, and in distinct ballots the person voted for as Vice President, and they shall make distinct lists of all persons voted for as President, and of all persons voted for as Vice President, and of the number of votes for each, which lists they shall sign and certify, and transmit sealed to the seat of the government of the United States, directed to the President of the Senate;—The President of the Senate shall, in the presence of the Senate and House of Representatives, open all the certificates and the votes shall then be counted;—the person having the greatest number of votes for President, shall be the President, if such number be a majority of the whole number of electors appointed; and if no person have such majority, then from the persons having the highest numbers not exceeding three on the list of those voted for as President, the House of Representatives shall choose immediately, by ballot, the President. But in choosing the President, the votes shall be taken by states, the representation from each State having one vote; a quorum for this purpose shall consist of a member or members from two-thirds of the states, and a majority of all the states shall be necessary to a choice. And if the House of Representatives shall not choose a President whenever the right of choice shall devolve upon them, before the fourth day of March next following, then the Vice President shall act as President, as in the case of the death or other constitutional disability of the President. The person having the greatest number of votes as Vice-President, shall be the Vice President, if such number be a majority of the whole number of electors appointed, and if no person have a majority, then from the two highest numbers on the list, the Senate shall choose the Vice President; a quorum for the purpose shall consist of two-thirds of the whole number of Senators, and a majority of the whole number shall be necessary to a choice. But no person constitutionally ineligible to the office of President shall be eligible to that of Vice President of the United States.

AMENDMENT XIII (1865)

Section 1.

Neither slavery nor involuntary servitude, except as a punishment for crime whereof the party shall have been duly convicted, shall exist within the United States, or any place subject to their jurisdiction.

Section 2.

Congress shall have power to enforce this article by appropriate legislation.

AMENDMENT XIV (1868)

Section 1.

All persons born or naturalized in the United States, and subject to the jurisdiction thereof, are citizens of the United States and of the State wherein they reside. No State shall make or enforce any law which shall abridge the privileges or immunities of citizens of the United States; nor shall any State deprive any person of life, liberty, or property, without due process of law; nor deny to any person within its jurisdiction the equal protection of the laws.

Section 2.

Representatives shall be apportioned among the several States according to their respective numbers, counting the whole number of persons in each State, excluding Indians not taxed. But when the right to vote at any election for the choice of electors for President and Vice President of the United States, Representatives in Congress, the Executive and Judicial officers of a State, or the members of the Legislature thereof, is denied to any of the male inhabitants of such State, being twenty-one years of age, and citizens of the United States, or in any way abridged, except for participation in rebellion, or other crime, the basis of representation therein shall be reduced in the proportion which the number of such male citizens shall bear to the whole number of male citizens twenty-one years of age in such State.

Section 3.

No person shall be a Senator or Representative in Congress, or elector of President and Vice President, or hold any office, civil or military, under the United States, or under any State, who, having previously taken an oath, as a member of Congress, or as an officer of the United States, or as a member of any State legislature, or as an executive or judicial officer of any State, to support the Constitution of the United States, shall have engaged in insurrection or rebellion against the same, or given aid or comfort to the enemies thereof. But Congress may by a vote of two-thirds of each House, remove such disability.

Section 4.
The validity of the public debt of the United States, authorized by law, including debts incurred for payment of pensions and bounties for services in suppressing insurrection or rebellion, shall not be questioned. But neither the United States nor any State shall assume or pay any debt or obligation incurred in aid of insurrection or rebellion against the United States, or any claim for the loss or emancipation of any slave; but all such debts, obligations and claims shall be held illegal and void.

Section 5.
The Congress shall have power to enforce, by appropriate legislation, the provisions of this article.

AMENDMENT XV (1870)

Section 1.
The right of citizens of the United States to vote shall not be denied or abridged by the United States or by any State on account of race, color, or previous condition of servitude.

Section 2.
The Congress shall have power to enforce this article by appropriate legislation.

AMENDMENT XVI (1913)
The Congress shall have power to lay and collect taxes on incomes, from whatever source derived, without apportionment among the several States, and without regard to any census of enumeration.

AMENDMENT XVII (1913)
The Senate of the United States shall be composed of two Senators from each State, elected by the people thereof, for six years; and each Senator shall have one vote. The electors in each State shall have the qualifications requisite for electors of the most numerous branch of the State legislatures.

When vacancies happen in the representation of any State in the Senate, the executive authority of such State shall issue writs of election to fill such vacancies: Provided, that the legislature of any State may empower the executive thereof to make temporary appointments until the people fill the vacancies by election as the legislature may direct.

This amendment shall not be so construed as to affect the election or term of any Senator chosen before it becomes valid as part of the Constitution.

AMENDMENT XVIII (1919)

Section 1.
After one year from the ratification of this article the manufacture, sale, or transportation of intoxicating liquors within, the importation thereof into, or the exportation thereof from the United States and all territory subject to the jurisdiction thereof for beverage purposes is hereby prohibited.

Section 2.
The Congress and the several States shall have concurrent power to enforce this article by appropriate legislation.

Section 3.
This article shall be inoperative unless it shall have been ratified as an amendment to the Constitution by the legislatures of the several States, as provided in the Constitution, within seven years from the date of the submission hereof to the States by the Congress.

AMENDMENT XIX (1920)
The right of citizens of the United States to vote shall not be denied or abridged by the United States or by any State on account of sex.

Congress shall have power to enforce this article by appropriate legislation.

AMENDMENT XX (1933)

Section 1.
The terms of the President and Vice President shall end at noon on the 20th day of January, and the terms of Senators and Representatives at noon on the 3d day of January, of the years in which such terms would have ended if this article had not been ratified; and the terms of their successors shall then begin.

Section 2.
The Congress shall assemble at least once in every year, and such meeting shall begin at noon on the 3d day of January, unless they shall by law appoint a different day.

Section 3.
If, at the time fixed for the beginning of the term of the President, the President elect shall have died, the Vice President elect shall become President. If a President shall not have been chosen before the time fixed for the beginning of his term, or if the President elect shall have failed to qualify, then the Vice President elect shall act as President until a President shall have qualified; and the Congress may by

law provide for the case wherein neither a President elect nor a Vice President elect shall have qualified, declaring who shall then act as President, or the manner in which one who is to act shall be selected, and such person shall act accordingly until a President or Vice President shall have qualified.

Section 4.
The Congress may by law provide for the case of the death of any of the persons from whom the House of Representatives may choose a President whenever the right of choice shall have devolved upon them, and for the case of the death of any of the persons from whom the Senate may choose a Vice President whenever the right of choice shall have devolved upon them.

Section 5.
Sections 1 and 2 shall take effect on the 15th day of October following the ratification of this article.

Section 6.
This article shall be inoperative unless it shall have been ratified as an amendment to the Constitution by the legislatures of three-fourths of the several States within seven years from the date of its submission.

AMENDMENT XXI (1933)

Section 1.
The eighteenth article of amendment to the Constitution of the United States is hereby repealed.

Section 2.
The transportation or importation into any State, Territory, or possession of the United States for delivery or use therein of intoxicating liquors, in violation of the laws thereof, is hereby prohibited.

Section 3.
This article shall be inoperative unless it shall have been ratified as an amendment to the Constitution by conventions in the several States, as provided in the Constitution, within seven years from the date of the submission hereof to the States by the Congress.

AMENDMENT XXII (1951)

Section 1.
No person shall be elected to the office of the President more than twice, and no person who has held the office of President, or acted as President, for more than two years of a term to which some other person was elected President shall be elected to the office of the President more than once. But this Article shall not apply to any person holding the office of President when this Article was proposed by the Congress, and shall not prevent any person who may be holding the office of President, or acting

as President, during the term within which this Article becomes operative from holding the office of President or acting as President during the remainder of such term.

Section 2.

This article shall be inoperative unless it shall have been ratified as an amendment to the Constitution by the legislatures of three-fourths of the several States within seven years from the date of its submission to the States by the Congress.

AMENDMENT XXIII (1961)

Section 1.

The District constituting the seat of Government of the United States shall appoint in such manner as the Congress may direct:

A number of electors of President and Vice President equal to the whole number of Senators and Representatives in Congress to which the District would be entitled if it were a State, but in no event more than the least populous State; they shall be in addition to those appointed by the States, but they shall be considered, for the purposes of the election of President and Vice President, to be electors appointed by a State; and they shall meet in the District and perform such duties as provided by the twelfth article of amendment.

Section 2.

The Congress shall have power to enforce this article by appropriate legislation.

AMENDMENT XXIV (1964)

Section 1.

The right of citizens of the United States to vote in any primary or other election for President or Vice President, for electors for President or Vice President, or for Senator or Representative in Congress, shall not be denied or abridged by the United States or any State by reason of failure to pay any poll tax or other tax.

Section 2.

The Congress shall have power to enforce this article by appropriate legislation.

AMENDMENT XXV (1967)

Section 1.

In case of the removal of the President from office or of his death or resignation, the Vice President shall become President.

Section 2.

Whenever there is a vacancy in the office of the Vice President, the President shall nominate a Vice President who shall take office upon confirmation by a majority vote of both Houses of Congress.

Section 3.

Whenever the President transmits to the President pro tempore of the Senate and the Speaker of the House of Representatives his written declaration that he is unable to discharge the powers and duties of his office, and until he transmits to them a written declaration to the contrary, such powers and duties shall be discharged by the Vice President as Acting President.

Section 4.

Whenever the Vice President and a majority of either the principal officers of the executive departments or of such other body as Congress may by law provide, transmit to the President pro tempore of the Senate and the Speaker of the House of Representatives their written declaration that the President is unable to discharge the powers and duties of his office, the Vice President shall immediately assume the powers and duties of the office as Acting President.

Thereafter, when the President transmits to the President pro tempore of the Senate and the Speaker of the House of Representatives his written declaration that no inability exists, he shall resume the powers and duties of his office unless the Vice President and a majority of either the principal officers of the executive department or of such other body as Congress may by law provide, transmit within four days to the President pro tempore of the Senate and the Speaker of the House of Representatives their written declaration that the President is unable to discharge the powers and duties of his office. Thereupon Congress shall decide the issue, assembling within forty-eight hours for that purpose if not in session. If the Congress, within twenty-one days after receipt of the latter written declaration, or, if Congress is not in session, within twenty-one days after Congress is required to assemble, determines by two-thirds vote of both Houses that the President is unable to discharge the powers and duties of his office, the Vice President shall continue to discharge the same as Acting President; otherwise, the President shall resume the powers and duties of his office.

AMENDMENT XXVI (1971)

Section 1.

The right of citizens of the United States, who are 18 years of age or older, to vote, shall not be denied or abridged by the United States or any State on account of age.

Section 2.

The Congress shall have the power to enforce this article by appropriate legislation.

AMENDMENT XXVII (1992)

No law, varying the compensation for the services of the Senators and Representatives shall take effect until an election of Representatives shall have intervened.

Bibliography

Allen, Gary. *None Dare Call It Conspiracy*. Seal Beach, CA: Concord Press, 1971.

Bastiat, Frederic. *The Law* (1850). Translated by Dean Russell, Irvington-on-Hudson: Foundation for Economic Education, Inc., 1950.

Brain-Washing (A Synthesis of the Russian Textbook on Psychopolitics). Fort Worth: Truth, Inc., n.d.

Collier, Robert. *The Law of the Higher Potential 1947*. Tarrytown: Book of Gold, 1947.

Congressman Louis T. McFadden on the Federal Reserve Corporation (Remarks in Congress, 1934). Boston: Forum Publishing Company, n.d.

Friedman, Milton. *A Program for Monetary Stability*. New York: Fordham University Press, 1959.

Friedman, Milton and Rose. *Free to Choose*. San Diego: Harcourt, 1980.

Goetsch, David L. and Archie P. Jones. *Rules for Conservative Radicals (How the Tea Party Movement Can Save America)*. Powder Springs: White Hall Press, 2012.

Greider, William. *Secrets of the Temple: How the Federal Reserve Runs the Country*. New York: Simon & Schuster Inc., 1987.

Hamilton, Alexander, James Madison, and John Jay. *The Federalist Papers*. New York: NAL Penguin Inc., 1961.

Hazlitt, Henry. *Economics in One Lesson*. Manhattan: Harper & Brothers, 1946.

Kurland, Philip B. *The Founders' Constitution*. Chicago: University of Chicago Press, 1987.

Paul, Ron. *End the Fed*. New York: Grand Central Publishing, 2009.

Roberts, Archibald E. *Emerging Struggle for State Sovereignty*. Fort Collins: Betsy Ross Press, 1979.

———. *The Most Secret Science*. Fort Collins: Betsy Ross Press, 1984.

Rothbard, Murray N. *The Case for a 100 Percent Gold Dollar*. Auburn, AL: Ludwig von Mises Institute, 1962.

———. *What Has Government Done to Our Money?* Auburn, AL: Ludwig von Mises Institute, 1963.

————. *America's Great Depression.* Auburn, AL: Ludwig von Mises Institute, 1963.

————. *The Case Against the Fed.* Auburn, AL: Ludwig von Mises Institute, 1994.

Schiff, Irwin. *How Anyone Can Stop Paying Income Taxes.* Hamden: Freedom Books, 1982

United States Government Printing Office. *Constitution of the United States of America, Revised and Annotated.* Washington, DC: 1938.

von Mises, Ludwig. *Human Action.* Auburn, AL: Ludwig von Mises Institute, 1949.

Welch, Robert. *Republics and Democracies.* Belmont: A speech first published as an article in the October, 1961 issue of the monthly magazine, American Opinion

Made in USA - North Chelmsford, MA

09.21.2020 1352